FAITH AND STRUGGLE ON SMOKEY MOUNTAIN

HOPE FOR A PLANET IN PERIL

Benigno P. Beltran

ORBIS BOOKS
Maryknoll, New York 10545

Founded in 1970, Orbis Books endeavors to publish works that enlighten the mind, nourish the spirit, and challenge the conscience. The publishing arm of the Maryknoll Fathers and Brothers, Orbis seeks to explore the global dimensions of the Christian faith and mission, to invite dialogue with diverse cultures and religious traditions, and to serve the cause of reconciliation and peace. The books published reflect the views of their authors and do not represent the official position of the Maryknoll Society. To learn more about Maryknoll and Orbis Books, please visit our website at www.maryknollsociety.org.

Copyright © 2012 by Benigno P. Beltran, SVD

Published by Orbis Books, Box 302, Maryknoll, NY 10545-0302.

Manufactured in the United States of America

Library of Congress Cataloging-in-Publication Data

Beltran, Benigno P., 1946-
    Faith and struggle on Smokey Mountain : hope for a planet in peril / Benigno P. Beltran.
        p. cm.
    Includes bibliographical references and index.
    ISBN 978-1-57075-975-8 (pbk.); ISBN 978-1-60833-210-6 (ebook)
    1. Church work with the poor—Philippines—Manila. 2. Church work with the poor—Catholic Church 3. Poor—Philippines—Manila. 4. Poor Religious life. 5. Philippines—Religious life and customs. I. Title.
BX2347.8.P66B45 2012
261.8'3250959916—dc23
2012014317

To my parents, Benigno Bala Beltran, Sr.,
and Concepcion Matugas Preagido,
who taught me, by their lives of faith-fullness and joyful hope,
that the universe is kind and that in the end, everything is grace.

CONTENTS

INTRODUCTION

WE REJOICE IN HOPE (ROM. 12:12)

We need to be on fire again,
for our hope is no longer an easy hope.
We live in a culture of despair
within which Pentecost can no longer be taken for granted.
Hence we must take upon ourselves the burden of the times
and refuse to make the Holy Spirit a piece of private
    property
but a spirit that matters.

—Mary Jo Leddy

Smokey Mountain was a huge garbage dump in the heart of
the city of Manila, Philippines. Several thousand tons of garbage
collected from all over the metropolis were dumped on Smokey
Mountain every day. More than 25,000 people scavenged in the
trash heaps in order to survive.

I lived for more than thirty years on Smokey Mountain. It
was an awesome experience—at once tremendous and terrifying,
fascinating and repugnant, energizing and enervating. It was an
experience filled with unspeakable sadness but also with passion and deep meaning. It was a journey through the heart of
darkness, a pilgrimage through the crucible of despair to emerge
into joyful hope in the end.

Global problems lay siege to our globalized world. Smokey
Mountain is a metaphor for a planet slowly choking with plastic
and all kinds of garbage in its cities and oceans; its rainforests
denuded, and arable land turned into deserts; with thousands of
species of plants and animals facing extinction; its life-support
systems poisoned by pesticides and toxic wastes; gasping for

breath in cities smothered by smog and noxious fumes; with more and more human beings living ever closer to each other, as resources quickly disappear. The image of Smokey Mountain, a trash heap that burned continuously for more than fifty years until it was closed in 1995, is a horrifying symbol of a planet in peril.

But the story of Smokey Mountain is also a metaphor for hope. It depicts the will to survive, the grit to sustain family and community, the ability to create joy while living in abject poverty. The scavengers refused to be beaten down by cruel circumstances and dreamed of a better life. They struggled mightily against government bureaucracy so that the dump site could be rehabilitated and houses built for their families. They banded together so that they could earn a decent livelihood and unite for a common purpose to help other poor people. Smokey Mountain is a point of light at the end of the tunnel that might teach others a few lessons in hope.

The scavengers' story is a small contribution to the global justice movement sweeping the world like brush fires today, from Tahrir Square in Egypt to Zuccotti Park in New York, a movement that has justice and democracy at its core. Their struggle is connected to the integrity and solidarity of ordinary people across international borders who are creatively infusing globalization with a more democratic spirit. The image of huge crowds of ordinary people facing down legions of police and soldiers protecting the enclaves of the rich and powerful who run the world has powerfully ignited the imagination of many around the world.

Each one of us has an obligation to give hope to this planet; we owe it to our own humanity. In the words of Lewis Thomas, "The idea that all men and women are brothers and sisters is not a transient cultural notion, not a slogan made up to make us feel warm and comfortable inside. It is a biological imperative."[1] This biological imperative is the locus of an ethical consciousness that insists on universal compassion. The context of the biological imperative is a universe in a continual process of becoming "with all its sham, and its drudgery and its broken dreams," a universe whose meaning can be fully revealed only in the future, a universe where one lives in hope and expectation. Giving hope to a planet in peril is indeed a biological imperative; even more, it is a moral imperative, a cosmic imperative. We see so many dreadful images daily that we become numb to their horror: victims of terrorism, environmental disasters, hunger and disease. No act of faith in the future should be made that would not be able to provide grounds for hope in the face of children dying before their time, children whose limbs are torn apart by terrorist bombs and land mines, children whose lungs become black due to pollution in the ecosystem. We need images of hope to counteract the images of horror we see on television, in newspapers, and on the Internet every day.

There is something wrong with us. Albert Einstein commented that we have become technological giants but ethical pygmies. The world spends a trillion dollars a year for military weapons, for example, while a billion human beings earn only $1 a day. Everyday, 26,000 children die from hunger and preventable diseases in the least developed countries. That comes to 182,000 a week and to 9,490,000 children dying every year. A small percentage of what the world spends for weapons of destruction can feed and educate all the children in the world and provide them with health care. Providing clean water for everyone on the planet would cost only $20 billion.

The most urgent task for humanity is to preserve the biosphere for future generations, to share the wealth of the earth, and to live together in harmony. We have to recognize the planetary dimension of the ecological crisis, summon the moral vision and fortitude to collaborate through aggressive societal action on a global basis in order to blunt climate change and other problems that plague our planet. To accomplish this, we have to engage in vigorous and rigorous dialogue concerning crucial issues of the global and digital age. We have to ask these questions together: what does it mean to be a human being, what should our core values be, where do we want to go from here, and what kind of society do we want to build for the children now and those still to be born?

We are confronting a looming apocalypse of unprecedented magnitude; the extinction of the human race is now a distinct possibility. We are on a countdown to global disaster, planetary collapse, world catastrophe.[2] Despite overwhelming scientific evidence of artificially induced climate change, many continue with ways of living way beyond the planet's limits.[3] We maintain our addiction to fossil fuels because we are afraid that it might crimp our lifestyles.

We have to face the bitter truth about the present global political economy: it is unjust, it is unsustainable, it is unstable, and it hurts very many people. While this has triggered outrage in many, we have yet to move from the "conscientization phase" to the "outrage phase" to the "hope phase." We should not stop at explanations of how this state of affairs came about. We should rely on courage, creativity, and compassion, and we should compete in doing good. It is not enough to describe the problems of the world; something should actually be done about them. Now.

We have to radically change the way we relate to the earth. The need for a planetary and democratic conversation about what kind of values will allow us to survive is crucial. Let us try to find the way out together on this planet where we use a billion plastic bags a year and only 1 percent of them are recycled; on this planet, where there is already an island of plastic in the Pacific Ocean called the Great Pacific Garbage Patch, one hundred meters deep and twice as large as the state of Texas; on this planet, where there are thousands of garbage dumps like Smokey Mountain, especially in the less developed countries. Several million people depend for their survival as trash pickers in these dump sites, while a fortunate few in richer countries use twenty times more resources than those in the poorer parts of the world. If they go on with their profligate ways, we will very soon need three or four more planets.

HOW CAN OUR WORLD BEST AVOID
DESTROYING ITSELF?

Wild, dark times are rumbling toward us, and the prophet who wishes to write a new apocalypse will have to invent entirely new beasts, and beasts so terrible that the ancient animal symbols of St. John will seem like cooing doves and cupids in comparison.

—Heinrich Heine, Lutetia

I wrote this book for all my friends in other parts of the world. They often asked me what it was like to live in a garbage dump with the overpowering stench and the smoke and the huge rats, the cockroaches and the buzzflies; why I chose to do so; and what was the end result of all those years of working with people who had to scavenge among trash heaps in order to continue to live. The most common question was simply "How was I able to survive for thirty years in a garbage dump?" I wrote this book to answer these questions but also to clarify my own choices and justify my taking up space in this already crowded planet.

This book is also for those partners and allies who look upon my faith and organized religion, in general, with derision but who nevertheless help me in educating the child scavengers, creating jobs to empower women in the slums. They believe it is the right of these poor people to have a decent life. Many of them are very good human beings, and they are convinced they can be good without God.[4] I would like to explain to them here the reasons why I do what I do. I would like to describe a personal vision of what it means to believe in God in the modern world and why I think it is the most rational thing to do. Believers are not required to crucify their intellect when they respond to God's call to renew the face of the earth. My faith is all I have in obeying the biological imperative and making this a better world than when I first came to it. It is the most vital part of my life—the faith that God our Father acted in Jesus through the power of the Spirit for human beings and for the universe as a whole.

Most of all, I write this book for the young people who have touched my life, those who listened to me when, as a disc jockey, I played rock music on a radio program for teenagers, those I taught in universities and theological schools, those who beat me in video games all the time, those who participated in the retreats and recollections I conducted, and the young people who worked with me in the garbage dump. Many of the young people I have met around the world are yearning for a greater purpose. They tell me they are worried about the legacy they are leaving. They want to be remembered for the quality of their human relationships, and their ability to look after those around them, and not for their beauty, power, or influence. They are afraid they will spend their lives without offering the best they can give to the world. They are searching for a vision of a world to which they can fully give their lives. I hope the vision for the future discussed here will inspire them to still greater things and speak somehow to their idealism and their need for freedom and personal achievement, because their views will redefine who and what a human being is, how humans will see themselves and their place in the scheme of things.

The story of the scavengers and slum dwellers provides ample reasons to hope. After years of nonviolent demonstrations and prayer rallies, of fasting and novenas, countless rosaries and Holy Hours before the Blessed Sacrament, the people of Smokey Mountain attained their objective of having the dump site closed and housing built for them. They now live in medium-rise housing with very cheap monthly amortization. The strategy the scavengers followed to nurture hope in the face of abject poverty in the garbage dump was to raise consciousness (*itaas ang kamalayan*), strengthen relationships (*patatagin ang ugnayan*), and allow shared vision to integrate (*pag-isahin ang adhikain*) raised consciousness and strengthened relationships through the core values of integrity, solidarity, and creativity. The long-term goals chosen were integral human development, social justice, and a sustainable future. These issues are what this book is all about. Smokey Mountain is a testament to what an integral transformative practice can accomplish in a universe God made to make itself, the one and triune God "who makes all things new" (Rev. 23:5). This book is a reflection on the inward journey I made together with the scavengers.

OUTLINE OF THE BOOK

Chapter 1 describes my inner pilgrimage as I made the garbage dump the sanctuary of my solitude. This interior journey shaped the way I chose to conduct my personal life and my journey from horror to hope. It filled me with a sense of despair and discovery, of isolation and inspiration, as I came face to face with the reality of life on top of a mountain of garbage. I also describe here the day-to-day life in the garbage dump, the drudgery of having to live on what others throw away.

Chapter 2 shows the way I engaged in prophetic dialogue with the scavengers. It also portrays how they understand the world and what they are doing to inspire hope.

Chapter 3 depicts the vital religious experience of the scavengers as points of departure for doing theology in dialogue with militant atheism and scientific materialism. It will also point out the differences in the languages and worldviews of East and West that structure the way people think about God, the world, and themselves. These profound differences have to be faced if there is to be hope for the planet.

Chapter 4 recounts the efforts of the scavengers to organize functional microsocieties for joint community performance to help build the society we want. It shows how a cadre of networked people burning with the desire to promote justice, peace, and the integrity of creation can make significant impacts on their communities and contribute to the building of a global political economy based on justice and the common good.

Chapter 5 is a reflection on the various conversions—intellectual, moral, and spiritual—I underwent after thirty years on Smokey Mountain and in prophetic dialogue with the new science. It will also describe the personal transformation that happened to me in the garbage dump in the attempt to forge a theology of the Trinity as I moved to higher levels of awareness in the quest for a transcendent purpose to existence.

This book is sacred to the memory of all those who suffered and died because of humanity's stupidity and greed, to all the babies dying before their time or growing up maimed because of the dioxin in their mothers' milk, to the scavengers and ragpickers all over the world whose life spans were considerably shortened by the smoke and the pestilence and disease coming from open dump sites.

This book is also a call to compassion for all the lost, the least, the last among the children of Mother Earth. Perhaps their agony will strengthen in us the resolve to make Mother Earth a more just, more peaceful, healthier society for tomorrow's children today. If we fail, we will not be the moral and worthy ancestors they will remember with honor and gratitude. For as Dietrich Bonhoeffer, the German pastor martyred during the time of the Nazis, said, the ultimate test of a moral society is the kind of world it leaves to its children.

There is an urgent need for hope for this planet in peril—hope for those living in grinding poverty in developing countries and hope for those boring themselves to tears in the developed world, hope that will enable everyone to find meaning to life and history. For Christians, hope is participation in the ongoing creation of the universe. Our hope is rooted in the earth, in this fragile blue planet, because the earth is the Lord's and the fullness thereof (Ps. 24:1).

Every day, urged on by this hope, we discover new truths, we awaken dormant potentials for self-transcendence, we craft more integral visions that lead farther and higher into the spiral of complexity and consciousness in an evolving cosmos. If you do not hope, you will not find what is beyond your hopes, wrote St. Clement of Alexandria. With the eyes of our hearts enlightened, we may know what is the hope to which God has called us (Eph. 1:18).

Hope is a conscious choice. The way we opt for hope is by working towards achieving a world of justice, peace, and a sustainable future. We have to provide the world with a hope that is a radical waiting, an eager longing, and a joyful expectation. We do this in an evolving universe moving towards a collective future where God will be all in all (1 Cor. 15:18). Let us all join together to build the kind of society the children and young people deserve, and provide vital signs of hope to this planet in peril.

It is the only planet we have.

Fr. Benigno P. Beltran, SVD
Divine Word Seminary
Tagaytay City, Philippines

NOTES

[1]Lewis Thomas, *The Fragile Species* (New York: Collier Books, 1992), 95. Thomas wrote that it is a moral obligation, driven by deep biological impera-

tives, to consider everyone as our brother and sister. It is also mandated by the conventional, cultural view of human morality because we are a compulsively social species (ibid., 80).

[2]See Lester Brown, *Plan B 3.0: Mobilizing to Save Civilization* (New York: W. W. Norton, 2008). Strictly speaking, it is us and other living beings who are in peril. It will only be disastrous for living beings who will be wiped out by the global climate catastrophe if we will not do something about it. The planet will go on orbiting the sun for around five billion more years according to scientific calculations. See Oliver Morton, "Our Planet Is Not in Peril," in *What Is Your Dangerous Idea?* ed. John Brockman (New York: HarperCollins, 2007), 50-53. Morton thinks the most important thing about environmental change is that it hurts people; the basis of our response should be human solidarity.

[3]Mary Hillman with Tina Fawcett and Sudhir Chella Rajan, *The Suicidal Planet: How to Prevent Global Climate Catastrophe* (New York: St. Martin's Press, 2007). Bill McGuire thinks it is not yet too late, but time is running out, in his book *Seven Years to Save the Planet: The Questions . . . And Answers* (London: Weidenfield and Nicholson, 2008).

[4]See Greg Epstein, *Good without God: What a Billion Nonreligious People Do Believe* (New York: William Morrow, 2009). Epstein prefers to call these nonreligious people humanists, who strive to live well, build community, live up to ethical values and lift the human spirit without belief in transcendent reality. See also Rodney Stark, *What Americans Really Believe* (Waco, TX: Baylor University Press, 2008). Stark's data show that many of those who do not attend religious services nevertheless believe in God.

Chapter 1

GOD AS CLOUD OF UNKNOWING

WELCOME TO THE GARBAGE DUMP

The cities of the future, rather than being made of glass and steel as envisioned by earlier generations of urbanists, are instead largely constructed out of crude brick, straw, recycled plastic, cement blocks, and scrap wood. Instead of cities of light soaring toward heaven, much of the 21st century urban world squats in squalor, surrounded by pollution, excrement and decay.
—Mike Davis, *Planet of Slums*

Like a fossil preserved in paleolithic rock, the day I first came to Smokey Mountain is embedded in my mind forever.

It was like landing on an alien planet. It took a tremendous act of the will not to retch and void my stomach because of the smell of the decaying garbage. It hit me like a punch in the gut. The overpowering stench, the unbearably sickening sweet-sour smell of putrefaction was hideous and fascinating at the same time. The smell clung to my clothes and skin and was difficult to wash away. It made my stomach curl up like an armadillo protecting itself from a predator's assault. The burning dump site easily brought to mind the imagery of fire and sulphur described in the Book of Revelation where the beast and the false prophet are consigned before the millennial reign (Rev. 19:20; see also Gen. 19:24). I was reminded of what the prophet warned when "the earth shall be completely laid waste and utterly despoiled" (Isa. 24:3).

The sense of asphyxiation from the suspended particulates in the air was unbearable and made my chest ache as the smell of human refuse burned into my nostrils. Even more painful was the sight of the men, women, and children poking into garbage heaps for a living, retrieving broken bottles, plastics, pieces of metal. After years of theological studies in Rome, I suddenly came face to face with the anarchy of desperation, of fear and resignation among people who survive on what others throw away. And the smoke from the constantly burning trash rose up like a great cloud of unknowing, mocking all the knowledge I had acquired in the Eternal City.

Millions of flies and cockroaches and mutant rats (huge!) competed with 25,000 scavengers for survival—25,000 men, women, and children who had been trampled upon, squashed, obliterated, condemned without trial to be a stinking class of human beings, carrying their rattan baskets like beasts of burden: people who had been lied to, deceived, duped, and spat upon all their lives. Hundreds of scavengers were figuratively crucified in the garbage dump, their hands and feet pierced by rusty nails and broken bottles while they searched for tin cans, scraps of paper and plastic bags, and climbed up their own Calvary.

Swarms of huge greenback flies strafed the piles of reeking refuse while worms of various colors crawled on the decaying detritus. I did not know how to keep the horseflies away from the chalice when I celebrated Mass that very same day with the scavengers in their tiny chapel. I did not know what to do with those that got into the wine in the chalice. While I celebrated God's bounty in the Eucharist, I was surrounded by starving children with swollen bellies, many with pus-encrusted eyes, skins covered with boils. I winced every time they took my hand and touched it to their foreheads in reverence. In my desolation, I raised the host as far as I was able, in my mind raising it higher than the summit of the garbage mountain, beyond the clouds and the stars, beyond the farthest quasar and supernova in the observable universe. "On an altar surrounded with flies, accept, O Lord, this sacrifice."[1]

As I approached the center of the dump after the Mass, I stood transfixed in the smoldering heat, deafened by the roar of the bulldozers and garbage trucks, with the scavengers shouting to

be heard above the din and the horrifying smell of decay assault-
ing my nostrils. I saw the scavengers with big wicker baskets
slung by a strap to their foreheads or shoulders following the
bulldozers, dodging the garbage trucks and each other. They used
hooks with handles to hoist the garbage into their baskets. They
were very skillful in choosing which kind of plastic or piece of
garbage to pierce with their hooks and place in their baskets
with one graceful swing.

I was not able to adjust to what my eyes were telling me. I
was assailed by a panorama of garbage of all kinds of shape
and color: tin cans, pieces of metal, broken glass, discarded
home appliances, battery containers, CDs and radios, battered refrigerators, and broken television sets, various kinds
of dead household pets, piles of human and animal excrement,
soiled baby diapers, used feminine sanitary napkins, flea- and
bedbug-infested mattresses and pillows, blood- and pus-soaked
bandages, rusted scalpels, medical syringes and dextrose bottles,
spoiled food, rotting fruit and vegetables. And plastic, plastic,
plastic everywhere bearing witness to human wastefulness in
all its horror.

All hail, the throw-away society!

I looked at the scavengers again, and thought of all the
tenderness and sensibility and ideals and poetry and song of a
race with deep feelings and fiery passion compressed in upon
themselves, bound inward by a constricting wall of frustration
within the communal confines of the garbage heaps. Ravaged
earth and wasted lives—that is the story of the garbage dump.

Smokey Mountain, what has not been devoured in your de-
monic furnaces by pollution, despair, disease, insanity, hysteria,
and tuberculosis?

THE JOURNEY INTO SOLITUDE

*I praise what is truly alive, what longs to be burned to
death . . . and so long as you have not experienced this:
to die and so to grow, you are only a troubled guest on
the dark earth.*

—Johann Wolfgang Goethe

It was a very long journey that led from the rainforest where I was born to the garbage dump where I chose to live for more than thirty years. Many people have asked me why I chose to stay on Smokey Mountain. They assume that I had a choice. I always tell them it was there among the poorest of the poor that I had to work out my own salvation in fear and trembling (Phil. 2:12). I did not go to Smokey Mountain to save the scavengers; I went there so that the scavengers could save me.

I was born in the rainforests of Mindanao soon after the guns of World War II fell silent. My father fought in the war against the Japanese Imperial Army. He was caught, tortured, forced-marched to a concentration camp and almost died of dysentery. As soon as he was released, he joined the guerillas. He met my mother, a nursing aide at a makeshift hospital, when he contracted malaria in the jungle. She gave him "Atabrine" for the illness. They got married and gave their first son the nickname "Brine." I think I am the only person named after a medicine for malaria.

My parents joined thousands of impoverished families who lost everything in the war. They dreamed of building a future in that Land of Promise of Mindanao in the south. A large number of dirt-poor peasants who wanted their own land, hungry and sick with malaria and dysentery, tried to eke a living out of the rainforest where we settled after the war. The slash-and-burn style of farming they used exhausted the soil as it destroyed habitats of plants and animals.

I experienced very early on the poverty, the constant conflict, and the destruction of the environment. And yet it was an idyllic childhood. I remember racing water buffaloes with my friends at the periphery of the jungle, unmindful of the crocodiles in the swamps and the pythons coiled in the underbrush. I can still remember the feeling of wonder and awe induced by the majesty and transcendent beauty of the web of life when we ventured deep into the rainforest. I passed through to a new level of consciousness, filled with mixed emotions of fear and fascination in the fetid swamps. It was like being in a cathedral or basilica. I can easily understand the feeling of Charles Darwin who, when asked towards the end of his life what was the most extraordinary experience he had, replied that it was in a rainforest when he just sat there and felt that "there must be more to man than the breath in his body." In his field journal, he noted this when he was in a rainforest in Bahia, Brazil, in April, 1832: "Sublime devotion the prevalent feeling . . . Silence. Hosanna."[2]

After high school, I was rudely transplanted to the asphalt jungles of Manila in 1961 to study Electronics Engineering at the University of Santo Tomas. Shortly before graduation, suddenly discovering a big black hole imploding in my chest that I thought was in the shape of God, I decided to become a Divine Word missionary and volunteer for the bush missions in Africa.[3] I was so happy to be accepted that I spent most of my free time praying in the seminary chapel. The provincial superior then, Fr. George Heinemann, SVD, from Prussia, became worried and called me to his office. He inquired whether I heard voices and saw visions. I said no, I experienced nothing extraordinary. If I had said yes, I would have been sent home at once. But truthfully, I saw no angels and demons when I prayed. Sometimes it even felt as if I was talking to myself in the dark.

The novitiate in Tagaytay City, where we learned to pray and deepen our spiritual life, was one of the happier times in my life. The novice master, Fr. Alphonse Mildner, SVD, taught me that holiness is doing ordinary things extraordinarily well. He noticed that I was in danger of twisting the gentle words of the Nazarene into threats and moral demands verging on self-righteousness with my fasting and long hours in prayer. One does not have to differentiate oneself in a religious community through long hours of prayer and fasting, he gently reminded me. Before the triune God, it is enough to simply be. I quickly abandoned the quest for sanctity through excessive fasting and long hours of prayer, but not the quest for inner certainty. I wanted to be absolutely certain God was really calling me to be a priest. I wrote Padre Pio of Pietrelcina, Italy, who was known for his miracles and later proclaimed a saint, to ask whether I really had a vocation to the priesthood. He wrote back that I should just pray that the will of God be done.

On June 23, 1973, with twenty-four other classmates, I was ordained a priest forever. I volunteered to be sent to Africa. My hopes turned to ashes in my mouth when, instead of being sent to Africa, I was told to teach in the seminary. Under the vow of obedience, I was sent to the Pontifical Gregorian University in Rome to study for a doctorate in Systematic Theology. Systematic Theology is the rational inquiry into the *nexus mysteriorum* (the network of mysteries) to ensure coherence and consistency. It sees the vision of faith as a grand and unifying struggle with the very nature of the universe and the one and triune God. It is the search for appropriate ways to understand religious experience and connect it with other knowledge, including knowledge that science gains from observing the world. Systematic Theology is the effort to put religious beliefs into a coherent intellectual system. The task of the systematic theologian is to purify the language of faith as history moves towards the future, in the face of the changes that history brings. Ultimately, theology is the attempt to describe an intense personal experience of mystery.

But after writing hundreds of pages of my dissertation, with hundreds of footnotes in several languages, I felt that something was standing between me and my sense of wholeness. I became terrified that my life would become unrecognizable. I sensed that the road I was taking was not wide enough to sustain my well-being. Years of study had honed the ability to dissect isolated words with such intense application that I often lost interest in their relevance. I became puffed up by the academic pretense of disinterestedness and dis-involvement, and desired only to be totally objective in order to arrive at the truth.[4]

HEART OF DARKNESS

Those who think that they believe in God without passion in their heart, without anguish of mind, without uncertainty, without doubt, without an element of despair even in their consolation, believe only in the God Idea, not in God Himself.
    —Juan Miguel de Unamuno, *The Tragic Sense of Life*

I was tired of the world. Most of all, I was sick and tired of myself.

I did not find the enlightenment that I thirsted for in the books that I read. I wanted practical knowledge of how to bring my faith in God into my heart. I wanted to understand where this yearning for light in the midst of the darkness in me came from. Does the universe have a purpose? Does science make faith in God obsolete? Were my parents right in teaching me that despite earthquakes, tsunamis, hurricanes, and ten-kilometer diameter meteorites slamming into the Yucatan Peninsula, the universe is kind and full of grace? How could I prove beyond a reasonable doubt that there is a beyond that transcends the vagaries of fate and all human delusions?

Overwhelmed with the certainty that I was doomed, I was left teetering at the unseen edge of a dark infernal abyss. Everything became dry and hard as if all graciousness had withdrawn from the universe. This lasted for weeks, an obscure ache that was both mental and psychological—a festering angst, a lingering sense of cosmic futility, some sort of free-floating anxiety that had no specific cause.[5] I was celebrating the Eucharist daily, reciting morning and evening prayers with my religious community, and studying theology in the Eternal City in the shadow of the Vatican. Why did the anguish become even more bitter and intense? I had terrifying visions of what hell might be like—not fire and brimstone but a loss of the capacity for joy, a narcissistic dread and anxiety, unrelieved, going on and on forever.

After I finished my studies in Rome, I visited holy places in India. In the Shantivanam ashram in Tamil Nadu, I met Fr. Bede Griffith, OSB, a very holy and learned man who served as a spiritual guide. The people in the ashram wanted to inculturate Christian faith into Hindu culture. I visited many Hindu temples, stretching out to touch the flame from the Brahmins' lamps and transfer its blessings to my forehead. One full meal a day, a vegetarian diet, and hours of chanting by the Cauvery River refreshed my drooping spirit.

It was while watching the cremation pyre of an untouchable by the banks of the Cauvery River that I thought of staying with people whom the world has forgotten, people whose lives mirror the powerlessness and the vulnerability of the carpenter from Galilee, and among whom I too could become vulnerable and powerless and therefore totally dependent upon God. I felt

I needed these people to help me find the courage not to flee from my own brokenness, to keep me from mistaking classroom talk about the Trinity for real openness to the triune God in prayer. I wanted to fashion my own hermitage and pitch my tent among these people so that I could hide from the world, square off to my doubts, plunge deeply inward and dwell in the gentle, healing presence of the holy and triune God. This, I thought, was the only way I could finally understand and come to terms with the contradictions that assailed me and my priesthood.

Thomas Merton wrote that theology really happens in relations between people. What is holy in our midst has something to do with the odor of dung on a stable in Bethlehem, the fruity taste of wine on the table at Cana, and the smell of dried blood on the cross at Golgotha. Theology is also a discipline in worship and adoration. I would know it by living life with the poor inside their shanties, not by poring over volumes of forgotten lore in musty libraries and sterile lecture halls. I needed the poorest of the poor to call me back to the truth about myself. Only then could I connect theology to personal holiness and social transformation.

I decided to pass over to the Trinity in the poor and come back again to Father, Son, and Spirit in myself. Returning to the Philippines, I crossed the divide, passed over to the scavengers on Smokey Mountain, and made the garbage dump the sanctuary of my solitude.

THE THROW-AWAY SOCIETY

A society in which consumption has to be artificially stimulated in order to keep production going is a society founded on trash and waste, and such society is a house built on sand.

—Dorothy Sayers

Residents of Metro Manila throw away more than three times their weight in garbage each year. Thirty percent of the garbage remains uncollected to rot in the streets. When the rain comes, the uncollected garbage gets stuck in the sewers and canals, polluting the streams and rivers, and providing breeding places for rats and mosquitoes. Much of the rest of it ended up at Smokey Mountain.

The gigantic pile of garbage was not only a test of how much my olfactory nerves could take. It was also a probing of the heart, an examination of my fundamental allegiance. It was very difficult to engage in theology while seeing the scavengers collecting food out of trash cans from fast food restaurants, taking out the meat that was left, cooking it again and eating it afterwards. After so many years, I can still smell the rotting meat and the fat they fry it with sizzling in their cooking stoves. In light of this misery, what is the focus of my ultimate concern? In whom do I really place my trust? Evagrius Ponticus, a fourth-century monk, wrote that a theologian is someone whose prayer is true. Could I call myself a theologian at all after years of study in Rome and was my prayer true? Origen, a third-century theologian, wrote that it is a fearsome task to talk about God, even if what you say is true. I was not even sure whether the things I taught in theology class or the homilies I gave in the garbage dump were true at all.

Often when I lay awake at night, I felt that the garbage dump was a malignant being putting me to the test, trying me out, tightening the barbed wires wrapped around my heart with each passing moment to see when I would turn and run away. I wanted to run away constantly, but as I blessed and unctioned with holy oils the dead bodies of stillborn children thrown into black plastic bags, the bloodied, frail bodies of young people run over by bulldozers, the bullet-riddled bodies of suspected criminals and rebels thrown into the trash heaps, it seemed as if I heard a distant, divine voice say, "This is my body."

I was continually enveloped in an aura of dislocation, instability, and strangeness, especially when the scavengers behaved as if I was not there. Sometimes I felt I was actually invisible to the scavengers, a stranger in a strange land. I felt I was observing them from another dimension of the space-time continuum. Many of the scavengers had never seen a priest in a white cassock set foot in their dreary landscape, much less eat with them inside mosquito nets to keep the flies away from the food. I did not know what to say to them; so in the beginning, we studiously avoided each other.

I spent a lot of time meditating before the flames of the burning garbage. When I stared long and hard into the fire, I stood mesmerized. There was something mystical, hypnotic, and atavistic about it. I often saw figures of dragons, dinosaurs, troglodytes, and other kinds of monsters whenever I peered long enough into the flames. Most times, the whoosh of the burning garbage, punctuated by the explosion of aerosol cans, reminded me of the primordial fire that engulfed the entire cosmos a few nanoseconds after the Big Bang. In that primeval explosion 13.7 billion years ago came all the elements of the stuff we are made of, along with everything that ends up in the garbage dump.

Observing the garbage from multiple levels of meaning, I picked up a piece of plastic. Behind it, I imagined the factory and the workers that produced it, the chemicals and the refinery, the oil wells and the drilling machines, the bacteria by the trillions and the organic material that decomposed, the formation of planet earth and the stars that died in order to produce the different elements in it. Behind every piece of plastic in the garbage dump is the whole universe. In the suffocating heat of the crackling inferno, the deathly smell, the continuous din of garbage trucks vomiting their load, I was reminded that Smokey Mountain was a metaphor for a world gone terribly wrong.

The scavengers have a special term for the smoke coming from the burning trash. They call it *asap*. It has particulates that irritate the eyes and cause labored breathing, often suffocation in infants and very small children. It also causes acute and chronic asthma, bronchitis, emphysema, and constriction of the bronchi and tissue damage of the lungs. The particulates are also very potent carcinogens. Studies have shown that some two hundred human diseases, ranging from cerebral palsy to testicular atrophy, are linked to pollutants like these. It was estimated at the 1992 United Nations Conference on Environment and Development that more than four million children die from waste-related illnesses each year.

The scavengers' practice of manually breaking fluorescent lightbulbs to get the metal inside causes mercury in the form of vapor to escape into the environment. Inhaling mercury vapor is damaging to the brain and the central nervous systems as well as to the kidneys and the liver. Ozone is produced when the particulates in the *asap* react with hydrocarbons and nitrogen oxides under the influence of sunlight. At ground level, ozone is a destructive gas that can burn the inner lining of the lungs. Dioxins, one of the most deadly family of chemical compounds known so far, are created when other compounds are burned. Dioxin has been found in the milk of mothers living in garbage dumps. In effect, the mothers are poisoning their babies with their own milk. The milk they give to their babies would be banned by the food safety laws of developed nations if it were sold as a packaged commodity.

The dump continuously burned during the dry season due to the methane build-up that caused fires and explosions. Large amounts of chlorofluorocarbons were released into the atmosphere by spontaneous combustion, enlarging the ozone hole, contributing to global warming, emitting toxic particulates that caused disease and blackened the lungs. The toxic, blackened leachate spilled into both rivers adjoining the dump site, polluting the bay and poisoning marine life. Escaping landfill gases increased the incidence of bladder cancer and leukemia, and caused a high incidence of birth defects among the scavengers.[6]

What happens to things after they are consumed? Garbage has to go somewhere. You do not throw garbage away because there is no "away." Unless you throw it to another planet.[7] The garbage dumped on Smokey Mountain came from somewhere else, even from other countries. You create a culture of obsessive consumerism, then you have to make the land and the seas and rivers the repository of your waste; you create an environment where birds disappear, along with the frogs and the bees and the butterflies; you create an environment where children are born with compromised immune systems, where people's health is ravaged by toxins in the land, the rivers, and the air. Instead of just doing research on a cure for cancer, therefore, we need to look at our relationship with the earth and the consequent lifestyle we lead that cause cancer because we cannot create society apart from the rhythms and pulses of nature, unmindful of the connectedness that characterizes everything in the cosmos.

The world is more sensitive than we can ever imagine. Chaos theory suggests that systems are so sensitive to the slightest input that the smallest disturbance will totally change their future behavior. We cannot foresee what terrible consequences a single garbage dump can have for living things on earth. In a universe where the flap of a butterfly wing in Manila can affect a tornado in Oklahoma, even an inconsequential act, like throwing out a piece of plastic, can have tremendous consequences for the whole planet. Imagine what a garbage dump like Smokey Mountain is doing to the global ecological system. But it takes two hundred years for plastic to degrade, and garbage dumps and oceans are far away. Time and distance take away the immediate connection of the act of throwing garbage irresponsibly and the terrible consequences to the ecosystem resulting from it, and therefore our moral sense is weakened.

Creation is continually being crucified by our greed and insensitivity. We have been brainwashed to consume specific products manufactured under specific brands, and then we throw the garbage into the dump. With half of the wasted food in the United States thrown into landfills and burned in incinerators, the billion poorest in the world can be fed.[8] The wealthy produce the most garbage, and the poor suffer the greatest consequences. The scavengers were not responsible for the toxic wasteland they had to inhabit and live from, but they helped lessen the amount of stuff we place in our dump sites and landfills. They provided a vital social function by taking out all the usable plastic and metal for recycling, saving valuable resources. Scavenging to survive, they served society. But scavengers are at the lowest socioeconomic rung and endure persecution that is often motivated by the public's revulsion at the mere sight of them.[9]

Nature recycles everything. Nothing is ever wasted. Only human beings produce waste, trash, garbage, refuse, rubbish. As self-employed workers, scavengers helped sustain the very economy that marginalized them in the first place. Recycling of refuse is a very labor-intensive activity and contributes substantially to employment generation. If waste recycling and reprocessing are fully developed, more than 2 percent of the urban population could be employed. However, recycling should not be done by scavengers who live in slums, lacking basic needs such as water, sanitary facilities, electricity, health care, and a clean environment. Without gloves, rubber shoes, or protective clothing, the scavengers become prey to a host of diseases. Smog, dust, particulates, and airborne pathogens in the air cause respiratory illnesses. Skin diseases occur due to infection of cuts and wounds.

If, as Wendell Berry posits, we have become incapable of denying ourselves anything, then all that we have will be taken from us. We are now sowing seeds of malignancy in our children as we destroy the ecosystem, for instance. Children are now born with 287 chemicals in their bodies, many of them endocrine disruptors.[10] Endocrine disruptors affect the reproductive and gender-related systems in our bodies. They also cause, among others, declining intelligence quotients; behavioral abnormalities; breast, testicular, and prostate cancer; hyperthyroidism; obesity. Because of epigenetic inheritance, it would take several generations to recover from the impact of a toxic planet.

When we were novices in the seminary, a story from the Desert Fathers told of how a disciple asked the master how he could find God. The master led him to a river, pushed his head under the water, and held it there until he fought his way to the surface for air. The master told him, "When you want God as much as you then wanted air, you will find him very quickly."

Fighting to catch my breath in the suffocating miasma of the dump, I desperately wanted God to exist, because if there were no God, this would be an unkind, remorseless universe. I had to focus on the age-old question of the absence of God in the midst of the scavengers' terrible suffering. There will be no meaning to the misery of these scavengers and the death of millions who perished in concentration camps, gulags, and killing fields if God were a delusion and there was no divine retribution. It would mean that mass murderers will get away with it. There is no point in being good and avoiding evil in a universe that is "neither good nor evil, neither cruel or kind, but simply callous—indifferent to all suffering, lacking all purpose."[11] Morality then becomes relative, the end justifies the means, and whoever has the gold rules or whoever has the commandos, the cruise missiles, and the aircraft carriers.

When there was a garbage avalanche that buried several

scavengers, the few seconds it took for the mountain of trash to slide down on the hovels below etched into my mind the idea of the fragility of the planet and of my own transitory life. I quickly learned how fragile life is, how easily lost. Seeing the scavengers die horrible deaths, I was touched to the core by intimations of my own mortality. I knew in the marrow of my bones how precious life is, how rare it is. I learned that faith must teach us humility and respect for life, all life, from conception to death. Such an insight hours of reflection in the idyllic ambience of the seminary would never have produced.

The garbage dump told me I would not last forever.

At the beginning, I stayed at Smokey Mountain only on weekends. I slept in a small chapel. I was afraid to contend with the horror, the terror, and the furor if I decided to live full time in the dump site. Thinking of the lost potential of these people placed me in a constant state of puzzlement. I often returned to the seminary sick with grief. Why this monstrosity of human degradation among innocent, inarticulate people who could not even tell one another adequately of their frustration and their dreams? The scavengers were human beings like me; they bled when pricked and they laughed when tickled, but they lived in shacks and shanties made out of cartons, wooden packing cases, and discarded sheets of corrugated metal, no bathroom and toilet, without running water and electricity, in shacks and shanties where sometimes eighteen people took turns sleeping in the night. I had a comfortable room in the seminary much larger than their hovels.

I always went back to the seminary to teach theology with my head full of hissing cobras. I felt it was not a life-sustaining path for me to merely deliver theological lectures to class after class of seminarians who were either bored out of their ears or had no deep interest in the issues I wanted to confront. I wanted my theology to make a difference in the lives of real people. My mind kept touching the edges of new, self-defining thoughts. The entire geography of my life had been transformed by strange insights, but no one had given me a new map.

I had to make a choice again and again between remaining a professor of theology, ignorant but comfortable in my room in the seminary, or seeking the truth about myself and the certainty of being ambushed by pain in the dump site. The physical toll Smokey Mountain took on my body was considerable, but its assaults on my mind and soul were even more horrendous. I was standing in a dark cloud of unknowing where, as Zen teaches, there is no place to stand.

When I was not able to stand the dichotomy any longer, I built a small hut on Smokey Mountain and dwelt among the scavengers.

REMEMBRANCES OF THINGS PAST

A society capable of naming itself lives within its stories, inhabiting and furnishing them. We ride stories like rafts, or lay them out on the table, like maps.
    —William Kittridge, *The Nature of Generosity*

The old folks still remember a time when the area around the garbage dump was surrounded by a beautiful shoreline. The beaches were pristine and the sunsets majestic and glorious.

Aling Marina was born in 1925 in Isla de Balut. Her mother, Pilar, who came from Bulacan, was only three years old when her parents died. Her aunt brought her to Balut. They lived near the shore in a place called *Kolorum*. Vicente Saturnino from Baguio woocd and married Pilar in 1924. They built a house by the sea, which was connected to other houses by wooden pathways. Aling Marina was born shortly afterwards. She remembers falling asleep as a little girl listening to the crashing of the waves under the house.[12] The dump site was then a peaceful village dotted by a few thatched huts. Fishermen sailed the rivers and Manila Bay in their frail outriggers. They always had plenty of fish to bring home. One could even fish from the wooden piers or gather seaweeds, mussels, oysters, clams, and sea cucumbers along the seashore. It was called *Barrio Magdaragat*—Fishermen's Village.

Aling Marina still remembered very clearly: "We were always taking a bath in the sea for hours on end with our friends. We only went home when the sun set like a big red ball of fire on Manila Bay." She remembered collecting a lot of starfish and listening to the murmuring of the sea by holding conch shells to her ears. One could still peer at the starfish and the seaweeds below several feet of aquamarine water then. She told me that they could still see the bottom of Marala River and Estero de Vitas while riding bancas to visit friends and relatives in the other villages. On Sundays, people from the other districts of Manila held picnics on the shore. They went home only when it was dark. Everyone had enough to eat then.

The peace of the village was shattered by World War II. Aling Marina remembered watching the dogfights of fighter planes over Manila Bay as a young girl, the planes sometimes plunging into the water in balls of fire. She also remembered seeing dead bodies washed up on the beach. When Bataan fell, Manila was declared an open city. The Japanese built a big garrison near Aling Marina's home.

After the war, she and her husband built a house near the sea once again. The area was called "Quonset" after the structures built by the Americans during liberation. A daughter, Normelita, was born in 1946. Aling Marina often brought her for picnics on the beach with her relatives.

The city government started dumping garbage in 1954. From then on, Aling Marina recounted, as the heap of garbage grew, more people who earned their livelihood before as fishermen came to work as scavengers. There were a lot of fights and riots. Gang wars erupted. Criminals roamed the alleys at night. The fishing ground became polluted by the garbage. Untreated sewage poured into the two rivers north and south of the barrio. The water became dark and turgid. It emitted a foul odor that caused vomiting in people with weak stomachs.

It was either a foreign journalist or a Norwegian missionary who called the dump site "Smokey Mountain," sarcastically comparing it to the Smoky Mountains in the United States. It became a regular stop for foreign journalists, especially after Ferdinand and Imelda Marcos were deposed. The sordid plight of hundreds of scavengers on Smokey Mountain made an interesting comparison with the three thousand pairs of shoes in Malacañang Palace. Tourists came to gawk at the scavengers in the trash heaps as if looking at exotic fauna in a zoo.

I talked to Aling Marina shortly before she died. She sighed wistfully, "They cannot restore this place to its former beauty, Father Ben." She believed it was a sacrilege, a grave insult to the Creator, when human beings destroy the beauty of the world. The memories of Aling Marina on Smokey Mountain portray the undeniable, unsustainable and yet politically untouchable long-term challenges Filipinos are facing today—rapid depletion of resources, exploding population growth, corrupt politicians, economists worshipping the free market calling for even more industrialization and urbanization, and more and more garbage. We have to be able to summon the will, the archetypal energies in the depths of our being, to bring forth the capability to face these challenges caused by the clash of worldviews. The older folks' memories of its former beauty should inspire us with the courage to undertake the moral responsibility to save the earth for future generations and remain faithful stewards in conserving the earth's resources and fertility from generation to generation.

THE BEGINNINGS OF SMOKEY MOUNTAIN

Why do men then now not reck his rod?
Generations have trod, have trod, have trod;
All is seared with trade; bleared, smeared with toil;
And wears man's smudge and shares man's smell: the soil
Is bare now, nor can foot feel, being shod.
        —Gerard Manley Hopkins, "God's Grandeur"

When the city government of Manila started dumping garbage in the village in 1954, the residents found out that money could be made by selling plastic scrap and other recyclable items. Scavenging thereafter began in earnest. The increasing influx of migrants from the provinces soon exerted tremendous strain on the amount of recoverable trash. The residents became threatened by the rush of newcomers who soon outnumbered them. Fights broke out afterwards over the rights to a particular section of the garbage heap. Spears, jungle bolos, *Indian pana* (a kind of arrow propelled by slingshot), and *sumpak* (homemade shotgun) were the usual weapons used during a "riot." The Tagalogs were members of a gang called *Sigue-Sigue*, and the Visayans belonged to the OXO gang. From fighting over trash, the gangs fought over territory. Vendetta then took over and even more people died. The whole district of Tondo became notorious because of these gang wars, a notoriety that remains to this day. Garbage, gangs, and drugs were a potent recipe for violence.

Basura in the vernacular means garbage. A *basurero* is a professional trash picker, a scavenger poking among piles of plastic, pieces of metal, discarded cathode ray monitors and cellphones, rags, bits of broken furniture and mattresses, tin cans, broken lamps, decaying fruit and vegetables, and household appliances mixed with the bodies of dead animals decomposing under the tropical sun. The usual day began by waking up very early when one's turn to scavenge was during the daytime. Those whose turn was to scavenge during the night trekked home to take their turn to sleep. There was very little capital outlay needed: a steel hook, a large wicker basket or sack, perhaps rubber boots, and the *basurero* could join the throng to pick the trash. They then cleaned and sorted it, had it weighed, brought it to be sold to junkshop owners, rested a little, and then went back to work.

As soon as the trucks dumped their load, hordes of *basureros,* heads and faces covered except for the eyes, fell on the garbage like vultures upon a carcass. Everyone raced and scrambled to pick and pry and poke for tin cans, pieces of metal and rubber, bottles and plastic jugs, jute and cement sacks, cardboard, or pieces of bone. Others kept what they scavenged as raw material for rags, dustpans, toys, picture frames, or pendants. Still others burned the rubber and plastic covering of electric wiring to get the copper inside. The *basureros* also got building materials for their shanties, firewood, and the occasional food, sometimes partly rotten, often with parts already teeming with maggots, from the trash heaps. Sometimes, they chanced upon a valuable item, a piece of jewelry, an envelope with money inside perhaps, sometimes a handgun or a usable cellphone. There was also a lot of business with forks and spoons and cooking utensils thrown away with the garbage.

The usual family on Smokey Mountain was crowded in an improvised arrangement of plywood, iron sheets, cardboard, and cloth. Pieces of rock and rubber tires were placed on the roof to keep it from being blown away by the wind. A few hovels were fenced with rusty bedsprings. Everyone lived in a single room—cramped, dirty, and very hot. The hovels were clustered close to one another. These *barong-barongs* take only a few hours to build. In a single night, hundreds of these hovels can spring up in an illegal settlement area. The bolder ones stole electricity from the poles, climbing them at night to loop strands of wire around the fences. Several of them were electrocuted. The current was so weak when it reached the shanties they had to buy bulbs of 110 volts, instead of the usual 220 volts. Since their shanties were on the periphery of the dump, the *basureros* did not have to travel far or spend money for transportation. They did not pay rent on the land or income tax on their earnings, but the huts built close to the sea were easily carried away by waves during typhoons. Those at the edge of the garbage heap sometimes got buried in the avalanche of trash when heavy rain poured down from the top.

Jumpers were those who leapt on top of the garbage trucks going the rounds to collect the trash bags. Jumpers needed physical stamina and a sense of balance as they jumped from truck to truck. They often fell or got crushed during accidents. It was a physically exhausting job, but it gave them first pick over the garbage. The weaker ones followed in the wake of the bulldozer at the dump site and were sometimes run over. The smaller boys went around the streets of the city with pushcarts (*kariton*) and scavenged for recyclables while the garbage was still piled in the streets. They usually went out after dark in twos or threes. Outside the dump site, they had to face the humiliation of being called "garbage people," looked down upon as scum of the earth, and suspected of being thieves and criminals.

Sometimes the police impounded the pushcarts and even burned them. There is a law against scavenging in the streets because the scavengers scatter the garbage, making the streets even dirtier, according to the police. The pushcart boys often became victims of extortion. They were also easy prey for drunks and drug addicts who asked for their hard-earned money or beat them up without provocation. In spite of the dangers, the *kariton* boys persisted in roaming the streets for garbage because they have less competition. Others roamed the streets in sidecars, a sort of tricycle, so that they do not become too conspicuous and invite scorn or suspicion.

A former *kariton boy* who shifted to being a jumper recalled some of his experiences to me: "During the rainy season, we were always drenched to the bone. Our clothes just dried on our bodies. I can still remember the storms during the rainy season and the blinding dust of summer, the cold of the nights and the smell of the garbage piles. Once we even found a dead person among the heaps of trash. We slept in our pushcarts when we got too tired. Our only blanket was our weariness and our pillow the garbage we picked up. If the streets were flooded, the water sometimes reached up to our waists. Our pushcarts floated in the water!"

He blew on the wood fire to cook the rice in a stove, and then continued: "When we arrived at the dump site, we had to push the carts in the muck. Worms squirmed up our legs. Only the thought of my wife and children who would have nothing to eat would give me strength to reach the junkyard and sell my stuff to the buyer. We never had enough money for necessities. My little boy died due to an infected navel. He only lived for eight days. It was too late when we brought him to the clinic."

He was once caught by the police for carrying a concealed weapon. He always carried one, he says, to protect himself from drug addicts. He had to borrow money to pay the bribe so that there would be no court hearing. He laments, "Sometimes you try to live a dignified life, and people prevent you from doing so. But perhaps all this is the will of God."

Many scavengers struggle to maintain their integrity in very difficult situations. One scavenger remembered his brother who was buried in a garbage avalanche. They were able to dig him out in a few minutes. He survived. His mother was not as lucky. It took them several hours to dig her out because they had to look for a payloader. She was already dead when they dug her out. He also remembers how lightning killed several of his companions as they were sifting the ashes by the sea to look for coins, pieces of metal, and other items to be sold.

The *manlilibis* are those who sift through the ashes of the burned garbage or pan the effluent near the water. They use a pick to loosen the garbage, which is only partially rotten or burned. They then burn it again to look for coins, bones, metal, copper, glass shards, tin cans, or aluminum with their scavenger's hook after pouring sea water on the ashes. "Sometimes I came upon pieces of gold and jewelry after sifting the ashes through a wire mesh," one of them remembered. "That was the way our world turned. We had to endure the heat of the sun, the smoke from the burning garbage, and we inhaled dust and ashes. We did not give up. We endured all this in order to live an honorable and dignified existence (*mabuhay ng marangal*). It is better than to be a robber or a thief." They told me, quoting an old Filipino proverb, "What is the use of eating in a golden plate if one is made to vomit blood?" They would prefer scavenging with a clear conscience, they said.

Junk shop dealers are the relatively affluent in the dump site. Many of them started as scavengers. By dint of hard work and thrift, they were able to save some capital to buy things from the other scavengers, jumpers, pushcart boys, and the panniers. They were able to sell to the factory owners directly. When they were able to own several pushcarts, they acted as feudal lords. They lent money to the other scavengers in need, who were then forced to sell their stuff only to them at a much lower price, of course. They were able sometimes to buy second-hand trucks.

Living among these people easily strips from one's life all superfluities and petty distractions; it is relationships that matter most to them. The harmonious negotiation of interpersonal affairs with the extended family brings reassurance, recognition, and even material rewards. Although they accept handouts, what they really want is not pity but respect. They are willing to pay for housing or land. Contrary to stereotypes about the indolence of the Filipinos, the people on Smokey Mountain work very hard. They have to work very hard, because it takes a long time of scrounging in the trash heaps to find a kilo of aluminum cans they can sell for a pittance, especially if they have to compete with hundreds of other scavengers. They carry heavy loads of baled plastic or cartons down the slippery slopes of the dump to the weighing scales of junk shop owners at all times of the day and night. They do it for their loved ones, so the work is not so hard, they told me.

Choices define us—they are all that we can call our own. Even scavengers make their own choices to define themselves. Scavengers, pushcart boys, jumpers, panniers, and buyers—denizens of Smokey Mountain. They all say they should not only be called the poorest of the poor, but the purest of the poor. They could easily have been criminals, but they chose to endure the smell of the garbage dump in order to feed their families. The *basureros* believe that those who do not value, above all, the interest of the group or the extended family lose their *pagkatao*, their essential human quality. Scavengers always resented the fact that they are seen mostly as criminals, dirty people with infectious diseases, thieves, prostitutes, or drug addicts, when most of them only want to find their own place in the sun.

WOMEN OF THE DUMP

To my sister Hildegard and all her sisters, past, present and to come, in a hope that their wisdom will cease to be repressed, ridiculed, forgotten and otherwise excluded from church, society and culture, so that the earth might be blessed and mutuality might be the law of the land.
—Matthew Fox, Foreword, *Mystical Visions of Hildegard of Bingen*

Women constituted a very vulnerable sector in the garbage dump. Apart from scavenging, they survived by their wits as manicurists, domestic helpers, street vendors selling all kinds of things, or selling lottery tickets for illegal gambling called "jueteng." They said they were forever teetering at the edge of survival.

Because they were poor and because they were women, women scavengers on Smokey Mountain were doubly oppressed. They had no medical insurance, social welfare, or benefits of any kind. Often they had to resort to faith-healing or go to quack doctors when they or their children got sick because they could not afford to go to a hospital or buy the medicines. They had to work twice as hard to help their families survive, to compensate for the lack of male employment opportunities, and then do the household chores. Some went to work as domestic helpers abroad. Many of them were duped by the employment agencies and were saddled with even more debt. Others were physically abused or raped. They had to come home through the charity of other people or the government. The men found work irregularly as construction workers, living in makeshift barracks at the site, or as stevedores on the pier. Then when the work was finished, they went back to scavenging again. Or they pedaled a "sidecar," a sort of a pedicab, owned by another person who they had to pay a daily quota. Since there were too many of these in the line, they slept or drank and gambled while waiting for passengers.

Apart from scavenging directly, the women and the little girls also washed bottles scavenged from the dump. Sometimes they baled plastic bags, or cut rubber interiors used to bind fish basins. They also ran food stalls and small stores in the dump site. Others gathered slop from the dump site to feed a few pigs they raised at the back of their shanties. When a half-rotten piece of fruit was found, they cut out the rotten part and ate the rest. After a hard day of scavenging, they still had to do the household chores. The women had to fetch water from far away and pay ten times more for their water than the rich in gated communities. And then they give birth in the squalid circumstances of their hovels, the baby literally wrapped in swaddling clothes and rags. When I blessed their still-born children or their babies who died before their time, I tried to reconcile this with the joy the Lord cited when the child is born after the birthpangs of the mother.

Sometimes the women got beaten up by a drunken husband when there was little food on the table. I have blessed the bodies of men stabbed to death by their wives who were no longer able to endure the beatings of their live-in terrorists. I wondered what the husband was thinking while beating up his wife. And I wondered how the women could take it. "I can stand the pain, Father Ben," one told me while I looked at the body of her husband that lay sprawled on the floor with a deep knife wound in the chest. "It is the humiliation before my children that I can no longer endure." It is a wonder there are not many more men killed in the same manner. Most men in the dump site do not have much of an inner life to speak of—it is all work, being with their drinking buddies, and watching the fights or basketball on television. Perhaps the ones killed by their wives did not even understand why their wives did it.

My pity soon turned to awe as I saw the women's indomitable spirit and gritty determination to survive, even prosper sometimes, in the face of society's neglect and even hostility. They reminded me always of the Gospels comparing the love of the triune God to a woman searching for a lost coin (Luke 15:8-10), or a woman baking bread (Luke 13:20). I was also reminded of the widows' mite when they placed blackened coins that they had picked up from the burning trash in the collection box during Mass.

There was a lot of entrepreneurial activity going on in the slum areas and in the dump sites, but the women earned so little. The economic activity going on in the dump site was all informal, all below the radar of those who calculate the nation's gross domestic product. The best way to fight poverty is to unleash the potential of women like these informal entrepreneurs. The most effective way to help the women scavengers to increase their income is to bring profitability to their informal enterprises. If their energy can be released by providing them with added opportunities, a way out poverty can be found. Women from poor communities all over the world might still save the global economy.

THE GARBAGE CHILDREN

Children are the world's most valuable resource and its best hope for the future.

—John F. Kennedy

On an ordinary day, hundreds of children and young people could be seen competing with adults over the garbage. Sometimes they were run over by the trucks and bulldozers. If the muck was soft enough, they survived, usually as invalids. They also sometimes fell into the burning pits and got their feet burned. According to a report entitled "Findings on the Worst Forms of Child Labor," submitted by U.S. Labor Secretary Hilda Solis on December 15, 2010, the Philippines is where the "worst form of child labor continue to exist, perpetuating a cycle of poverty and often denying children the chance to attend school and learn the skills they need to become productive adults." The report indicates that the exploitation of Filipino children happens mostly in prostitution, pornography, and the sex tourism industry, as well as in agriculture, domestic work, drug trafficking, and child soldiering.

The dignity and integrity of the human person is seen clearly in children. The right to survival of children and infants in the dump site was always in the balance, since children were most vulnerable to disease and malnutrition. Often parents forced their children to scavenge in order to augment the family's income. The very young often got sick from extreme heat and exhaustion. They were constantly exposed to hospital waste like used syringes, blood, and body parts thrown into the dump. They were also exposed to mercury vapor pollution when they break toxic lamps to get to the metal inside. Mercury is highly toxic and, if ingested, inhaled, or absorbed through the skin, can damage the brain and the central nervous system and cause other serious diseases. The children had little protection from harmful influences like drug addiction and a culture of crime. They were sometimes physically assaulted and sexually harassed. Their childhood had been stolen from them. They had been dumped like garbage in the trash heaps.

There was a high incidence of upper–respiratory tract illnesses, such as bronchitis, asthma, and pneumonia, due to the smoke from burning garbage. Aside from infection and malnutrition, the deaths of child scavengers were mostly due to parasitic diseases and diarrhea. The local health department is chronically too underfunded and understaffed to make much of a difference. The children were first brought to shamans and quack doctors, and then brought to the hospital only when it was often too late to save them. If they did not die early, the children in the garbage dump also faced a shortened life span due to chronic, weakening or incapacitating illnesses. Child scavengers suffered from cuts, scratches, and burns incurred while working in the dump site. They were run over by bulldozers every now and then. Some had their skulls bashed in by back-hoe shovels. Still others were buried by an avalanche of decomposing garbage.

Drunken, violent fathers, negligent mothers, physical abuse, even incest added to the suffering of the young scavengers. It was very difficult not to weep while bringing abused little girls and boys to the social welfare, their faces bereft of all feeling. Their backs, arms, and legs were covered with scars and bruises, proof of lives that had only known pain and despair.

Many infants died stillborn. Often the little ones did not survive to their fifth year. According to a 1990 UNDP report, the infant mortality rate for the Philippines is sixty-six deaths per one thousand births. An estimated 4,500 women die every year because of complications from pregnancy and childbirth. The rate was much higher on Smokey Mountain for infants and mothers. As I looked at the little children playing in the muck, I always wondered how many of them would reach the age of five. Disease would kill many of them. Those who survived, lacking protein due to undernourishment and because of pollution, would have low intelligence quotients. A measles epidemic would sometimes kill thirty babies within two weeks. I have lost count of the infants I blessed in their coffins, perhaps two or three every week sometimes. I played with them one day, and the next they have been embalmed, lying so innocently in their cheap coffins or cardboard boxes. Sometimes I saw lice crawling on the faces of the little girls as they lay dead in their hovels, and it was almost more than I could bear. I could not even conceive the depths of the parents' anguish. The children were all that they had.

I explained to the parents that there were already too many people in the world, and the resources of the environment were stretched to the limit. The mothers said, however, that they wanted to have many children because they thought many would die anyway, so they conceived many times in hopes that some of them would survive into adulthood. They also needed children to help with the household chores, take care of the smaller ones, and work with them in the dump site. Parents also needed their children to take care of them when they got old (there is no such thing as social security in garbage dumps). Still, I always asked why the burden of planning the family was laid on the shoulders of the women alone.

Lewis Thomas has noted that the population problem is

part of a system of problems that has to be solved in a logical sequence. The poor have health problems because of poverty and malnutrition, which are partly the result of overpopulation, which in turn is the result of disease, poverty, and malnutrition. Their worldview and understanding of family also have to be considered. Thomas says that the massive population explosion already under way and beyond control is based in large part on the reproductive drive among people now deprived of almost everything except reproduction itself.[13]

The African statesman Julius Nyerere once noted that "the most powerful contraceptives are the confidence by parents that their children will survive." If development goals do not consider seriously the problems of social justice, birth control devices and techniques will continually be ignored by the poor. The vicious circle then endlessly revolves around the population explosion and diminishing resources. And development agencies will go on spending fortunes on condoms and IUD's to give to them, forgetting that they are poor therefore they are many, not the other way around.

DEATH AND DYING IN THE GARBAGE DUMP

*Nothing that is worth doing can be achieved in our
    lifetime,
Therefore we must be saved by hope.
Nothing which is true or beautiful or good makes
    complete sense
In any immediate context of history;
Therefore, we must be saved by faith.
Nothing we do, however virtuous, can be
    accomplished alone.
Therefore we must be saved by love.*
                                    —Reinhold Niebuhr

Omay was a *kariton boy*. One morning, his body was found along the highway beside his pushcart. He had been badly beaten, then stabbed many times with an ice pick, and strangled with a piece of plastic rope. His body bore marks of horrendous torture. There were rumors that Omay had a string of criminal offenses. It was another case of "salvaging," the Filipino euphemism for termination with extreme prejudice, extrajudicial killing, or summary execution. The funeral parlor asked for $4,300, more than $100, an enormous sum for scavengers. Omay's neighbors and relatives had to run an instant gambling joint to raise the money from the *tong* (percentage of winnings) collected to augment what little alms they were able to beg. Some went to ask for donations from relatives in other parts of the city. They ran away with the money afterwards. As the scavengers say, *patay na, pinapatay pa*—already dead but still being killed. A few days later, when I came to bless Omay's coffin, his relatives discovered there were already worms on his feet. The agents for the funeral parlor assured them the embalming was good for fifteen days. They lied.

It always takes a long time for the dead to be buried on Smokey Mountain. The city government buries the dead for free in a common plot within twenty-four hours after death, but the scavengers want to be with their dead for at least a few days. Asked why they do not avail themselves of the free burial, an elderly scavenger said to me, "We already live like rats when we are alive. At least, we should be buried as human beings." They often wait for close relatives to come from afar before the funeral date is set. The funeral thus becomes an important social event. It is a time of deep emotional sorrow. They want a private plot in the cemetery, not a pauper's grave, so that they can visit on All Souls' Day, every November 2. They bring food and drinks to offer on the tombs of their dead relatives on that day. And that is why even if it costs a fortune, the scavengers on Smokey Mountain make the sacrifice of borrowing money from loan sharks so that in death, at least, they are made to feel they are also human.

Life was cheap among the trash heaps. The open dump site was not only a dumping place for garbage, but also of dead bodies. I blessed the bodies of those who were "salvaged" during the martial law era—people terminated with extreme prejudice either by government authorities or criminal syndicates. Sometimes the bodies were still warm; at other times, the face and the extremities were already partially eaten by rats. I blessed the nameless, faceless victims like Omay who were not important enough to warrant a byline from the newspapers and sympathy from society at large. They had laughed and cried, known terror and pain. They had families and friends who would mourn and miss them. Many of them were innocent of the crimes imputed to them, but no trials were ever held in a court of law.

The dead sometimes remained unburied for weeks, and the cadavers turned different shades of green and gray. Molds and fungus grew around their eyes and lips. Fatty liquids coagulated under their coffins. There were nights after a day blessing cadavers that I had nightmares of the rotting bodies tied to each other with blue plastic rope floating above me while I struggled to rise to the surface of the fetid *estero* (large canal), gasping for breath, lungs burning, the oil on the surface of the effluvium aflame. I often woke up drenched with sweat, almost delirious, after nightmares like these.

Yeshua bar-Yosef did not just die, he was brutally murdered in Golgotha, just like all those people whose corpses were dumped on Smokey Mountain. We fool ourselves if we try to gloss over the terrifying fact that Christ died in bitter agony in a garbage dump outside the gates of Jerusalem. He experienced the most cruel form of death in order to show us how insignificantly mortal we are and how terrible sin must be if that was the price he had to pay. He came into history in complete weakness to unmask the illusion of power of those who murder others without being called into account for it.

Lasting peace, enduring justice, and a future that is without threats can only come when the reign of God arrives in its fullness. In the meantime, those who pay the price of achieving some kind of social transformation can gaze upon the Cross of the Nazarene, consoled by the shared faith in the one who was crucified for humanity and will reign eternally. To approach God in the cloud of unknowing is not a popularity contest. Those who hunger and thirst for justice will often suffer persecution and might even lose their lives. The greatest lessons that life teaches always involve great loss. Beneath the surface, where loss discloses itself, is where one must begin the journey into solitude to reach God's dazzling truth as one breaks through the cloud of unknowing. The cloud of unknowing symbolizes the ultimate unknowability of God.[14] It also symbolizes the quantum indeterminacy of reality and the openness of the future in an ongoing process of cosmic evolution. This openness overwhelmingly suggests that the universe is about something, that there is a meaning to it, and we are part of whatever future there will be, death notwithstanding.

GRIEF, TERROR, AND RAGE

> *God guard me from those thoughts men think*
> *In the mind alone;*
> *He that sings a lasting song*
> *Thinks in a marrowbone.*
>   —William Butler Yeats, "A Prayer for Old Age"

After some time among the scavengers came the anger—a terrible, unyielding rage whose power and intensity surprised me. I was already an angry seminarian during the time of the conjugal dictatorship of Ferdinand and Imelda Marcos, having experienced first-hand during summer camps the oppression of the peasants by the military in the countryside and the profligacy of many of the absentee landlords living in gated communities in the city. I endured the tear gas of the police as we manned the barricades during demonstrations and rallies against martial law. Many of my companions in those rallies, consumed by their own anger, disappeared without a trace after they took up arms and joined the Communist rebels in the mountains. The temptation was always there to make a whip of cords and, like the Galilean consumed by zeal for his Father's house (John 2:17), drive the people responsible for the dying of the children in the garbage dump and the thieves pillaging the resources of my country out of this planet, to the farthest black hole billions of light years away.

When Mother Teresa visited the dump site, she told me, "Father Ben, no one should live as scavengers on Smokey Mountain because the Philippines is a Christian country." A country where a few hundred families control political and economic power can hardly be called Christian, even if more than 90 percent have been baptized. The scavengers in the garbage dump are not alone in their misery. Thirty-two million Filipinos, out of a total population of ninety-five million, survive on less than $1 a day in a land rich in natural resources. But unlike Mother Teresa, very few seem troubled by this stark reality of injustice, just as very few are troubled by a mountain of garbage rotting in the very heart of their city. I think that if politicians, scientists, religious leaders, and corporate decision makers had scavengers as neighbors, they would do much more and sooner to solve the problem of global poverty. If they could see the black vomit and greenish excrement with intestinal parasites deposited by the children from the slums in the driveways of their gated communities and beachfront mansions, in their laboratories, cathedrals, and corporate offices, I believe the scandal of global poverty would be solved in no time at all. Moral responsibility can be more easily responded to in face-to-face relationships between the global elites and the people affected by their decisions and their ways of life.

I kept trying to convince myself again and again that what I was doing made a difference in the lives of the poor somehow. The anger and the inner torment snarled and snapped inside my heart like molting pythons and wounded crocodiles stalking the fetid swamps of my childhood as I lay awake at night. I heard in my brain the bulldozers and the screams and the babble, together with the smoke burning its way into my throat. That, in itself, let me know how alone I was as I grappled with the suffering, the sadness, and the dying. There I was, afraid of the "otherness" of the scavengers, coming from Rome with a theology based on God as the *Ipsum Esse Subsistens* (the Being whose essence is to exist), trying to grapple with the findings of quantum physics about "becoming" and searching for ways faith in the Trinity could be explained in that new view of reality, which sees relationships as all there is in the universe.

How alone can one feel?

But like a bolt of lightning, it also struck me that we are always alone. It is unfair for me to burden the scavengers with taking away this aloneness. No person, no thing in the universe will be able to "live up to our absolutistic expectations," wrote

Henri Nouwen. It is enough to gain access into the other's inner world. But still, nearness does not guarantee this intimacy. We can only love the human race by loving particular human beings who cannot totally be trusted to love us in return or never abandon us. I had to reflect on how best to relate to the scavengers as the "other," because there was a still small voice that constantly warned me, "Don't get too close. They will go away or die and then your heart will be broken." We are always afraid that we will be engulfed by emotional closeness, torn apart by personal intimacy, by betrayal or by abandonment when the "other" leaves or dies. No connection, no danger of emotional pain.

In my pastoral work in the dump, it was not so much spending time in careful planning but in coping with the unforeseeable and the chaotic, depending on serendipity to lead to new opportunities or new terrors. Simple presence and attention were difficult to achieve; there were always children to bring to the hospital, fights to mediate, and many other distractions. Unpredictability, disequilibrium, loss of control and the occasional chaos when rival gangs rioted characterized my life in the garbage dump. I also had to shield myself from the daily horrors I encountered just to be able to continue to function. I was able to understand the seeming callousness of scavengers as they cracked scatological jokes while crowding around a murder victim thrown into the garbage dump. When all of a person's life is spent just surviving, there is no time for etiquette and polite conversation.

The scavengers regularly found fetuses wrapped in rags or placed in boxes thrown away by their mothers. As soon as they were born, they were asphyxiated and thrown away. Some looked so beautiful, they took my breath away. The scavengers remarked that they would have won in a Miss Universe contest if they had grown up. The smaller ones in black plastic bags must have come from abortion clinics. The scavengers solemnly buried them at the edge of the dump site or brought them to me to be blessed. There were so many through the years that I was often tempted to remove the sandals from my feet for the dump site I was standing on was "holy ground" (Exod. 3:5). It was the hallowed burial place of countless innocents. Numberless futures ended on Smokey Mountain because mothers abandoned all hope for the children in their wombs.

It is the infants' wails I hear from afar when silence fills the air in the dead of the night, dead babies moaning in low, miserable voices at the back of my brain. The desperation of my nightmares (in vivid colors) always involved fire—being a passenger on a plane with engines on fire, or trapped in a building with the flames licking my heels as I try to escape. I often dreamed of dying children locked inside burning buildings in the middle of killing fields and concentration camps. I listened helplessly to their tortured lament, now rhythmic, now raging, relentlessly calling on me to save them from the flames. The sound and images of scorched infants haunt my sleep with these desperate, disordered dreams, dreams that wash away large chunks of my soul each night. The infants' screams I hear in my dreams seem even louder and agonizing whenever I am tempted to just run away from the horror of it all.

I was always afraid on Smokey Mountain, even if I tried my best to hide it. Pure, visceral fear gripped my insides as I caught glimpses beneath the placid exterior of a people who looked very gentle, of the potential for violence that their ready smiles denied, and of the capacity to inflict pain that lurked just beneath the surface of their laughter. And yet among them, there was a culture of compassion. They helped each other in difficult times. This culture of compassion did not extend beyond what they considered their territory, however. The people across the two rivers bounding the dump site were considered mortal enemies. The cycle of violence and vengeance fueled hatred for decades. The peace in the dump site would now and again be shattered by the blast of a homemade shotgun or the commotion caused by another stabbing incident or by a platoon of policemen with Armalite rifles coming to seek and destroy, without benefit of due process, another suspect hiding in one of the hovels. Sometimes I collected the empty cartridges and placed these on the altar to remind myself always of the way Jesus died.

I was always terrified of catching a disease and passing it on to the confreres in the seminary, especially after I joined a wake for someone who died of an infectious disease. A few confreres who worked in the dump with me contracted life-threatening infections and had to leave. I was horrified when a dermatologist once suspected a blotch in my skin as the beginnings of leprosy. But in my most intimate moments, when I was honest with myself, my greatest fear was not of a violent death or of infectious diseases. It was encountering the alien "otherness" of the scavengers that I was really afraid of. We are always afraid of those who are different from us, perhaps because it undermines the centrality of the self. We are afraid because encountering the other means we will somehow be changed. I used my "otherness" as a priest to shield myself from real encounter with the scavengers because of this fear. But in the end, I realized that even if I was constantly afraid, I did not have to be dominated by my fear.

The children were something else. They laughed with such heartbreaking sincerity that I forgot my terrors for a moment, their smile like gentle raindrops falling upon a parched earth. I was never afraid of them, even when those with terrifying skin diseases touched my hand to their foreheads. I was expecting that the horrors of living in a garbage dump would be visible in the children, that the squalor would sculpt their faces, chisel their bodies into angles of rage and dread, and paint a morbid sheen of desolation in their eyes. Instead, I was surrounded by smiling faces, their eyes calm pools in which were reflected the depths of a gentleness like a flight of butterflies in the moonlight. These were the same kind of children's faces I saw in the dump sites of Mumbai and Johannesburg; among the poor in Anacostia and Washington, DC; in Roxbury, Boston; in Nairobi, Kenya; and in many other slum areas I visited.

The gentleness of the gaze of these children and their smiles condemn us all.

HOPE SPRINGS ETERNAL

At a time of world food shortage, of financial turmoil, of old and new forms of poverty, of disturbing climate change,

of violence and depravation which force many to leave their
homelands in search of a less precarious form of existence,
of the ever-present threat of terrorism, of growing fears
over the future, it is urgent to rediscover grounds for hope.
—Pope Benedict XVI, Easter Message, April 12, 2009

In my dark night and existential dread, I turned to the poor
and yearned for meaning. Living with the poor, I yearned for
justice. Turning towards the immensity of the universe, I yearned
for God. But I found out God is a hidden God.

Where my passion for shalom intersected with the misery
of the scavengers, I found myself immersed in a great cloud of
unknowing. I had to leave behind ideas, images, and symbols,
and learn how to approach the divine humbly in fear and trembling. The intense longing for the transcendent that held me in
its grip came face to face with the incomprehensible mystery
of the triune God in the squalor of the garbage dump. And in
the encounter with the cloud of unknowing, I discovered hope.

I am extremely fortunate to have been given a glimpse of the
scavengers' world of meaning and faith, the world in which they
lived their lives and died their deaths without complaint or fear.
Their existence in the midst of squalor was a powerful witness
to me of a hope much more vital than mine, a hope that sees
them through the darkest night. I say this not only after having
lived with them for thirty years, but also after hearing countless
confessions when they bared their wounded spirits and were
made whole again by my blessing. I am also fortunate to have
been their companion as they fought for justice and a sustainable
future for their loved ones. In light of prophetic dialogue with
them, I realized that theology should not only be a *fides quaerens
intellectum* (faith seeking understanding), a purely cognitive approach to theological inquiry. In today's world, theology should
also be linked to social concerns as *fides quaerens justitiam* (faith
seeking justice), *fides quaerens pacem* (faith seeking peace) ,and
fides quaerens vitam (faith seeking life).[15]

It was the scavengers who taught me how to hold on to the
frustration and the tension between learned ignorance and
theology as a discourse on God. Dionysius the Areopagite, a

mystic writer in the sixth century, declared, "At the end of all our knowing, we shall know God as the unknown." After thirty years among the scavengers, I finally learned in the marrow of my bones that the ultimate in human knowledge, as St. Thomas Aquinas wrote, is to know that we do not know God. But in the darkness of this faith, I discovered hope.

Hope is a way of knowing things beyond the empirical, it lies beyond reasoning and cannot be adequately expressed in words, much like the entanglement of quarks and the leptons of quantum physics. In the midst of the cloud of unknowing, hope believes that the holy and triune God is deeply engaged in all of human history in the context of an emergent cosmos. In light of worldwide poverty, widespread terrorism, and environmental degradation, this hope is being challenged today to question the basic assumptions of the prevailing, predominantly Western worldview: the assumption that human beings have the right to completely subdue and dominate the whole of creation, the myth that consumption equals happiness and fulfillment, the unbridled avarice that victimizes people who are already oppressed and disenfranchised, and the unquestioning belief that technological innovation and greater production are inherently good.

Jürgen Moltmann wrote that the future is a mode of God's being. I believe that this understanding of God as future is one of the most important Christian contributions to the conversation about how our global crises should be confronted and the motivation for a prophetic stance to question the basic assumptions that are so destructive of the future of the planet. At the center of our destructive orientation and our wastefulness is the desacralization of life that is overwhelming the life-support systems of Mother Earth. This is deeply rooted in the way we look at God, ourselves, and the cosmos. Theology has to examine how the Western way of looking at the world has helped cause this destruction of ecosystems. Listening to the earth helps us to listen to each other. Then we can make the link between justice and the environment that divides the rich nations from the impoverished and debt-ridden countries. Then we can extend our compassion to all those who are struggling to survive on the planet, especially the poor, the deprived, and the oppressed. Human beings have to live in hope to enter into higher dimensions of consciousness; towards integral development; towards justice, peace, and the integrity of creation.

In his encyclical *Spe Salvi*, Pope Benedict XVI declared that, "Redemption is offered to us in the sense that we have been given hope, trustworthy hope, by virtue of which we can face our present: the present, even if it is arduous, can be lived and accepted if it leads towards a goal, if we can be sure of this goal and if this goal is great enough to justify the effort of the journey." Without this kind of hope, human beings would cease to build the earth, and in the chilling prophecy of Teilhard de Chardin, humanity would perish either through nausea or revolt. It is only in the cloud of unknowing that life can be lived in wonder and creativity, in mystery and ambiguity, in openness and flexibility, in expectation and hope for a future beyond all imagining. The ultimate ground for my hope therefore is the one and triune God ever hovering beyond the horizons of time and space, beckoning me and the scavengers, all human beings and the whole universe, ever onward and upward towards the new heaven and the new earth.

We are what we are because of what we choose to become. We choose to become according to the hope that we have. Hope is a choice, a moral imperative necessary for commitment and success. It is an arduous task. It remains wishful thinking if it does not bear fruit in the face of trials and difficulties, in the face of concentration camps and garbage dumps, in the face of melting polar caps and suicide bombers. We have to take a stand to make concrete the hopes of tomorrow by thinking of all the children yet to be born, lessening our environmental footprint, minimizing our use of the earth's resources, helping the poor, simplifying our way of life and building peace. We have to take the future seriously because tomorrow is our responsibility—we are morally bound to care for the future. We mortgage the future if we shirk from this duty to build the earth and defend life. By following the triune God through the cloud of unknowing into the emergent future, we can provide hope for this planet in peril.

NOTES

[1]Dr. Alejandro Roces, National Artist for Literature, shared with us this poem he wrote after attending Mass in the garbage dump.

[2]See Krista Tippett, *Einstein's God: Conversations about Science and the Human Spirit,* (New York: Penguin Books, 2010), 108, in her interview with James Moore, the biographer of Charles Darwin. Darwin described himself as an agnostic, but I think it was because of the death of his children. He could not reconcile a beneficent deity with evil in the world, especially when his daughter Annie, the apple of his eye, died in 1851 when she was only eleven years old. Sometimes Darwin also claimed that he was a Theist.

[3]My journey paralleled that of Warnie Lewis, the brother of C. S. Lewis, who finally came back to faith as a result of "a conviction for which I admit I should be hard put to find a logical proof, but which rests on the inherent improbability of the whole of existence being fortuitous, and the inability of the materialists to provide any convincing explanation of the origin of life." See Clyde S. Kilby and Marjorie Lamp Mead, eds., *Brothers and Friends: The Diaries of Major Warren Hamilton Lewis* (San Francisco: Harper & Row, 1982).

[4]This is contrary to what St. Thomas Aquinas already argued in the twelfth century—we cannot understand God separate from verification because he cannot be understood the way we understand physical objects. Our understanding of God follows our interaction with God—*lex orandi, lex credendi* (the law of prayer is the law of theology). But I had become so infected by the Western cultural need for certainty and its intellectual hubris that again, I easily forgot.

[5]The monks who went to desert in the early centuries described this state as *acedia*—apathy, boredom or torpor, the serious malady of being unable to care. They spoke of *acedia* as paralysis of the soul, as tedium and despondency, bitterness of spirit and utter despair. Kathleen Norris believes that "much of the restless boredom, frantic escapism, commitment phobia, and enervating despair" that plagues the modern world is the ancient demon *acedia* in modern dress. As we are desensitized by ever more intrusive distractions, as we lose the ability to care about what is truly important, we suffer from *acedia*. See Kathleen Norris, *Acedia & Me: A Marriage, Monks and a Writer's Life* (New York: Riverhead Books, 2008).

[6]Soil analysis of the dump site done in 1993 showed heavy methanogenic activity and the presence of persistent organic pollutants (POPs) such as pesticides and poly-chlorinated biphenyls (PCBs). Heavy metals were also found in heavy concentrations, such as chromium, lead, arsenic, zinc, cadmium, cobalt, copper, nickel, and barium. There were also traces of dicyclohexyl phthalates, a substance used to produce plastic suspected of disrupting endocrine functions and harming the liver. These chemicals disturb the normal hormone-controlled development of humans and animals, affecting gender and reproduction.

[7]For an exploration of the economic, geographical, and ecological per-

spectives of garbage and the culture of waste disposal, see Elizabeth Royte's *Garbage Land: On the Secret Trail of Trash* (New York: Back Bay Books, 2005). Royte followed the route of the garbage from her kitchen in Brooklyn to landfills, incinerators, and other means of garbage disposal in answer to the question "Where does it all go?" See also Heather Rogers, *Gone Tomorrow: The Hidden Life of Garbage* (New York: New Press, 2005).

[8]See Tristram Stuart, *Waste: Uncovering the Global Food Scandal* (New York: W. W. Norton, 2009). See also Jonathan Bloom, *American Wasteland: How America Throws Away Half of Its Food (And What We Can Do about It)* (Cambridge, MA: Da Capo Lifelong Books, 2010).

[9]Anneli Rufus and Kristan Lawson, *The Scavengers' Manifesto* (New York: Penguin Books, 2009), 71.

[10]See Jane Houlihan et al., *BodyBurden: The Pollution in Newborns* (Washington DC: Environmental Working Group, 2005).

[11]Richard Dawkins, *River Out of Eden* (New York: HarperCollins, 1995), 96.

[12]Some of the stories cited here have been recounted in Benigno P. Beltran, *Smokey Mountain: Ravaged Earth and Wasted Lives* (Manila: Divine Word Publications, 1994). See also some reflections of ecology in light of the garbage dump in Benigno P. Beltran, *Muellberg und Umweltkirche: Interkulturelle, theologische, pastorale und paedagogische Perspecktive auf den Philippinen* (Berlin: Lit Verlag, 2007).

[13]Lewis Thomas, *The Fragile Species* (New York: Scribner's, 1992), 82.

[14]See James Walsh, ed., *The Cloud of Unknowing* (New York: Paulist Press, 1981). The book was written by an unknown English monk in the fourteenth century and depicts how human knowing has no power to pierce the cloud of unknowing that separates God from humanity.

[15]These new ways of doing theology were explained by Rev. Fr. Antonio M. Pernia, superior general of the Society of the Divine Word (SVD), during his talk at the Divine Word Seminary, Tagaytay City, on the occasion of the Centennial Celebrations of the SVD in the Philippines. Fr. Pernia, the first Asian to be superior general of a major religious congregation for men, commented that these new ways of doing theology become necessary by virtue of the demographic shift of the church to the global south.

Chapter 2

GOD OF THE POOR
AND THE OPPRESSED

A STRANGER AMONG MY PEOPLE

But yield who will to their separation,
My object in living is to unite
My avocation and vocation
As my two eyes make one in sight.
Only where love and need are one,
And the work is play for mortal stakes,
Is the deed ever really done
For Heaven and the future's sakes.
   —Robert Frost, "Two Tramps in Mud Time"

Aling Inday, the nickname of Enriquieta Escarda, was a woman scavenger from Bacolod City. *"Ang buhay ko sa simula pa ay isang pasang-krus"* (my life from the beginning has been a carrying of the cross), she told me when I visited her one evening in her shanty. A sadness that ages the heart had made her look older than her years.

The day she arrived on Smokey Mountain, she went up to the trash heaps with an iron hook and a basket. It was difficult competing with men who were stronger and faster and then returning home to help in the washing of the clothes and the preparation of the food. With fierce and stark simplicity, she talked about her life as a scavenger, the gnawing hunger when there was nothing to scavenge, the vicious fights and the knifings, the dead bodies of salvaged criminals and insurgents dumped in the rubbish heaps. She remembered seeing a few dead babies thrown in the garbage cans. She placed them in milk boxes, prayed over them, and buried them in the dump.

"*Nakaraos din sa awa ng Diyos*" (We were able to survive with the help of God). How will she survive when she is old and alone? "*Pag-iisipan kong mabuti,*" she murmured softly. "I will think very hard about it."

When she became too weak to climb up the mountain of garbage, I asked her to help in the church, cleaning the chapel and preparing the materials for the Mass. She spent most of the day praying. When she became weaker still, she dropped my chalice while preparing for the Mass and broke it. It had a gold interior and a fiberglass exterior. I only put glue in it to bind the pieces together to remind me of what St. Boniface said: "In the olden days, priests had wooden chalices and hearts of gold. Now they have chalices of gold and hearts of wood."

Aling Inday has since died of tuberculosis, but she died happy. The housing project the scavengers fought for was finished, and she was given a unit. She told me she was very happy to die no longer an alien in her own country. She told me before she died that she only lived to serve God's people. Her lungs were slowly being eaten by bacilli, but her heart, like many women in the garbage dump, was burning with love and the strength to endure. It will be poor people like her who will bring back integrity to this broken world.

Massive poverty and the misery of the scavengers like Aling Inday challenged me to make the poor an indispensable element of my religious and moral reflection: "We are dared to source our theological questions from the existential ones they raise, to shape our questions in conjunction with their frames, to find answers that will satisfy not only our minds but also their hearts."[1] Our theological concerns must be developed from the questions and needs of the poor. This dialogue, this welcoming of the "other," involves openness, vulnerability and risk, struggle, and pain. The move from conversation to action that affirms and celebrates "otherness" in word and deed involves even more vulnerability, uncertainty, and pain.

Who are the poor on Smokey Mountain? Why do they do

what they do? How do they look at life? How do they understand reality? What are the modes of thought and understanding
characteristic of people living off and on the trash heaps? Why do
they not rise up in revolt against the venal politicians who fool
them come election time and the ostentatious rich who flaunt
their wealth? What do they consider a life well lived?

I found that everyone had a gripping story to tell if I took the
time to listen. Actually, for the first few years I did little else but
listen—and watch. I lived with the scavengers; ate with them;
learned their languages; observed their customs; and talked with
them at great length, exchanging jokes and laughing with them in
gut-busting guffaws late into the night as I joined them in wakes
and birthday parties. I spent many happy moments listening as
the women took the lice out of each other's hair, entranced by
their humor and recoiling at the crudity and rawness of their
language. My seminary training did not prepare me to deal with
women and children who can outcurse a sailor.

Decay, disease, despair, destitution, and degradation are com-
monly associated with the garbage dump. But there were a lot
of very interesting and very human characters once I started
listening. A former burlesque queen who gloried in having men
gaze at her body when she was young and then, when she grew
old, was forced to sell it for less than what it costs to buy a liter
of bottled water, often told me, "I should have managed my
money better, Father Ben." I listened to a top commander of
the Communist rebels visiting relatives in the dump recounting
his exploits against government soldiers, his face drained of all
expression. He kept quiet when I reminded him that those soldiers were fellow human beings forced to join the military out
of poverty, like some of his relatives. They had nothing to do
with the government abuses and plunder he was so angry about.

There were countless interesting lives and I listened with
fascination as the scavengers recounted them. My world was
enlarged by stories of pain and humiliation, of healing and hope
from worlds different from my own. I listened to the stories of
ex-convicts, whose bodies were full of tattoos and scars, nar-
rating their experiences with gang wars and riots in their prison
cells. "I have done a lot of bad things, Father Ben, but I never
fouled my own nest," one gang leader told me, as he touched my

hand to his forehead in respect. They did their "thing" far from the garbage dump, far from where their families and relatives lived. I wish the rest of humanity would also think that way of their home—planet Earth— and not defile it. Often I had to bless the bullet-riddled bodies of these felons brought home after a gun battle with the police. And then I had to ask around for money, so that they could be buried with dignity, or try to help their families after they were put in prison. The guys who rob you with guns and knives often pay for it with their lives. Those who steal billions of dollars with laptops often get away with it.

The fifteenth general chapter of my religious congregation defines prophetic dialogue as the deepest and best understanding of the call to mission. Prophetic dialogue is carried forward through interaction with people who have no faith community or religious affiliation, the poor and marginalized, those of different cultures and people from different religious traditions or secular ideologies.[2] Prophetic dialogue with the poor means rejoicing in the goodness we find in them. We accept with gratitude what they have to offer. We accept their virtues and admire them, we accept their brokenness with compassion, and we hope we can learn more about God from them. Prophetic dialogue is an exercise in the disciplined practice of listening; thus, it is both a spirituality and a method.

Prophetic dialogue is the dialectic between commitment and openness. Every point of view needs to be given a fair hearing. We open up to the "other," not only to understand her or him, but to understand ourselves in the "other." It creates space for the encounter of commitments, a space where we can be distinctly ourselves in relationship with people who do not necessarily believe the same way we do. Prophetic dialogue is where the stakeholders enter into each other's world, grow in consciousness and understanding, strengthen their connectedness, and collaborate in transforming the planet. It seeks mutual understanding, not total agreement, between people whose meanings and values, creeds and interests might be vastly different. In his encyclical *Ecclesiam Suam*, Pope Paul VI declared that "dialogue is the new way of being Church." Dialogue is speaking our hopes, expressing our fears, and mutually understanding and sharing our vulnerabilities. In discovering our common humanity, we should be ready to be surprised by the "other." We create understanding without dominance or submission. This mutuality can lead to collaboration in the transformation of the world.

Prophetic dialogue is the call to extend the self to the other in hope, especially in these times when our futures have become inextricably intertwined. Dialogue and hope are always associated with communion. Prophetic dialogue is possible only when I acknowledge the scavengers' integrity that cannot be reduced to my perceptions and desire to help. It means I and they belong to a community of interconnection and mutual transformation. It is the sharing of knowledge and the sincere expression of what one stands for, what one stakes his or her life for. It is the exchange of ideas and feelings, the sharing of feedback for communal enhancement. It is discussion, listening, engaging, caring, and trusting. It requires life-on-life interaction and collaboration.

The most difficult thing that I had to do during the whole time I stayed in the dump was to bridge the divide that separated the scavengers' world from mine. I was looking at the scavengers from the perspective of an outsider most of the time.[3] I felt the life of the scavengers running adjacent to my own, on a different dimension altogether, positing a certain obliqueness that left me always interpreting and simplifying their way of looking at the world. I felt a deep compassion for them, yet they seemed so remote and unreachable. In engaging in prophetic dialogue with them, I soon found out that I was a stranger in my own country. The scavengers arrived at a truth directly, and their conclusions were often based on keen instinct and intuition. When I asked how they arrived at such a conclusion, they became uneasy, unable to answer, such as I would be if a blind person asked me to describe one of the paintings of Monet.

Prophetic dialogue is based on collective respect and collaboration born of trust. It was very difficult for me to understand and trust the scavengers when there was something I perceived as urgent, and they told me the equivalent of "Don't just do something, sit there!" But most often, they solved the problem. When I wanted to do battle with the government to have the dump closed and housing provided, they suggested that we all pray and discuss it. They planned their prayer rallies for what seemed to me like ages, but in the end they triumphed.

From this I learned an essential lesson: in figuring out how to solve poverty, the first thing to do is to ask the poor how it should be done, to engage in dialogue with them, to try to understand their point of view.

The more I tried to clarify the scavengers' mode of thinking, the more I felt that it was not only dialogue with the poor I was engaging in. It was almost a dialogue at the same time with people of another culture and of another religion. I discovered that the scavengers' inner world was more complex than it appeared at first glance. I wanted to discover what their ultimate concerns were and where they looked for answers to fundamental questions. I persisted and went on asking them what they think God was like, what they think God required of them, and what they wanted out of life. They told me that life is a mystery—*mahiwaga ang buhay ng tao*. A human being has to live with the mystery, they told me. The vastness of the ocean, the starry skies, the endless stretch of the heavens all touch something eternal inside us and remind us of the mystery of life. The more we discover the mysteriousness of life, the more profound our worship, the richer our spiritual life, the farther we journey into higher dimensions of consciousness.

How can I be pastor to these people when they see the world differently?[4] There was one saving grace—my jokes. I made the scavengers laugh. I honed the timing of my punch lines by trading jokes with them, and we laughed with abandon late into the night. Laughter is the human being's response in the face of the juxtaposition of incongruities we experience as spirit-matter in the world. Laughter bridges different worlds and makes prophetic dialogue less complicated. Laughter signals a shared understanding of the world, so it is foundational to interdependence, intimacy, and likemindedness. We laugh, therefore we are.[5]

During many conversations, Bible sharings, and surveys, I asked the scavengers what they consider the most important questions in life. They summarized these in three questions: What does it mean to be a human being? How can we live together as brothers and sisters? How can we give the children a good future? Their answers can be summarized in three principles from which we drew the core values of integrity, solidarity, creativity: *pagpapapakatao* (becoming human), *pakikipagsandiwaan* (being one in spirit with others), and *pagkamakasaysayan* (being historical). We tried to base these values on faith in the Trinity in light of the unity, interconnectedness, and dynamism of the universe. We made *diwa*,[6] the root word of *sandiwa,* one in mind and heart, into an acronym for *damdamin* (feeling), *isip* (thought), *wika* (language), and *adhika* (passionate intention, dream, or ambition). *Sandiwaan* meant shared humanity and shared destiny.

Pagpapakatao for the scavengers means becoming all that one can be, constantly striving for wholeness and the fullness of life. It also means having unchanging principles to live by while adapting to the changing times. *Pakikipagsandiwaan* is dynamic connectedness with other human beings as brothers and sisters. *Pagkamakasaysayan* means that the world is historical—it had a definite beginning and will someday end. Human beings are historical too with a past and with a future. They need to be creative to adapt to changing circumstances. For the scavengers, historicity means *isaloob ang kahapon* (put the past in your innermost being), *isapuso ang ngayon* (put the present in your heart), and *isadiwa ang bukas* (put tomorrow in your spirit). As historical beings, we are duty bound to create a positive human future and fulfill our destiny as loving, thinking, relating, and dreaming human beings. In light of these questions and the fast changes in the world they perceive, we decided on the values of integrity, solidarity, and creativity as the most crucial in order to live more humanly in an evolving world.

While I catered to the understanding of "person" as an individual substance of a rational nature, identity among the scavengers was always understood as shared identity. Filipinos understand themselves as beings in relation. Their languages have many words for being in relationship: *pakikipagsandiwaan, pakikiisa, pakikisama, pakikitungo, pakikisalamuha, pakikisangkot, pakikialam, pakikisali, pakikipagkapwa.*[7] They are more prone to say "we" instead of "I." The people on Smokey Mountain do not define themselves apart from each other. Their understanding of themselves is characterized by the intense experience of the self as a member of a group rather than as a separate ego. The poor have no exaggerated sense of their own importance and no exaggerated need of privacy. Ego boundaries blend with others, and identity is dependent on the extended family. They are intuitively aware that everything is interconnected. They also have a strong sense of place, dividing the dump site into subsections as their territory. People are known by their family and location in the dump, and by their dialect. I spoke four of the Filipino languages, so I was accepted by many groups as one of their own, even as a relative by some because we had the same family name. For a long time, different families took turns to feed me breakfast, lunch, and supper every day in my hut, and they were very happy to do it.

In an environment where urbanization has brought about knowledge of a framework of laws, of formal and contractual relationships, the consciousness of the people in the garbage dump remained rural. Self-definition is still deeply relational. The Filipino is characterized by a relatively unindividuated ego, a dependent subjectivity. There is no word in Filipino languages that corresponds exactly to "individual" in the Indo-Germanic languages. To be is to be in relation. "To thine own self be true," is foreign to the understanding of the scavengers. "To the family be true" would be closer to their thinking. And that is why they bear a lot of children. This is apart from the need for a large family to scavenge more items or as insurance for old age. They really love children—there are no homeless kids in the garbage dump. Somebody else will always take care of them. They also turned a deaf ear on the church's teaching of responsible parenthood and continued to bear children they could hardly feed, much less send to school. Agencies distributing condoms and birth control pills discovered they were not used. The condoms were blown up as balloons for birthday parties.

There were a lot of children, but very few mothers knew about family planning. The few who wanted to could not afford to buy contraceptives. Others bought indigenous contraceptives from sidewalk vendors. These are made of roots and tree barks. But even if these were given free, the majority wanted to have children and nurture them. They continued to have as many children as they could so that a few would survive to adulthood and care for them in their old age. They did not listen to my homilies on responsible parenthood and natural family planning as taught by the Catholic Church. I found out, however, that where we were successful in giving women access to education and health care, they had fewer children than their mothers. In slum areas all over the world, the attack on standards of self-discipline and fidelity in family relations is undermining the values of the extended family. Strong families and communities are needed to help foster individual virtue and the freedom this virtue allows. Our family life ministries in the dump site sought to strengthen family ties, but it was an uphill struggle to define the ultimate in terms of spiritual and societal transformation in the face of the onslaught of advertising from the mass media.

Child-rearing techniques among the scavengers teach the children early to avoid confrontation and to know their place in life. They are taught respect and submission to morally superior people, to parents and priests, teachers, and others who occupy positions that merit respect. Now television, films, and video games use sex, violence, and material excess to lure young viewers into accepting the worldview their offerings assume. The free market treats the child not as an immature dependent, but as an autonomous adult, the object of advertising and marketing strategies tempting them with pleasures against which the child is defenseless. Freedom is understood as freedom from any restraint on immediate urges and desires. Ultimate satisfaction will come from increasing consumption of things. The parents on Smokey Mountain now have a harder time teaching traditional values like respect for elders and relating harmoniously with others in the face of this brainwashing.

Smokey Mountain was a network of relationships and mutual interdependence. In the garbage dump, the scavengers were never alone. They equated being alone with being sad. The tradition of mutual self-giving and reciprocity was very strong. An inner sense of solidarity bound them together. Neighbors banded together and helped each other in order to survive. One mended shoes, another cut hair, everybody shared food and other necessities. Smokey Mountain was a real community of shared lives toward a shared good in the midst of smoldering trash. The poor expect little from competition and much from cooperation. The rules remain unwritten, and relationships are based on status. People who rely on the good will of their neighbors usually also tend to act morally in view of reciprocal relations. Their greatest fear was to be considered an outcast. It was their social networks that helped the scavengers create a sense of meaning and safety in their lives in the garbage dump. Their primary value was solidarity, the oneness of the *loob*, of one's inner being with the community.

The people of Smokey Mountain believe in the basic inequality of each person. Superiors are destined to lead and protect, inferiors must obey. Inferiors must be grateful and behave according to their status, respecting the honor and dignity of the superiors. One is born into one's place in the scheme of things as destiny dictates. They think that somehow they are deserving of their fate. They blame fate for their being poor, for having no education at all, no skills, and no decent work. They are prey to petty exploitation and have to pay extortion money to local gangs and syndicates for permission to put up their hovels or sell cigarettes or vegetables because they are unable to organize as pressure groups to protect themselves. They want no confrontation because they believe that to be poor and oppressed is their destiny. The denizens of the dump site do not resent the opulence of the elite because they think that is their own place and it is their fate to be rich. While they live in slums like anthills in density, they do not envy the homes of the postcolonial elites with gardens and swimming pools and large open spaces. Their own destiny is to be scavengers—it is written in the palm of their hands and dictated by the wheel of fortune.

The scavengers are highly dependent on the extended family for a sense of identity, reassurance, and emotional well-being. When I bring the children to a fast-food chain, they only eat half of the hamburger I buy for them. They tenderly wrap the other half in tissue paper and bring it home to their family. They know not only their dependence on God and on powerful people, but also their interdependence with one another. The family members of the godparents at baptism become members of the extended family system. The circle of trust, however, is very narrowly conceived as valid only to this extended family. Their "we" does not extend to the whole community, much less to the whole nation and to the whole planet. They bear grudges for a long time and the whole family or clan would become embroiled in the fight. I often had to wade into the midst of petty quarrels and constant bickering, to act as referee or lightning rod.

The scavengers' view of time is different from the Western understanding of history, which is based on the idea of time as a measure of duration. In this view, time is like an arrow always pointing to what is to come. History would then be the categorizing of the sequences of events, then analyzing their causes and effects. The scavengers' view of time is cyclic. It is based on the *kairos*, the opportune time. The people of Smokey Mountain believe in fate and exert great effort to align themselves to its flow and bear the consequences stoically when they fail. The slum dwellers are memory-oriented. Their sense of history is shaped by memorable events; "My first child was born during Typhoon Ondoy," they would say. It becomes difficult for people in government to record birth dates and death certificates in the dump site. This imprecise view of what is past, present, and future makes it hard for them to be on time. Even the conjugation of tenses in Filipino languages reflects this imprecision.

Being with the scavengers made me see history in a new way. I believed, like them, that a universe without a transcendent dimension cannot save me from my own brokenness and fragility, from the cosmic vertigo of absolute emptiness and chaos. The scavengers' passion for song and music gave me insights into the way they viewed history and of the interpenetration of time and eternity. This view transcends the geometric analogies of the Western understanding of time structured by the vision of linear progression. Viktor Zuckerkandl, a philosopher of music, explored this paradox beautifully in *Sound and Symbol*: "Every melody declares to us that the past can be there without being remembered, the future without being foreknown—that the past is not stored in memory but in time, and that it is not our consciousness which anticipates time but that time anticipates itself." All the instruments become one in the remembering, listening, or performing the music, which is wholly in the present and fills consciousness entirely. Hearing a melody, according to him, is hearing, having heard, and being about to hear, all at once.

Religious symbols are used to legitimize familial relationships. Believing is not divorced from belonging. Their religious devotions are used to ask for good fortune, to influence luck for the family, or keep everyone safe from harm and provide for their needs. Their traditional values stress the importance of enduring human attachments. While unfettered choice and economic freedom is the ideal in developed countries, the preservation of the family is more important among the people in the dump. Many of them would prefer to remain destitute rather than break up the family. They often say that money makes one poor. They told me that happiness is the fruit of inner harmony rather than satisfied ambition or the possession of material things. They judge their wealth by the depth of their relationships with others. Instead of seeking power and control, the scavengers seek wisdom and the joyous acceptance of whatever comes. Into this community of relationships I came, with the objectifying mind-set I use to construct reality, and I felt a stranger in it.

The poor rest their security not in things but in other human beings—they have very little sense of privacy. They cannot stand being alone for long. It is this lack of privacy that is difficult to bear when one lives in a slum area. Your life becomes open to their scrutiny. They come knocking at your door at all times of the day, especially when you are doing something else. They will wait for a long time if you were out. They laugh and smile as if they had no care in the world. When I fell down a hole in the dump site, my white cassock was drenched in mud up to my waist. To my utter consternation and their delight, they laughed at me and said, "Now you can truly be our priest, because you smell like one of us." Living with these people whose view of reality was different from mine, I knew that I had come home, but I had come home to an even stranger self.

A few years ago, I took the StrengthsFinder questionnaire, intending to use it for our out-of-school youth. The results showed my strengths to be Futuristic, Input, Learner, Self-Assurance, and Strategic. A picture of what tomorrow would look like keeps pulling me forward, and I lived with people who were more interested in the past. I collect information—words, facts, books, quotations. I could not stand not knowing, and I lived among people who seldom read. I am drawn to the process of learning more about many things, and I lived among people who were satisfied with learning only which kind of plastic would sell for how much. I am confident in my ability to take risks and meet new challenges, and I lived among people who have been stomped down so often they did not believe their lives made a difference. I can play out alternative scenarios and choose the best path to the chosen goal, and I lived among people who seldom see the consequences of their decisions.[8] I believe the best way to succeed is to find out what the goal is and choose the best way to achieve it—feelings, fantasies, and vain imaginings are irrelevant—and I lived among people whose emotions rule their thinking. By temperament and training, the defining strategy for me was to confront problems directly, and I lived among people who intuitively understood what Sun Tsu wrote in *The Art of War*: The best general is he who wins without fighting.

I always knew I was the wrong guy to minister to the scavengers.

TO BE IS TO BE IN RELATION

> *. . . and nothing was burning,*
> *nothing but I, as that hand of fire*
> *touched my lips and scorched my tongue*
> *and pulled my voice*
> *into the ring of the dance.*
> —Denise Levertov, "Caedmon"

The interpersonal world is the primary source of emotional gratification for the people on Smokey Mountain. Their understanding of being is fundamentally relational, as being with. Communally shared meaning and intersubjective values maintain social cohesion. The scavengers cannot see themselves independent of their relationships. The tone and context in which a statement is made affect its meaning. Their passion for smooth interpersonal relations makes them use euphemisms extensively. It is almost impossible to get a straight answer from them—they do not want to hurt the feelings of others. Often they give answers that they imagine will most likely please the one asking the question. They share the Asian sensibility that seeks harmony and balance. This stems from the feeling of belonging and being rooted—but also because one's very survival in the trash heaps depends on it. Self-esteem derives from "face"—how a person is perceived by others. They are averse to direct confrontation. This brings with it the tendency to conformity, shyness, and unassertiveness to maintain smooth interpersonal relations. A good deed, like an insult or a slight, is etched in stone in their hearts. They will also bear malice forever. They can tolerate a lot of aggravation and will usually wait a long time before they will hit back. Wild buffaloes cannot stop them from taking revenge when their patience runs out.

The scavengers have a keen sense of gratitude. Once a grenade was thrown at the rectory by a minion of a drug dealer who did not like our programs to wean the youth from drugs. It was a Belgian fragmentation grenade, which luckily failed to explode. I woke up in the middle of the night to see men with their machetes and homemade guns surrounding the convent to watch over me. Many of them were the favorite targets of my sermons against the evils of drinking, carousing around, and gambling with fighting cocks. And there they were, willing to lay down their lives for me—"Greater love than this." I wept bitter tears as Simon Peter did after he betrayed the Galilean and the cock crowed three times. They watched over the rectory for a long time afterwards. They said they were paying a debt of gratitude because I helped send their children to school or brought their sick relatives to the hospital. Two or three came to me in the dead of the night and said they were going to kill the people who were giving me a hard time. I told them never to do it, frightening them with hellfire and all the eternal punishments I could think of to convince them to desist.

The scavengers love drama and gossip, and they spend hours before cheap television sets gawking at movie stars and following up on the latest soap opera. They can also tolerate a lot of noise—a dog howling the whole night and disco music that busts the eardrums do not bother them at all, while I toss around in my bed, especially during times when my chronic bronchitis acts up, gnashing my teeth at their insensitivity. In times like these, I perform mind-centering exercises to calm my spirit and drift off to an uneasy sleep. Sometimes I just put on my headphones and listen to the music of Anton Brückner and Gustav Mahler. Lewis Thomas wrote that listening to Mahler's Ninth Symphony made him think of death, death everywhere, the dying of everything, the end of humanity through thermonuclear bombs and radio-active clouds.[9] Mahler's Tenth Symphony (he was dying when he wrote the piece and asked that it not be published) makes me think of oceans covered in garbage and whales choking on plastic, of glaciers calving in the Antarctic and melting fast in the Himalayas. It reminds me that Greenland is melting at an unprecedented rate, faster than any model can predict. This does not help my insomnia very much.

The scavengers are still waiting for a warrior on a white horse who will save them from oppression and poverty—they have little regard for their own strength and initiative. They vote for movie actors and television artists during elections in the hope that they will save them from poverty. They therefore become easy prey for patronage politics—the corrupt, money-driven partisan electoral exercise conducted every three years. The scavengers expected at first that I would be giving handouts like a politician each time they lined up at the convent door. It took a long time for the idea to sink into their minds that I had nothing to give out. Some of them think that whenever politicians or white people from America or Europe come to visit, they will leave millions of dollars for them.

The scavengers are on friendly terms with fate. They face any trial in life with great calm and equanimity. In the grip of grief or before a painful surgical operation, they generally show little fear. They are adjusted to the unforeseen and accustomed to the unexpected. If times are good, they enjoy it. If times are bad, they endure it. They live for the moment, seldom make plans, and are often improvident. They prize conservation more than innovation. They build their hovels on dangerous ground and trust that God will watch over them. Their faith provides them with a strong reassurance and peace that passes understanding. I anointed with the oil for the sick many of those who were dying. They all died peacefully, clutching their rosaries. I have seen hundreds of them die with calm assurance and tranquility of spirit. This is what I have observed about the relevance of faith in the lives of the scavengers: it provides them with the means to explain their place in the scheme of things. Faith gives them the power to endure misery, the strength to follow a moral code, and brings them together in community. It gives them hope for the future in this world and in the next, and so they face death peacefully. Their most common response to grief and painful experiences is resilience. I never saw anyone lapse into serious depression. They never even realized that they possess this kind of emotional strength.

The *basureros* seldom ventured out of the dump site for fear of being ostracized. Life was more secure among their friends and relatives. Children from the dump often came home crying after being cruelly teased by their classmates as garbage denizens, victims of bullying in school. I understood why when I noticed that people always moved away from me, reeking of the stench of burning garbage after a day in the dump, as I rode in jeepneys and buses. When I stole out of the dump to join the demonstrators during the People Power Revolution in 1986 against the Marcos regime, I passed by the scavengers in the dead of night with their flashlights scrounging the trash heaps. When I came back two nights later after Marcos was spirited away by American helicopters to the U.S. military base and on to Hawaii, it was the same sight I saw. Their lives are not bothered by any change of regimes as long as they have each other. They believe that their family structures are divinely decreed and part of the workings of a coherent universe, and their lives are part of a pattern that has been designed from eternity, so everyone has a stable sense of identity from birth to death. Their relationships shape their personal identity and self-respect—their "I" is structured by the "we" of the community, and morality is never a private affair.

The scavengers risk death when their houses are carried away by the waves or buried in garbage avalanches. They constantly risk eviction and demolition of their shanties. But for all their fatalism and resignation, they are most afraid of fire engulfing their dwellings, which are highly flammable. Sometimes, crime syndicates set fire to their shanties so that the land can be sold to other squatters. Fire trucks, if they bother to come at all, cannot negotiate the narrow alleys already filled with the fire victims running around, and so the flames race through the slums to burn the shanties completely to the ground. When a huge fire burned the neighboring slum and threatened an old warehouse we used as a chapel, everyone was so busy saving their meager belongings, I had to grab one of the fire hoses and douse the flames myself.

Cooking stoves are often the cause of fire in the slums. The candles and kerosene lamps the scavengers use often set the cardboard in their walls on fire. The World Health Organization estimates that indoor smoke kills a million and a half people each year and causes a host of illnesses—pneumonia, bronchitis, emphysema, tuberculosis, cataracts, cancers, heart disease, high blood pressure, and low birth weight.[10] It is also suspected of causing cleft palate and other deformities. Apart from causing a lot of fires, smoke from the cooking stoves of the poor pose a universal threat now that global temperatures have risen. As if the smoke from the burning garbage that turns the scavengers' lungs black was not enough.

Sometimes, when I woke up in the middle of the night, I realized the error of my thinking about the scavengers. The problem was not in their improvidence, fatalism, or resignation; it was in my impatience. In my belief that "the best way to predict the future is to create it," I wanted assurance of success—work among the poor should be above the governance of probability and chance. I wanted to hurry them up, I wanted visible results immediately, but they took their own sweet time. They operated on a different level of consciousness.

The scavengers do not live by the clock. They live mostly by the immediacy-of-experience principle, and one has to adapt to this if one is trained in German punctuality. I grit my teeth when they do not come on time for worship and meetings and they slowly trickle in, without any care in the world. "Blessed are the punctual for they shall be lonely," they seem to say to me!

Every person on Smokey Mountain has a doctorate in endurance. The poor can wait, because they have acquired a kind of patience born of acknowledged dependence on God. And here I was—carried away by a multitude of conflicting theories of personality, busy with too many demanding tasks, committed to too many projects, wanting to help everyone in everything, obsessed with the fetishism of immediate visible results —wanting to engage in prophetic dialogue with people who have the patience of the mountains. Filipinos educated in the Western system strive to insure themselves against the unknown. They cannot understand the improvidence of the poor and their incapacity for long-term planning because they look at the poor, as I did at first, as if they had no prior history, no racial memories, no collective unconscious.

Many people of good will, touched by pity for the children in the garbage dump, came to help, but many of them soon packed up and left in failure. I was often left holding the bag. Their set of meanings and values did not correspond to that of the meanings and values that inform the lives of the scavengers. Functionaries came to the dump site only every now and then. They were often not there when significant events happened in the community, events that shaped the world of the scavengers and how they view reality. Others who wanted to help ended up victimizing the scavengers. It is very difficult to help the poor when one's being is fragmented and afraid to enter into a relationship with the "other." Only when we are whole can we see others as a whole. I have tried to bridge this spirituality of the scavengers who are at home in mystery with the functioning of the cosmos, of its majesty and beauty, but it was tough going.

The poor on Smokey Mountain confronted me with my impatience and my being a control freak. In my sleeplessness over their misery and their fatalism, oppressed by the shadowy fatigue that I carry inside me like a garbage dump, I had not bothered to be grateful for the things that the poor have. The poor can distinguish between necessities and luxuries. The fears of the poor are more realistic and less exaggerated because they already know that they can survive great suffering and want. They even joke that God made the Americans rich because God had pity on them; he knew they were not strong enough to endure the deprivations of being poor.

THE THEOLOGY OF THE INARTICULATE

I have been summoned to explore a desert area of man's heart in which explanations no longer suffice, and in which one learns that only experience counts. An arid rocky dark land of the soul, sometimes illuminated by strange fires

which men fear and peopled by specters which men studi-
ously avoid except in their nightmares. And in this area I
have learned that one cannot truly know hope unless he
has found out how like despair hope is.

—Thomas Merton

Theology as faith seeking understanding is needed to strengthen the commitment of believers and make the proclamation of faith intelligible—building integrity, strengthening solidarity, and fostering creativity in a particular time and place. A theologian has to choose his or her dialogue partner and audience. The theology I wanted to do required a spiritual engagement in the world of poverty. It is the community of scavengers and their starving children that need my theology, not people whose main problem is how to lose weight. And so, instead of adding more footnotes to my books, I composed more songs and exchanged more jokes with the scavengers.

The scavengers of Smokey Mountain practice a kind of Catholicism based on tactile liturgy and mystical intensity. They rub religious images with handkerchiefs that they then touch to afflicted parts of the body as protection from harm or for strengthening their inner resources, always remembering to insert a coin in the slot and light a candle before shuffling to the altar on their knees.[11] I wrote about this thaumaturgical religiosity in my dissertation.[12] I always felt like I was engaging in prophetic dialogue with people of different religious beliefs. Filipinos believe that they always know more than they can understand, and they always understand more than they can say—truth for them is intersubjective and community oriented. They do not have complete trust in words to express the truth. So they dance and sing their prayers.

Although they come by the hundreds for Christmas and Easter celebrations, not too many came to the celebration of the Eucharist in the dump on Sundays. They preferred to go on pilgrimages and processions to places where miracles occur. So I decided to celebrate the Eucharist daily in their homes. The families gathered together, and we proclaimed the death and rising of Christ in their own cluster of hovels. And this is the point of the scavengers' faith—it instills in them a belief that in the end, light always defeats darkness. They might not understand much of what I tell them about the doctrines of the church, but this they understand, which is the main point of faith in Christmas and Easter. They see the world as a theophany, a revelation of God's power and majesty, a sacrament of the divine presence, which guarantees that light will not be overcome by darkness (John 1:5). And that is why they do not need therapists, tranquilizers, and sleeping pills to get them through the misery of their daily life in the garbage dump.

After I bless the dead using prayers from the Sacramentary, they perform their own rites, with much crying and speaking to the dead person and remembrances of joyful moments spent with him or her in the past. The prayers I pronounced were too bland for them. They needed a more emotionally intense form of liturgy and more of the fire and brimstone type of homilies. They concentrated more on the emotional charge and tone of the speech or homily, not so much on the content, so I had to compose religious songs and write poems so that my theology could be inscribed in their hearts to make sense of the agony and joy of the garbage dump. I also organized a dance troupe of children who performed the dances and rituals of the indigenous people to bring home the message that like them, everyone should live in harmony with the universe. I had a sculptor make an image of the Sacred Heart as Jesus the Scavenger, with a hook and a sack of trash, to express the all-powerful and undying love of Jesus for them. The scavengers attributed miracles to the image. They would not talk to me for a long time if the procession did not pass in front of their homes.

The scavengers live in a sort of magical reality where the sacred and the profane are congruent and overlap. In their mind there are no clear boundaries between the spiritual and the material realms, between the living and the dead. The scavengers value the interior modes of our humanity—compassion, caring, concern, wisdom, contemplative awareness, introspection, and intentionality. They value people who possess introspective perceptions and the ability to read the signs of the times. They are concerned with blessings, with power (especially against evil spirits), with safety from danger and misfortune, against the unknown, and in the face of the assaults of destiny. Much of their devotional practices are concerned with sacred energy and potency (amulets and charms), which can be harnessed if one says the right prayers, performs the right rituals, or invokes the right saint. Spells and incantations are uttered to control powers beyond nature and to heal diseases of the mind and body.[13]

The scavengers live in a world full of magic, miracles, saints, and never-ending transactions with the divinity. Sometimes they wake me up in the middle of the night to bless a person who has been possessed by a dwarf (there are white and black ones, they say) or by a saint or the Virgin Mary. I performed the exorcisms, all the while thinking of explanations from Western theories of deviant behavior for the symptoms exhibited by the person possessed. When they were healed, I had a lot of psychological explanations at hand while the scavengers attributed it to my priestly powers. After a man who cursed me died before the sun set, presumably of a heart attack, the people thought that anyone who did me harm would be punished up to the seventh generation. This way of thinking might be the reason I was not killed in the time I stayed in the garbage dump. It was like living in the radiant, magical reality of Ben Okri's *The Famished Road* or Gabriel Garcia Marquez' *One Hundred Years of Solitude.*

Like most Filipinos, the scavengers on Smokey Mountain live off a numinous experience of the presence of the divine that arouses sentiments of fear and fascination. They are at home in the darkness of unknowing. They sense and revere the nameless and ineffable. They are unafraid of the majesty of the everlasting glare. They always sense themselves as being in the presence of an ultimate mystery to which they give their deepest trust, through which all things are held together in tender loving care. They live a life suffused with the sense of mystery, of dread, and the relatedness of all things. Their desire is not so much to be illumined but to be overpowered and possessed by the divine. Their poverty and oppression dispose them to look for redemption and attune them to listen to any message of hope. They are therefore in the best position to discern whether the hope held out is an authentic answer to the human dilemma or not.[14]

The folk Catholicism of the scavengers has been influenced by their precolonial past and by the animism of their forefathers. It is a complex of beliefs and practices where human beings can negotiate with supernatural beings through rituals and special prayers. Their *panata* (religious vows) where they lash themselves with whips are reminiscent of the machismo of a precolonial warrior mentality and their animistic past. They believe there is power or energy in the universe that can be harnessed for their benefit through special words, incantations, and amulets. These potent words can heal, prophesy, destroy, maim, and kill. Magical spirits bestow blessings and curses that determine events.

In many ways, the people in the garbage dump still have a lot in common with the indigenous people and the hunter-gatherers in the mountains and in the rainforests. Apart from an animistic view of reality, the people on Smokey Mountain also react to everything emotionally. They exhibit the territorial instinct of the tribal community where cooperation and trust are only accorded to the members. If they had enough food, they would not work anymore. Many also gamble because of their belief in luck and good fortune. Some of the tribal attitudes and mentality the people of Smokey Mountain still exhibit are the blustering of the males and hostility and belligerence to outsiders; hierarchical thinking and excessive deference to the leader of the group, which leads to conformity and the herd mentality; the inability to question the hierarchy; the avoidance of risk; and looking back at the past instead of to the future.[15]

The consciousness of the people on Smokey Mountain seems to span several levels at the same time. Seen in the colored schema of the levels of consciousness drawn by Don Beck and Chris Brown, many of the scavengers are still in the archaic-instinctual beige level of basic survival.[16] They are also in the purple realm of the magical-animistic with their spells and superstitions within the magic-impulsive and sociocentric way of life. Because they belong to the church, they have also moved to the mythic order in the blue realm where life has meaning, direction, and purpose directed by an all-powerful, personal deity. A few of those we have helped send to college might have moved into the orange dimension of consciousness already, but they would comprise only about 1 percent of the population. A few of the mystical old women who spend their lives praying might have moved into the yellow integrative dimension or even into the turquoise holistic dimension, but they just smile at me when I ask them about it. They have no words to describe their religious experience and formless mystic consciousness.

Their religious consciousness gave the scavengers a transcendent courage that no ideology can ever bestow. When they later held rallies and demonstrations to pressure the government for housing and to press for the closure of the dump site, they always brought their images of the child Jesus and the Blessed Virgin— rocket-propelled grenades would not have diverted them from their path. They feel that words are inadequate to give praise to God, and so they dance with their images, just like their ancestors before their sacred groves and like the tribal communities in the mountains and the rainforests. Their gestures of creative movement in dance is an affirmation of the final victory of all human acts of creative beauty over acts of destruction, even over the ugliness of garbage dumps, the venality of corporate leaders, and the cruelty of concentration camps. From these inarticulate people I have learned that truth is the adequacy of consciousness to reality. I was immediately disabused of the notion that it will be my efforts and my eloquence that would save them. They themselves will have to widen the horizon of their possibilities in light of how they understand their world and their hope for what is to come.

And so, life has been, even in a garbage dump, a constant lesson in grace for me.

SEARCHING FOR GOD AMONG THE TRASH HEAPS

> A *man must go on a quest to discover the sacred fire in the sanctuary of his own belly, to ignite the flame in his heart, to fuel the blaze in the hearth, to rekindle his ardor for the earth.*
>
> —Sam Keen, *Fire in the Belly*

Faith is as natural to the scavengers as breathing. They have an intuitive understanding of the human need to believe in the transcendent and a strong evolutionary predisposition to believe in the divine. Their brains are hard wired for faith, partly because of their culture, partly because of their poverty. The poor know they are in urgent need of redemption. The omnipresent symbols of Catholicism in make-shift altars inside their hovels depict their deep feeling of intimacy and their belief in the easy accessibility, of the divine. When I told them that many people in Europe and America no longer believe in God because they think only matter exists, they could not imagine how that could be—the spiritual realm is more real to them than the physical world. They said the reason might be that Europeans and Americans suffer from too much knowledge—*sumobra ang dunong*. They told me that knowledge without humility leads one astray. I think it is the quest for absolute certainty and the dualism inherent in their worldview that contribute to the modern state of unbelief in the West. Unbelievers deny transcendence and spiritual intuition, thereby disenchanting their world in the process. They bash their heads against the steel cage of their constricted worldview in search of complete certainty and then call the blood objective knowledge, according to Ken Wilber.

The majority of the scavengers live in a world of uncertainty; they don't even know where the next meal is coming from, but they live lives full of joy and meaning because their faith provides them with fortitude and wisdom. For them, religion is not a matter of having correct beliefs in a system of doctrines; it is a matter of personal faith and experience. Their religiosity endows them with meaning and purpose in the midst of grinding poverty. Because of their faith, they look at reality as ultimately meaningful. Suffering for them is endurable because there is a moral order in reality. Thus, they accept life as it is, without grasping at if-only and what-might-have-been. They view day to day as a changing flux of similar events. Their faith buoys up their spirits, raises the level of their consciousness, strengthens their will to survive, and makes life worth living even in a garbage dump. They are at home in things of the spirit and alternative realms of reality.

The secular humanism that comes out of utopian material-ism, the myth of unlimited progress, gives way to the fever to consume, the gratification of desires, and the satisfaction of the instinct to possess. The scavengers, however, are rooted in life itself, living within their own element, like birds in the air that can never understand our fear of falling. When the poor have the

Gospel preached to them, it sounds like good news and not like a threat or a scolding. The poor can respond to the call of the Gospel with a certain abandonment and uncomplicated totality because they have so little to lose—they only have their faith and each other. I would find it difficult to live without my laptop and Internet connection. The scavengers would find themselves dead in the water without their loved ones. I build my life on pieces of wire and metal that connects me to virtual reality. They build theirs on living, breathing human beings. They are at home with ambiguity and uncertainty, so they are more adapted to live in an indeterminate universe than I am, with my quest for control and certainty. They seem to have made the uncertainty of the world around them an intuitive part of their daily life.

The faith of the scavengers is like the bamboo, inexorably growing in the midst of storms and earthquakes. It is faith that sustains them, faith that makes their center hold in the midst of trials, faith that makes sense out of the chaos of the dump. It is not only in pain and terror that they call on the Supreme Being. They call on God at all times, in times of joy and in times of sorrow. Their faith takes away the sting of adversity. Everyone believes in a beyond where they will be reunited with their loved ones after death. The scavengers have evolved to live in ambiguity because they believe in an unconditioned reality. Ambiguity is an intrinsic ontological characteristic of the universe, and the scavengers feel at home in it. Ambiguity and uncertainty are inevitable facts of their lives. The new physics forces everyone to come to terms with uncertainty, ambiguity, and the importance of context and relationship. The scavengers have always lived in that kind of world because they believe in God's promises. There are no atheists on Smokey Mountain.

The religious dimension of their folk Catholicism is often mixed with shamanistic and animist elements. The people expected me as their priest to be a miracle worker, healer, and exorcist. When the government decided to relocate the scavengers, the chapel was bulldozed, but the bulldozer emitted a lot of smoke and the drivers ran away. For them, this was a sign from heaven. They said they did not want God to be angry at them for destroying his house. When a fire that consumed more than two-thirds of the hovels in the dump threatened the church and the rectory, I knelt in prayer and extended my arms more in desperation than supplication. A gust of wind turned the fire in another direction, and the church and convent were saved. I was filled with awe and confusion, but the people thought it natural for a priest's prayer to be always answered. He is supposed to be close to God, and there I was still wondering whether God really answered my prayers or the wind turned due to some meteorological phenomenon.[17] I often envied them their instinctive intimacy with the Almighty, their innate capacity to get lost to God in prayer, while I wrestle with reconciling belief in the Creator God with the pulsars, quasars, and supernovas in outer space and the bosons, fermions, and gluons of subatomic physics.

The religious experience of the scavengers veers towards the pure immediacy of intuition or feeling. Supernatural intervention in human affairs is naturally expected in all areas of life. Faith healing and talk of apparitions are common, including belief in sorcery, witchcraft, and black magic; rumors of witches and evil spirits; and ghosts and goblins. Filipinos like to scare their children with stories of evil spirits more frightening than the fevered imagination of Anne Rice or Stephen King can conjure. Belief in miracles and the saints is very strong due to the local belief in the active role of the recently deceased in the lives of the living. Dead relatives are invoked in times of trouble and during times that call for consolation. All Souls' Day (celebrated on All Saints' Day!) is a big affair. The dead are not only accessible, they participate in the festivities. The scavengers, like most Filipinos, visit their dead in the cemeteries, bringing food for the dead and having a "fiesta," reminiscent of Neanderthals who buried their dead with flint implements, food, and flowers.

The material and spiritual realms form a single unified, coherent whole for the scavengers. Some of them reach heightened forms of consciousness in prayer by singing religious hymns very softly and, as an old woman told me, "allowing the melody to resound in the bone marrow." Doing theology in the dump site therefore means engaging in prophetic dialogue with Filipino culture and its thaumaturgical spirituality, its mystical predilection and sacred visions. It means going through the cloud of unknowing to encounter reality in its pristine form as perceived by the scavengers—beyond language, beyond ideas, beyond reason.

Because of their nondualistic view of the world and a language at home in metaphor and paradox, I do not find it difficult to speak about God's relation to the world and explain the notion of divine action in their lives. They are not bothered by the problem of evil, too, while I always have to ask why God does not punish those who throw their children into the piles of trash. I still have a lot of difficulty reconciling a benevolent deity with a wasteful and violent universe and especially a wasteful and violent human race. Sometimes I feel ashamed to belong to a species that killed more than 100 million of its own in last century's wars, as I think of the Jews gassed in concentration camps and those tortured and killed in Gulags and killing fields. I am also appalled by the number of species that were killed off by economic development without regard for the ecosystem.

I am always haunted by the thought that when global warming adds to the misery the slum dwellers already suffer and they cannot endure it anymore, they will just march towards the California-style homes of the elite, to their health clubs and shopping malls, their golf courses and nouvelle cuisine bistros. What if the denizens of the slums in Abidjan and Lagos and Nairobi, the dwellers of the *pueblos jovenes* in Lima and Mexico, the *favelas* of Rio and São Paolo, the *desakotas* of Jakarta and the slums of Mumbai and Dhaka, and the 200 million *leudong renkou* in the cities of China did likewise at the same time when all their hope is gone, after they have been stripped of everything except the resentment in their hearts and occupy the business districts and opulent suburbs? I have doubts though whether they will really rebel, because a global monoculture manipulates them day and night into passivity. They will find it very hard to question beliefs and ideologies because mass culture is being created to ensure the continuous obedience of the masses to market interests. On Smokey Mountain, they will also not rebel because they believe it is God who will set them free, not M-16s and Kalashnikov rifles.

A greater part of dump sites are areas that break God's heart, regions where crowding, loss of values, poverty, disease, and crippling powerlessness overwhelm hope. Disciples steeped in the theology of the Crucified God are needed to evangelize, empower, and equip the poor for self-determination. In the struggle for liberation in the garbage dump, we discover everything as vestiges of the Trinity. We discover the triune God as a God who sets people free if we view the scavengers as subjects, partners in the work to promote the common good. It is the poor and the oppressed, those who have nothing else they can put their trust in except the promises of the triune God, who are most open to the promise of an unimaginably new world. The poor are not passive participants in the quest for empowerment if they make use of their social capital and their networks. They live life in a spontaneous and flexible manner, wanting only to experience life and gain wisdom, instead of controlling it, in the effort to transform society.

Jesus talked about the poor in a series of parallel expressions: the broken-hearted, the oppressed, the hated, those who mourn. He called them blessed. "Poor" is taken in a very broad sense—the helpless, those without resources, the despised, and the ill-treated. His poor are those who realize that they need God. To go to the God of Jesus the Christ is to go to him in justice, for he is present in every starving, thirsting, imprisoned and humiliated human being (Matt. 25:45). The poor are blessed because the Kingdom of God is expressed in the manifestation of God's justice and love in their favor. The outcasts of society have been granted by Jesus the privilege of being the first citizens of the Kingdom. The high and the mighty may enter the Kingdom only by serving the poor, or else God will cast them down from their thrones (Luke 1:52).

Those who have passed through the cloud of unknowing caution us that because of our blindness, we should live in a community where our religious experiences and theological tracts can be evaluated. That is why I had to go to the garbage dump to clarify my motives. In the course of looking back at the years I spent working among and with the poor, I realized that I was often dislocated, I was challenged, I was provoked. I was often enraged, frequently humbled, and sometimes surprised, but I think I have purified my motives and strengthened my resolve. God can also be found in fear, confusion, pain, and in the face of death.

In the face of death, everything just falls away, all pride or fear of failure, leaving only what is truly important.

THE STRUGGLE FOR JUSTICE
AND A SUSTAINABLE FUTURE

*There is no change without the movement of action, no
movement without the friction of competing interests, and
no friction without the heat of controversy.*
> —Saul Alinsky

In 1983, the scavengers were relocated by the government to
Cavite, about forty kilometers away. Illegal settlers are always
considered troublesome elements, human trash, disposable
people whose shanties can be demolished for the sole crime of
being in the path of progress. Foreign consultants suggested that
the twenty hectares on Smokey Mountain could be made into a
beautiful orchidarium or a golf course. The soldiers came with
their trucks and the scavengers loaded their meager belongings.
When they arrived at the relocation site, they quickly put up
their hovels once again (they can do it overnight). The air was
clean and the grass was green, but since there was no provision
made for jobs or other amenities, they slowly trickled back to
the dump site and did what they do best—scavenged in the trash
heaps. We had to start all over again. I was seething with anger,
but the people accepted the whole thing with stoic resignation.

The community-oriented methodology to empower the people
of Smokey Mountain and promote a critical mode of thinking
clashed with the decisions made, sometimes with good inten-
tions, from air-conditioned government offices a few miles away.
Bureaucrats who never condescended to come to the dump site
had little awareness of the consequences of their decisions on the
lives of the poor. Development models structured according to
an understanding of the human being from the West were often
destructive and antidemocratic, and only served to prolong the
dependency syndrome among the poor they presumed to serve.

Being poor is not simply about lack of money. Ultimately, it
is a person's lack of feeling for the reality of his inner being. It
is this feeling that we sought to restore in our work with the
scavengers. A lot of community organizing had to be done. The
test of the community's strength came when there was a rumor

that they would be resettled again. In 1988, the government planned to relocate the scavengers once more. This was during the tenure of President Cory Aquino, motivated by a sincere belief that the government knew what was best. But the scavengers did not want the dislocation to happen again. We started to organize a massive rally.

On February 4, 1988, the Philippine *Daily Inquirer* filed this report about the scavengers' march to Malacañang:

> Thousands of residents of Smokey Mountain in Tondo marched to Malacañang to protest plans by the Metro Manila Commission to relocate them to Carmona, Cavite . . . as part of the (Commission's) Comprehensive Solid Waste Management Program . . . At the Smokey Mountain Community Center, residents assailed the MMC's lack of concern for their welfare and vowed to "defend to the death" their right to reside in the area. (The residents also) bewailed the lack of provisions for livelihood and housing of the new site, which were the failure of previous plans to relocate them.

Actually, the march to Malacañang did not materialize. The people were ready, their banners were prepared, the marshals were briefed. As they were making placards and mobilizing the populace for the march the next day, Ms. Bea Zobel, Ms. Merci Tuazon, and Ms. Carmela Borres happened to visit the dump to give a few boxes of apples to the children. When they learned of the planned demonstration, they hastened to President Aquino's home. Within the hour, they came back and assured the leaders that there was no cause for worry. I was called to the Office of the President the next day. President Aquino could not understand why the scavengers were averse to living in nice houses in a nice place outside the city. I told her the scavengers believed that Smokey Mountain was their home. Many of their children died in the dump site. They considered the place sanctified by those who died there.

President Aquino signed Memorandum Order 161-A directing the National Housing Authority (NHA) to conduct feasibility studies for a low-cost housing project for the scavengers On Smokey Mountain. The rest of the area was designed to be developed into an industrial site to provide livelihood opportunities for the scavengers. From that time on, the community was very clear on its objectives and never lost sight of its ultimate goals: housing and jobs; the dump site closed and rehabilitated; no more pollution of land, air, and sea. It was easy to focus energies afterwards on short-term activities that would lead to the fulfillment of goals in light of this shared vision for the future.

The scavengers were allowed to dream once more, but there were people who blocked the project. There is a kind of darkness that you have to undergo in engaging in prophetic dialogue with the poor—the realization that there will be people who will not wish you well. The more one is involved with the struggles of the poor, the more conflicts of interests one discovers. There will always be people who will be upset with what you do. They will block your efforts, question your motives, and cause you pain even if you have not done them evil. Some religious people thought that I was only prolonging the agony of the poor. Others attributed purely selfish motives to my search for God among the scavengers. Even other Christians did not understand what I was doing. They said I was a Communist because of our rallies and demonstrations. I was slandered and reviled by other religious groups.

It was very difficult to understand why, for defending the dignity of the poor, certain people would want you killed. I have met people who hated me on sight because I was a priest, a member of the Catholic Church, which they believe is an evil enterprise, a worshipper of graven images, the scourge of the earth because of its stand against abortion and contraceptives. They heap curses upon my head because of the Inquisition and the Crusades. They rail against many other pernicious doctrines, which I am absolutely sure the Catholic Church never held. As we battle global poverty, global terrorism, and global warming, we need to have a very strong hope to run the gauntlet of derision, insults, lies, hatred, and even threats of assassination from those who would like the poor to remain poor, from those who believe that others who do not share their faith are infidels, from those who think that global warming is one big scam, from those who hold us in contempt because they believe faith is a delusion. However, the most painful thing I ever experienced was the realization of the truth of the Lord's saying—our greatest enemies are those of our own household. Those who were supposed to be on my side caused me the greatest pain.

Social transformation will be a slow and messy process, chaotic and even dangerous. I have always misread and underestimated the animosity of others who did not wish me well just because I took the side of the scavengers. When the communities of the parish marched and rallied to force the government to provide them with medium-rise housing, people with vested interests organized other scavengers to ask for a house and lot for each family. The area of the dump site would not have been enough for the five thousand families for their kind of housing program. And the prices of the units would have been astronomical. They persisted, although they were a tiny minority. They had already made up their minds; they could not be bothered by the facts. I tried to explain, but they held rallies against me in the office of my provincial superior and in the house of His Eminence, Jaime Cardinal Sin.

The opponents of the housing program lambasted me in tabloids and newspapers, saying all kinds of nasty things. I had to go to court and sue them. Our lawyers won the suit and the justice of the peace trying the case ordered them to make a public apology in writing. But the damage had already been done. They smiled and shook hands with me, and going around with their big Bibles in hand, proceeded to destroy me continuously. I was seething with resentment, but I now realize that I should have shown greater compassion by not going to court and not worrying about the injustice done to me. I should have followed what Plotinus counseled: "Be kind, for everyone you meet is carrying a great burden." I tried my best to live out what Longfellow wrote: "If we could read the secret history of our enemies, we would find sorrow and suffering enough to dispel all hostility." I was given patience and forbearance by the teachings of Mahatma Gandhi and Martin Luther King, Jr., but most of all by the Galilean hanging on the cross.

The project proposed by the majority of scavengers was approved. As the scavenger families were transferred to temporary relocation sites, the other group fought the police with stones and homemade pistols. During the melee, one of the presidents of our Basic Ecclesial Communities tried to save the recyclables he gathered in the dump site. Ric Villorente took refuge in the chapel during the violent confrontation and was hit by a stray bullet. With spirit crushed, I celebrated his funeral Mass. I suddenly realized that I became a little less unworthy, because of the pain I experienced, to pronounce the words of consecration, "This is my body broken for many." Pain and brokenness can be a form of prayer and a profound source of insight and conversion. I found out that sorrow can be a way of worship, a path where a person can be drawn more deeply into the mystery of the Trinity's redeeming love masquerading as pain, loss, or failure.

When there were constant rumors of plans to have me assassinated and a fragmentation grenade was thrown at the roof of the convent, I ran to Cardinal Jaime Sin and asked for advice. He told me to sleep in our convent in town at night and do pastoral work in the garbage dump only in the daytime. I do not remember all the counsel he gave but I was so strengthened by the way he acted like a spiritual father that I went back to face death, if need be, heart in my throat, knees quavering, waiting for the gunshot that would end my life. I had to keep going because that's what I vowed to do to the best of my ability. I found out I need not become my fears. I did not romanticize them, I did not idealize them. I simply focused on what I was doing and willed the fear away. Sometimes you can be as strong as you act. Sometimes how you live your life is as important as how you face your own dying. The fear never goes away. Not for a moment. But the pain I experienced helped me to become more intensely myself.

The Archbishop of Manila, Luis Antonio Tagle, said, "It is interesting to note that quite often, Jesus was denounced as a violator of God's law when he showed compassion for the weak, the poor, the sick, the women, and public sinners. He offered new life to those considered impure by eating and mingling with them. He assured them that God was not distant and there was hope in God's loving mercy." Archbishop Tagle continued, "But he himself got no mercy from his adversaries, only ridicule for disobeying laws that were supposed to embody God's will. Jesus suffered on account of his self-offering for those loved by God. But he never wavered in his sacrifice. In the process he exposed the false gods that people worshipped, erroneous notions of holiness and the blindness of righteous people to the visitations of God. Jesus' sacrifice uncovered the link between the worship of false gods and insensitivity to the needy."

During those few times that I felt despondent, I remembered what St. Paul said—I have not yet resisted unto blood. It is a great consolation to know that other missionaries have suffered more, from the time of the Roman persecution to the present. The coming years will be characterized by many sacrifices and much suffering. Frederick Douglass said, "Power concedes nothing without a struggle. It never has and it never will." The journey into higher realms of consciousness and fostering relationships with others is not a picnic, but faith can surmount innate human greed, ferocity, and indifference so that the planet can survive. We need people whose altruistic genes are more evolved, like the martyrs, who were imbued with great compassion and caring. Strengthened by faith in the holy and triune God when they are tested, they can go on giving hope to this planet in peril.

HOPE IN TROUBLED TIMES

We work to win more widespread recognition and ap-
preciation of the dignity and inner worth of the human
person. We assist the poor and oppressed in such a way that
gradually they are able to arrive at better living conditions
by means of their resources and initiative.
                                        —SVD Constitutions, 211

More than simply experiencing the torments of a dying land, I have witnessed what the poorest of the poor themselves are doing to reverse the destruction of the environment and their struggle for justice, peace, and a sustainable future through creative education and evangelization. The people of Smokey Mountain have tried their best to mitigate the devastation of the planet by raising environmental awareness and fostering closer relationships with other people's organizations. They have chosen long-term objectives for their community development in order to attain the fullness of life, living in peace with others and helping to create a better world. They have sought to understand better what is it in their culture that stands in the way of their aspirations for a more just, prosperous, fulfilling, and dignified life—and what they can do to promote social transformation. They have discussed plans of action for protecting Mother Earth and creating an environment of care and concern. They join countless men and women, unheralded in slums and farms, who still recognize the sacred in the cosmos and respond to it in faith, hope, and love.

The people of Smokey Mountain have spearheaded a campaign to educate people in ecological responsibility so that they can do something to reduce, reuse, and recycle waste. Through the parish cooperative, they are trying to segregate recyclable and nonrecyclable items towards zero waste management in their homes. Biodegradable trash is shredded and mixed with enzymes to produce organic fertilizer. They are producing decorative and handicraft materials out of used paper, most of which is exported to their partners abroad. They are advocating for the use of technology to solve the garbage problem of the whole metropolis.

The waste management program of the parish cooperative was called the Smokey Mountain Resource Recovery Systems (SMRRS). The SMRRS received a garbage truck, two compressors, and two pressers from the Herz-Jesu Gemeinde from Oberhausen, Germany, for its waste management program. They also received three trucks from the embassy of Japan. The SMRRS ran a bioreactor that changed four tons of food waste into two tons of organic fertilizer in a few days. Close to 70 percent of the residents of the temporary housing were segregating their garbage, and the food wastes were brought daily to the bioreactor. The Department of Environment and Natural Resources through the National Solid Waste Commission donated a shredder, hammer mill, and pelletizer. The Department of Science and Technology, which donated the bioreactor, made plans with the SMRRS to construct a machine with a capacity of forty tons a day. The SMRRS also hauled the segregated waste from schools and malls of the City of Manila. Aside from being paid for the hauling, they also recycled plastic bags, cartons, and pieces of iron.

During the celebration of World Family Day, a million people gathered at the Luneta Park in Manila for the culminating liturgy. The parish cooperative, in collaboration with the Eco-Waste Coalition and other environmental nongovernmental organizations, fielded 120 volunteers from Smokey Mountain to man the garbage cans for separation into biodegradable and nonbiodegradable waste. Eight tons of garbage were collected, recyclables were sold to factories, and foodwaste was composted. Very little was thrown into the garbage dump. Once again, the people from Smokey Mountain had proven that with solidarity and political will, they can still win the race to save the planet. We can make our environmental footprints lighter by being creative and collaborative.

The Children of Mother Earth, the performing arts group of young people from the garbage dump, signed a memorandum of agreement with the Department of Environment and Natural Resources to reforest 135 hectares in Mt. Ayaas in the Marikina Watershed (about fifteen kilometers away from Smokey Mountain) from where Metro Manila gets its water. They are doing the reforestation in partnership with large business corporations wanting to protect the watershed. Remote sensing equipment from satellites showed that the greater part of the area's forest density cover is zero. Only thin grasses cover the slopes, and they die out during the summer months. The degradation was caused by *kaingin* (slash and burn method of farming) and charcoal production. They are advocating for the use of permaculture methods, biodynamic farming, urban gardens, and other healthy and sustainable ways of growing food near communities who eat it. The young people of Smokey Mountain have pledged to plant a million trees in denuded areas and nurture them to atone for the destruction of the environment the dump site has caused for more than fifty years. They have partnered with the Dumagats, the indigenous people living in the area, for the production of organic food. The young people are searching for a new spirituality that will no longer see human beings as the center of the universe, no longer believe that everything exists to fulfill their wants and needs.

The small victories the scavengers have achieved actualize the radiant hope that human beings will wake up from this ecological nightmare, from this unjust society and constant conflict.

The wounds of Mother Earth sound a serious warning and invite us to search for deeper sources of creativity and to espouse values appropriate to the challenges we face. It is from our inner dynamism that we will discover the strength and the patience to build a world glowing with vitality and harmony. Restoring the earth and preventing wasted lives is not only necessary for the planet and for humanity, it is also an integral part of finding our own identity and our own place in the scheme of things. This is the best way to fulfill the biological imperative—to engage in prophetic dialogue and situate the efforts of each inhabitant of the planet in the global networks that work for mutual emergence and enhancement towards a more encompassing hope for the future.

The scavengers on Smokey Mountain have borne the brunt of environmental indifference, but their story tells us that the future also holds the opportunity to heal the planet and our relationships with each other. There is tremendous opportunity to redirect our energy and resources for the future of the coming generations if we can get our acts together. Respect for life is closely related to respect for creation. Lack of respect for others is evident in many patterns of environmental abuse. It is insane to continue to lay waste the bounty of the planet in the name of consumption and corporate growth and then throw the waste into the heart of our cities and into our oceans. We have to realize that to wound the earth is to wound ourselves.

We have to look at the world in a new way. The culture of consumerism and the ideology of unlimited growth have driven the economic advances of the past century. That can no longer be, for as Edward Abbey, an environmental activist, once said, "Growth for the sake of growth is the ideology of the cancer cell." Indiscriminate material progress will destroy the earth, just as melanoblastoma lays waste the human body. An economic system that depends on ever-increasing corporate profits is suicidal. If it does not care for the environment, it will also care little about ruined lives left in its wake. The people of Smokey Mountain call on everyone to work towards reaching a new balance with the natural capital of the planet while continuing to expand economic opportunities for the billions of people who still lack a decent standard of living and those who have to scavenge in garbage dumps in order to continue to live. We have to live together in an ecological way where our needs can be met without destroying the biosphere. We have to engage in systemic transformation to address the structural causes of the ecological crisis and create sustainable economic and political alternatives.

In *Hope Dies Last*, Studs Terkel documented the stories of people who held on to hope in the face of unendurable odds. His book portrayed the indefatigable spirit and tenacity that human beings exhibit in the face of insuperable trials.[18] Hope is also born first, long before the baby sees the light of day. Hope is born first in the mother's heart, hope for a beautiful tomorrow for the child in her womb. Hope springs eternal and if it ever dies, it is because we have abandoned it.

Hope is a dynamic force that enables the poor to give them selves to the future. It provides them with unflagging energy and enduring strength to pursue their dreams of building a sustainable way of life. The point of talking about injustice and evil, of garbage dumps and climate change, is not to frighten us or beat us into submission but to inspire us to transform the world, to allow us to heal it and make it flourish. Hope is security in ambiguity and uncertainty. Groaning with longing is the language of hope (Rom. 8:18-25).

Frail human beings are capable of change, even radical transformation. We can imagine better worlds. We can, through vigorous and sustained effort, alter our dysfunctional tendencies. To care for the world and enter into its places of pain, our central concern should not be what we produce, not what we achieve. The fundamental issue is what we are as human beings, that we are in the universe for a purpose, and that we do have a future. Knowing who we really are bolsters hope that the world is open to infinite possibilities, possibilities we can dream about and celebrate.

And so, there is hope. The scavengers on Smokey Mountain have shown that we have more than enough reasons to hope for this planet in peril.

NOTES

[1] Dionisio Miranda, "What Will You Have Me Do for You?" in *Catholic Theological Ethics in the World Church*, ed. James Keenan (Manila: Ateneo de Manila University Press, 2008), 178. I was forced to dialogue with the poor because I found out personally that in the words of Brian D. McLaren, "the modern Western understanding of the Gospel was too often truncated, shallow, thin, bland, anemic, privatized, personalized, polarized and compromised." See Brian D. McLaren, "Church Emerging: Or Why I Still Use the Word *Postmodern* but with Mixed Feelings," in *An Emergent Manifesto of Hope*, ed. Doug Pagitt and Tony Jones (Grand Rapids: Baker Books, 2007), 148.

[2] For a discussion on prophetic dialogue, see Stephen Bevans and Roger Schroeder, *Constants in Context: A Theology of Mission for Today* (Maryknoll, NY: Orbis Books, 2004). See also Stephen Bevans and Roger Schroeder, *Prophetic Dialogue: Reflections on Christian Mission Today* (Maryknoll, NY: Orbis Books, 2011).

[3] I have read John Howard Griffin's *Black Like Me* (Boston: Houghton Mifflin, 1961) several times. He darkened his skin color with a chemical and traveled as a black man in the south of the United States. Although my skin was brown like the scavengers, their world was different from mine, and it took years before they allowed me to enter it.

[4] I have tried to compare this worldview with the worldview of the West when I taught at the Johann Wolfgang Goethe University in Frankfurt. The lectures have been published in Benigno P. Beltran, *Philippinische Theologie in ihrem kulturellen und gesellshcaftlichen Kontext* (Duesseldorf: Patmos Verlag, 1988).

[5] Dacher Keltner in his research on laughter at the University of California, Berkeley, says that our relationships are only as good as our histories of laughter together. See his *Born to Be Good: The Science of a Meaningful Life* (New York: W. W. Norton, 2009), where he shows that human beings have evolved positive emotions like amusement, gratitude, compassion and are hard-wired to be good.

[6] Some historians claim that *diwa* comes from the Sanskrit *deva* (shining one). In Hinduism, *deva* is any being possessing divine grace.

[7] Agnes M. Brazal, "Reinventing *Pakikipagkapwa*: An Exploration of Its Potential for Promoting Respect for Plurality and Difference," in *Fundamentalism and Pluralism in the Church*, ed. Dennis T. Gonzalez (Manila: Dakateo and De La Salle University, 2004), 50-70. Brazal understands *kapwa* as the shared inner self. *Pakikipagkapwa* refers to treating the other equally and justly.

[8] See http://www.gallupjournal.com and look for the StrengthsFinder Center. See also Marcus Buckingham and Donald O. Clifton, *Now, Discover Your Strengths* (New York: Free Press, 2001).

[9] Lewis Thomas, *Late Night Thoughts on Listening to Mahler's Ninth Symphony* (New York: Bantam Books, 1984), 165. Stephen Johnson, in *Mahler: His Life and Music* (Naperville, IL: Naxos Books, 2007), claims that the

Tenth Symphony "journeys through desperate longing, icy visions of death, and convulsive terror to final hope of renewal and peace."

[10]World Health Organization, Fact Sheet No. 252 (September 2011).

[11]Pastor Ed Lapiz, who founded the Day by Day Christian Ministries with churches in the Philippines and in other parts of the world, noted in his blog that Filipinos are a touching people. They have lots of love and are not afraid to show it. They almost inevitably create human chains with their perennial *akbay* (putting an arm around another's shoulder), *hawak* (hold), *yakap* (embrace), *himas* (caressing stroke), *kalabit* (touching with the tip of the finger), *kalong* (sitting on someone else's lap), etc. Filipinos, according to Lapiz, are always reaching out, always seeking interconnection.

[12]Benigno P. Beltran, *The Christology of the Inarticulate: An Inquiry into the Filipino Understanding of Jesus the Christ* (Manila: Divine Word Publications, 1988).

[13]For the cultural context of these "superstitions," regarding illnesses and their perceived causes, see Michael L. Tan, *Revisiting Usog, Pasma, Kulam* (Quezon City: University of the Philippines Press, 2008).

[14]See Monika Hellwig, "Good News to the Poor: Do They Understand It Better?" in *Tracing the Spirit: Communities, Social Action and Theological Reflection*, ed. James E. Hug (New York: Paulist Press, 1983), 122-48.

[15]See F. Landa Jocano's *Filipino Indigenous Ethnic Communities: Patterns, Variations and Typologies* (Manila: Punlad, 1998). See also F. Landa Jocano, *Filipino Prehistory: Rediscovering Precolonial Heritage* (Manila: Punlad, 1998).

[16]Don Beck and Chris Brown, *Spiral Dynamics: Mastering Values, Leadership and Change* (Cambridge: Blackwell Publishers, 1995). The growth in interior development and the evolution of consciousness in the human being as a hierarchy of needs or a series of stages have been the conclusion of many developmental psychologists, from Abraham Maslow to Jane Loevinger to Robert Kegan to Clara Graves, Juergen Habermas, and Cheryl Armon, Kurt Fischer to Jenny Wade, from Deirdre Kramer to Susanne Cook-Greuter.

[17]After I stayed for some years on Smokey Mountain, I read Graham Greene's *A Burnt-Out Case* (New York: Viking Press, 1961) and found parallels between my experience and that of the architect in the novel whose success has only served to fill him with boredom and disgust. He goes to a leper colony in Africa where the more he denies any spiritual motives for himself, the more others see God's work in him.

[18]Studs Terkel, *Hope Dies Last: Keeping Faith in Troubled Times* (New York: New Press, 2003).

Chapter 3

GOD AS FEARSOME AND ALLURING MYSTERY

LORD OF THE GARBAGE DUMP

FIRE. GOD of Abraham, GOD of Isaac, GOD of Jacob, not of philosophers and of the learned. Certitude. Certitude. Certitude. Feeling. Joy. Peace. GOD of Jesus Christ . . . Forgetfulness of the world and of everything except God . . . Grandeur of the human soul. Joy, joy, joy, tears of joy.
—Blaise Pascal, November 23, 1645

The rockets explode high in the air, showering multicolored stars in the darkness before the dawn. From the north of the dump site, the image of the Risen Christ atop the *andas*, a gaily decorated platform with long handles, is carried by the men on their shoulders. They dance with the image in unison with the beating of the drums. From the south, about a kilometer away, the image of the Sorrowful Mother, face covered by a veil of mourning, is placed in another *andas* festooned with flowers. It is accompanied by hundreds of women and children. The devotees, preceded by a brass band, move solemnly in procession. The lights from their candles and their murmured prayers rise up to the skies, inducing and sustaining a state of hope and fervor, deepening the sense of the numinous as the rockets continue to explode in the air.

The droves of scavengers are filled with joy, uplifted by the spectacle of victory over death and darkness as the two platforms meet under a *galilea*, a structure festively decorated with flowers and balloons. Little children dressed as angels sing hosannas to the Risen One. An angel is lowered down the *galilea* to take away the veil of the Sorrowful Mother. The veil is then tied to a clump of balloons with money in an envelope. It is a gift to the lucky person who will pick it up far, far away from the garbage dump. A hundred more rockets explode in the air. The choir of angels sings praises to the conqueror of death and darkness. The brass band and the drums with their frenzied beat try their best to drown the people's shouts of hosanna and alleluia. Then the people joyfully dance with the images in fervent devotion, the platforms swaying gracefully to the beat of the drums, everybody shouting and crying with overwrought emotions, the smell of sweat and body heat mingling with the smell of incense and burning candles.

It is the dawn of Easter and the scavengers are celebrating the Resurrection, sounding their collective hope for life everlasting. The celebration is called *Salubong*, the encounter between the Risen Christ and the Blessed Mother. It is celebrated in Catholic parishes all over the country at the dawn of Easter each year. On Smokey Mountain, it is also the celebration of the parish fiesta. It is a celebration of the meaning the scavengers discover in the community of faith and the reassurance of their rightful place in the universe: they have a right to be here. It is also the expression of their biological need to belong to a community with shared vision and values, shared grief and hopes that produce a sense of communion, giving continuity and dignity to their lives. Their rituals frame their identities and aspirations, and make vivid and substantial the framework in which life is to be lived. Their celebrations embody the sense of the presence of the transcendent in the world.

In the garbage dump, the power of faith to motivate and inspire through vivid narratives and collective acts of rededication remains undiminished; acts of worship remain a realm of wonder and creativity. This faith embraces the cloud of unknowing as a requirement for a deeper understanding of the mystery. The primal experiences of transcendence, revelation, love, death, and the hope of life everlasting are reinvigorated in the encounter with God as the fearsome and alluring mystery. Their religious ceremonies provide a sense of meaning and direction to their lives and propel them to a more transcendent realm of inner experience and purpose. Their rituals make them understand the ultimate mystery, the divine plan to bring salvation, communion, and fulfillment to the whole universe. For the scavengers, faith is not mainly intellectual assent to a body of doctrines; it is a whole-body experience, even going beyond the boundaries of the physical. The margins between life and faith, between consciousness and devotion, disappear in their joyful dancing.

The joy is almost palpable in this communitarian gesture of praise and worship to the Risen Lord. Nietzsche wrote that he did not have a high regard for Christianity because Christians look so unredeemed. If he were alive today, I would have invited him to come with me to the garbage dump during Easter celebrations. There exultation becomes an expression of the self-identity of the faith community of scavengers. They know the joy about rising again by dwelling in it in mystic surrender and sensuous abandon. This joy shows in their rapt and glowing faces as they celebrate their fiesta. They are completely absorbed by the ritual activities in their whole being. Some seem to be in a trance. In this grand conjunction of drums, of dancing and of ecstasy, of sunrise, and of hope was a wealth of experience I would not exchange for any other. For me, the meaning the scavengers discover in these celebrations is a clue that the universe is more than just the interactions of gluons and leptons. This meaning expresses something that is enduring in human beings: the hope that springs eternal at the core of our humanity.

Clad in my liturgical vestments as I join the people's procession, I become part of the dancing wave and experience, through their sacramental imagination, glimpses of divine glory. Through this dramatic manifestation of God's presence, through a deep receptive sensitivity to the divine, the scavengers are transported to another dimension inaccessible to me, a dimension that connects them to something that I can barely glimpse. Their religious activities become numinous symbols pointing to a transcendence beyond, to the presence of a mystery that both blesses and calls, allures and terrifies. It is during celebrations like these, as I gaze into the eyes of the scavengers in procession, that my hair stands on end. Their sense of awe and reverence, their total surrender to worship, terrifies me into silence. I am stunned, transfixed by what I cannot put into words.

Theological anthropology teaches that critical aspects of our humanity are mysterious, unquantifiable, and blessedly meaningful, just like the religious experience of the people of Smokey Mountain. During these celebrations, the scavengers experience the divine in such an intense, intimate way that their only appropriate response is worship and adoration, reverence and devotion. They are lost in an experiential communion before God the Father, who raised the Christ from death in the power of the Spirit. They are reimmersed in their Trinitarian faith as they stand in awe and fascination. They become part of something larger than themselves and are subsequently subsumed into the greater mystery. The scavengers become participants in the cosmic dance that imbues everything with grace and meaning. This sense of cosmic belonging experienced in ritual moments symbolic of the past, present, and future is reenacted, intensified, and realized sacramentally as the scavengers celebrate the truth they know about salvation and hope. Their faith enhances their primordial religious experience and heightens their sense of mystery.

Ritual and symbol are as necessary to the scavengers as food and water; they mark the scavengers as human and give them their identity as they journey in two worlds: in this world and in the world of promise and expectation. One scavenger told me his skull swells up in a grace-filled sense of immediacy and expansiveness to fill the whole world when he dances with the image of the Risen Christ during the Easter celebrations. The scavengers are profoundly, ecstatically, vitally, and joyously spiritual. They even fight among themselves as to who can help carry the platform where the image of the Risen Christ is placed during the Easter procession. Buoyed up by the ecstatic consciousness in their religious celebrations, I did not have to know how to define "mystery," as in *mysterium tremendum et fascinans.*

I just had to stand in awe.

In the afternoon of their fiesta celebrations, the scavengers bring out their religious images in procession once more. Even if it is a very small parish, the procession lasts more than three hours, with the dancing in place in several locations. There seems to be a collective consciousness that grips the participants and allows them to choreograph their dancing of the platform, which is made of stainless steel and weighs more than half a ton. Thus, it is also an ordeal—to participate in the dancing is a spiritual feat. The procession is almost like a mass ballet, a choreographed event. It is characterized by joy and profound transformation of the senses as barefoot participants take turns carrying the platform. The performance of ritual acts transports the scavengers into another mode of existence, to a different way of looking at and living in the world. The praise and worship they offer to the Risen Lord is both a response to the hope they discover and a celebration that they are empowered to respond to that hope. Moments of religious experience provide a time outside of the here and now in which the world becomes meaningful because it is seen in its ultimate context—communion with the deepest source of everything that is.

The same thing happens during religious celebrations in other parts of the Philippines. During the feast of Jesus, the Nazarene, in Quiapo, as many as three million barefoot penitents, almost all men, join the procession, which lasts up to eight hours. The Christ child in Tondo also attracts droves of dancing penitents in fluvial parades and street processions. In Cebu and in Antique, the same fervor and ecstasy, the same devotion and joy are expressed by devotees in the hundreds of thousands. Filipino religious experience is sometimes darkened by the doleful image of the *Santo Intierro* (the dead Christ), at other times highlighted by the joy of the Resurrection, but it is always an intense, communal celebration.

Comparative surveys have shown that Filipinos are among the most religious people in the world.[1] Their Christian faith provides them with the most powerful explanation of the world as they experience it. Joyful songs and dances heighten their religious experience during their celebrations and put them in a state of radical openness and trust. Their Catholic faith provides them with the symbols and ceremonies for celebrating and contemplating the sacred. They live their faith through their very lives, their breath, their words, and what is left silent. This faith gives substance to their hopes and reality to the unseen.

In their joyous celebrations, the scavengers are transformed into the mystery they celebrate.

In these celebrations, I experience a renewed understanding of *homo religiosus* (the religious human being). I also come face to face with the profundity and pervasiveness of my own religious feelings of numinosity and communion. At the same time, I always analyze my own religious experience using theoretical frameworks from Western theories of personality. I try again and again to reconcile the scavengers' religiosity with the findings of the cognitive sciences, philosophy of mind and psychology. And I envy scavengers who, without much effort, become one with all that is. They recognize not only signals of transcendence in their religious activities but hear trumpet blasts of God's glory and majesty. Religious experience connects their spiritual awareness with cosmic awareness; they believe the universe is one and everything is interrelated. Their religiosity is a unified system of meaning, binding their community through symbols, rituals, narratives, and celebration. Religion is not just a matter of personal belief for them. It also embodies social practices and worshipful celebrations that encourage personal experiences of immense emotional power.[2] One has always to speak about God to the scavengers in the context of this kind of worship and adoration. Theology has to be rooted in the very heart of these celebrations; otherwise it will become a rootless enterprise, alienated from its living subject, the religious experience of believers.

The scavengers see themselves as living in a universe permeated by spirit, by meaning, and by peace and beauty. They conduct their personal lives and organize their social order accordingly. Participating in these rituals, they believe that prayer and worship are life transforming and can lead to personal growth and self-transcendence. For the scavengers, religious rites mediate a power that makes life whole. Trust in a transcendent power is morally empowering for them. Their religious practices are not just rooted in the belief that there are spiritual beings. It is the path to obtaining creative spiritual power or to deflecting destructive spiritual power. They are guided by a way of looking at the world where imagination is more important than reason, myth is more important than history, and dreams are more important than knowledge.

In the numinous dimension of existence, one can only speak in symbolism, in myth, parable, story, and figures of speech as one is enveloped in the cloud of unknowing; one can only talk using models, analogy, allusion, paradox, and metaphor. Or better still, one can only dance for joy and join the universe in its cosmic choreography as one encounters the God who is a fearsome and alluring mystery. The spatial metaphor, for example, becomes inadequate when one talks about God. The temporal might be a better metaphor in light of Yahweh's *eyeh esher eyeh* (Exod. 3:15), which biblical scholars claim is better translated as "I shall be there as who I am shall be there." In the end, however, silence is the only proper attitude to take before God. God is beyond everything we can talk about.

The people on Smokey Mountain and Tondo are very poor. They are also deeply, enthusiastically, and joyously religious. Living with them revealed to me the more profound and manifold ways the poor respond to truth, beauty, and goodness, and to the mystery of suffering and glory of communing with God. For them, life and history are a medium for contemplating the things of the beyond if one knows how to read the signs. Their mystical intensity leads them to a sense of awe, devotion, and adoration, which is expressed in self-effacing rituals, sacrifice, and prayer. It helps them discover God's presence in all human events and his redemptive action in all human affairs. It helps them recognize that our nature is deeply wounded—something is out of sync, there is something wrong with human existence—and that we are in absolute need of being saved. We have to be saved from ourselves most of all. Without this need to be saved, it is very difficult to see God in the world. In the modern world, it is God that is put on trial, not the human being that recognizes the need to be redeemed.

Homo sapiens are biologically inclined to reflect on the deepest nature of their being human and to attempt to fathom the deepest secrets of the cosmos. They are constantly pushed to ask the why of things. Brain research has shown that we have a natural propensity for belief, even if evolutionary biology explains this as just another means for survival, a means of adaptation. This propensity becomes more intense in the midst of squalor and degradation; folk religiosity in the garbage dump is more intensely practiced and celebrated. When the scavengers speak of Jesus, Mary, and Joseph, they speak of persons they know intimately. The betrayal of Christ by Judas is as real to them as the betrayal of a relative to the police that happened the day before.

In the Philippines where church and culture have become virtually identical, the specific task of Christian theology has often been forgotten or eclipsed.[3] It is difficult to differentiate religion, state, and nation in the Philippines because Philippine history is the history of Catholicism. Now that the modern world is fast changing the relationship between church and culture, it is incumbent for theologians to draw theological implications from issues relevant to how life is lived in the Philippines today, especially among the poor. The challenges that the modern context in the Philippines raises for a communication and presentation of the Gospel that is understandable to the scavengers have to be faced. This integrating sacral worldview is celebrated more intensely during the Christmas season and Holy Week liturgies. It should provide a critique of the Western understanding of politics, economics, science, and art, which organize themselves as autonomous entities owing no allegiance to a higher power. The communal spirituality and incarnational faith on Smokey Mountain must speak against the view that religion and spirituality are a private affair, beneath the concern of public life.

The human mind yearns for patterns and meanings. The scavengers find these in their religious celebrations. In what follows I will attempt to describe the most significant religious celebrations of the scavengers as the context of meaning for their faith.

CHRISTMAS ON SMOKEY MOUNTAIN

God became human, in no way different from other human beings, to break through the walls of power in total weakness.

—Henri Nouwen

"And the Word was made flesh, and dwelt among us" (John 1:14). Whenever I read this verse, I always recall the words of

Bono, the rock star of U2: "The idea that there is a force of love and logic behind the universe is overwhelming to start with, if you believe it. But the idea that the same love and logic would choose to describe itself as a baby born in shit and straw and poverty is genius. It brings me to my knees, literally. To me as a poet, I'm just in awe of that. It makes some sort of poetic sense. It is the thing that makes me a believer."

Christian faith proclaims that because God loves the world, he sent his only begotten Son (John 3:16) who entered time and history and was born in a manger. Smokey Mountain is the ideal setting for this Christmas story. In no other place is the exaltation and glorification of the spirit of the child Jesus who was born poor more meaningful. In no other place can the residents really identify with the child that was born poor in a stable. I once wrote the lyrics for a song, *May Pasko ba sa Smokey Mountain?* (Is there Christmas in Smokey Mountain?). The song goes to note that the Christ child was also born poor, had no place to lay his head, and used rags for diapers, but the archangels and cherubim exulted in the heavens at his birth. The refrain ends:

> *There is Christmas even in a garbage dump,*
> *There is Christmas in Smokey Mountain!*
> *Even if we seem miserable to the eyes of other people,*
> *We more than make up for it by the splendor*
>   *of our dreams!*

Advent, the time of preparation for Christmas, is a season of contrition and anticipation. This is to prepare the faithful to understand how great a gift the Incarnation is and how this channels our hope towards the ultimate goal of existence. The Mexican *posada* (inn), which became the traditional *panunuluyan* (trying to find lodging for the night), has been given an added dimension on Smokey Mountain during the celebration of Christmas.[4] The scavengers do not just adopt the *panunuluyan*. They give it a Smokey Mountain touch. In their version, Joseph and Mary look for a place to spend the night in the rich subdivisions outside Smokey Mountain. Everywhere, they are turned away—by the rich, the powerful, the famous in society. Finally, the Virgin faints from hunger and weariness and it is the scavengers who rush to help. They let her ride on their pushcart among the tin cans and pieces of plastic they gathered and bring her to their humble shanty in the garbage dump where she gives birth to the Redeemer. Everyone has tears in their eyes afterwards, including me.

Christmas season in the Philippines officially begins with a novena of nine dawn Masses at 4:00 a.m., December 16, culminating in the *Misa de Gallo* on Christmas Eve. There are huge crowds during these dawn Masses. Christmas is a time for many people in the dump site to sell fruits and things they make for Christmas presents. The whole family joins together for the Midnight Mass on December 24 and then shares the food of the *noche buena* (the good night) afterwards. During the whole season, there is a heightened state of intimacy with the divine that is almost palpable. It is a celebration of the sacredness of humanity because the fullness of the Son of God, the Divine Word, was pleased to dwell in it. I have celebrated Christmas on Smokey Mountain for thirty years, and I cannot understand why Bertrand Russell wrote in *Why I Am Not a Christian* that fear, conceit, and hatred are the three human impulses embodied in religion, permitting men to indulge in their passions without restraint. Despite their sordid circumstances, the impulse I noticed among the scavengers was joy, humility, and fellowship, especially during the celebration of Christmas. The characteristic moods I noticed were predominantly those of reverence, exultation, and social harmony.

The Philippine Christmas symbol is the star lantern. Ten long and five short pieces of bamboo, rice paper, string, and straw are all one needs to make it. The star lantern decorates every home on Smokey Mountain. It is the sign that the Holy Family is welcome in each and every home in the garbage dump. Some decorate Christmas trees and add wads of cotton to represent snow. They also make a small *belen* (creche), with the images of the Holy Family and the shepherds. The scavengers experience God in an almost tactile way, wiping handkerchiefs on the image of the divine child lying in the *belen*, feeling the presence of the ineffable, numinous, holy God. For the scavengers, faith is a source of joy and consolation, of compassion and solidarity, of creativity in finding ways to remain human in squalid circumstances. These are felt more intensely during the Christmas season. They discover an incarnate, embodied knowledge of God, a knowledge that is corporeal (they say they can feel God), a knowledge that is active and transformative. They do not need logical proof that God reveals himself to human beings.

HOLY WEEK IN THE GARBAGE DUMP

There is in us an instinct for newness, for renewal, for a liberation of creative power. We seek to awaken in ourselves a force which really changes our lives from within. And yet the same instinct tells us that this change is a recovery of that which is deepest, most original, most personal in ourselves.

—Thomas Merton, Honorable Reader: Reflections on My Work

The culminating point in the liturgical life in the garbage dump is Holy Week. Holy Week is a celebration of God's saving activity, which embraces all creation and points to its fulfillment in the new heaven and the new earth. It is crucial for people of faith to know what truth is, what good and evil are, what the relation of truth to freedom is. The scavengers know the truth through these celebrations. The celebrations of Holy Week are the way the scavengers express the truth of their lives and their beliefs. It starts on Palm Sunday with the blessing of palms followed by a procession to commemorate Christ's triumphal entry into Jerusalem. The church keeps some of the palms blessed to be burned into the ashes used for the Ash Wednesday ritual, when believers are reminded that they came from the earth, they are completely dependent on it, and to the earth they shall ultimately return.

The rituals and liturgical services of Holy Week are designed to express sensually the mystery and awe of worship. They provide a communal context for the Christian knowledge of God. This involves the embedding of that knowledge with rituals and practices in creative and transformative action. An example would be the two very interesting rituals on Holy Thursday. In

most parishes, the priest washes the feet of twelve men represent-
ing the apostles. This is also done on Smokey Mountain. It was
always a source of amusement for me when I washed the feet
of the scavengers who came directly from scavenging to see the
water in the basin turn murky. I kissed those feet, sometimes with
suppurating pustules and thick scabs, as an act of abasement.
The twelve apostles then participate in the reenactment of the
Last Supper. There was constant ribbing as to who played the
role of Judas Iscariot.

The element of imaginative engagement and contemplative
self-abandon are even stronger in folk religiosity during Holy
Week. Good Friday is when the passion and death of Christ
are commemorated.[5] Good Friday tells the scavengers what it
means to be fully human in the face of death and mortality. It
confronts all of us with our destructiveness of the earth and
of human beings, and calls us to repentance and conversion.
It calls us to a new way of seeing the world and to adopting a
new ethical attitude towards it. The idea of redemptive suffering finds strong resonance in the hearts of the slum dwellers
because of their corporate understanding of our being human.
This communal understanding of redemption gives them social
stability and the courage to endure. It enables their families and
community to hold together.

The garbage dump is filled with sadness as the scavengers
wait for Easter. The scavengers go around the mountain of
garbage following the footsteps of Christ in the Way of the
Cross on Good Friday. This practice became more meaningful
to the scavengers after they learned that Calvary was a garbage
dump outside the gates of Jerusalem. Their imaginative engagement provides them with the ability to be present before the
all-encompassing presence, especially as the *Santo Intierro*, the
dead Christ, is brought around in procession. Those who are
oppressed find it easier to believe in redemption and liberation.
The triune God identifies with the oppressed so that all people
who believe will avoid all forms of oppression. The way to honor
the Crucified Jesus is to work for redemption from all kinds
of slavery—from sin, from economic and political oppression.

On Good Friday, some men whip themselves with lashes that
have broken pieces of glass tied at the ends. Some are literally

crucified in other parts of the country. Several scavengers also become flagellants in the garbage dump due to vows and promises made to God. I close the church during this time because they spill their blood on the pews and pavement. There is no need to lash ourselves, I tell the flagellants. Salvation means to be engaged and transformed by the Spirit's sanctifying mission and to be increasingly drawn into God's triune life. We have to fast from our frustrations and resentment and our anger and bitterness of heart, as we search for God in places where life is most threatened and death-dealing forces are hard at work.

The devotions of Good Friday are followed by the celebration of Easter Sunday with Holy Saturday being a time of silence and reflection. The scavengers await the resurrection with gratitude because the Redeemer who bore the sins of the world intended to bring human beings to share the divine life. The God disclosed in the Holy Week celebrations is the same God who called the Israelites out of Egypt, made flesh in Yeshua bar Yoseph, the same God who relates to the cosmos in the mission of the Spirit, the same God who opens the universe to a future that can ground the hopes of everyone in it.

NATURE AS A HERACLITEAN FIRE

Enough! the Resurrection,
A heart's-clarion! Away grief's gasping, joyless days,
    dejection.
Across my foundering deck shone
A beacon, an eternal beam. Flesh fade, and mortal trash
Fall to the residuary worm; world's wildfire, leave but
    ash:
In a flash, at a trumpet crash,
I am all at once what Christ is, since he was what I am,
    and
This Jack, joke, poor potsherd, patch, matchwood,
    immortal diamond,
Is immortal diamond.
                —Gerard Manley Hopkins,
                    "That Nature Is a Heraclitean Fire"

Smokey Mountain could not have found a more fitting patron than the Risen Christ. In the parish church altar before the demolition of their shanties, Christ was shown bursting forth from a *barong-barong* (hovel) in the midst of garbage into heavenly splendor, bursting forth from rottenness in ultimate triumph. The Resurrection is the keystone of Christianity. The Risen Christ is the embodiment of the ultimate transformative power in the universe that moves it towards fulfillment. This is a reminder of our common destiny and of the ultimate destiny of the earth, which also groans with longing for redemption (Rom. 8:28). I have witnessed every Easter amidst the throng of scavengers their overwhelming joy in Christ's rising again (2 Cor. 1:5).

In celebrating the Resurrection, the scavengers celebrate the presence of the Risen One among them, in the midst of the stinking garbage, at the center of their lives, at the center of their very being, at the heart of their community, at the heart of the universe. The celebration of these feasts through their worship and processions is their way of expressing their knowledge of the triune God—of the Father who raised his Son from the dead through the power of the Spirit. They believe that the Resurrected Jesus is present to human beings in a new way, a way different from his bodily presence before death. He is present to us in the Spirit in a hidden, but no less real, way, and we can live in the strength of his resurrection despite the ambiguities and uncertainties of this world.

Late in the afternoon, the images of the victorious Christ and Blessed Mother are marched in procession. The icons are again placed on a platform with long handles. Several people place the platform on their shoulders and dance with it. With the drums that quicken the blood and the shouts of the rejoicing throng, I am also filled with the sense of reverence and submission, of being pulled upward within a vast cosmos filled with light. I become overwhelmed by the feeling of the *mysterium tremendum et fascinans*, the primordial experience of God as the Wholly Other yet immanent in the Risen Christ, of the God who, in the raising of Jesus from the dead through the Spirit, makes all things new and ushers in a radically new future. Thus, faith in the Resurrection provides scavengers with an understanding of God and ourselves in light of our understanding of a universe that will be creatively transformed at the end of time. Christian faith invites believers to be embraced by the power of the future that has dawned in the Risen Christ. The Resurrection is faith's answer to the question of why there is anything at all rather than nothing, to the question of what it means to be human, and why we are here in the universe.

Joy is the hallmark of Christianity because it believes that salvation is the love of the Father who sends the Son who lives and dies and rises again. The Father sends the Spirit so that we may return to him through Christ in the power of the same Spirit. In their ritual gathering for Easter, the scavengers celebrate the timeless yearning, the eternal hope, the archetypal longing for redemption and fulfillment that the Resurrection exemplifies. Their religious celebrations are a disclosure of ultimate meaning and value. It is a time of wholeness, communion, and bliss celebrated in rituals in which they are completely absorbed. Scavengers long for something sensible, something they can see and touch; they long to bring the divine into the level of their fleshly existence. They experience God acting in direct, irrefutable ways through fits of ecstasy, miraculous healings, answers to prayer in mystic surrender, and sensual abandon. They never doubt, because of this experience, that each of them is important to God, intimately and personally important.

The joyful celebrations of the people on Smokey Mountain expand their capacity for mystery and help them become the kind of people God wants them to be—believers who are liturgically centered with a robust faith and a rigorous morality. They express their gratitude to the Father who glorified Christ, who in turn gives the Spirit so that we may be united to him and return to the Father. The death and rising of Christ reveal the truth about who God is—one and triune. Knowledge of the triune God in the sense of the Hebrew *yadha* (intimate knowledge) cannot be sequestered from the community of faith and its practices. The consciousness of a profound presence the scavengers experience during religious activities is suffused with a sense of the sacred and mystery. It is not only their different worldview that makes me feel a stranger in the garbage dump. It is mostly during their worship that I am filled with envy at their intimate sense of how God loves the world and human beings.

The spirituality of the scavengers is characterized by celebration, dance, ecstasy, and rapture. That is why the scavengers dance the image of the Risen One during their fiestas. To understand their world, one must understand how their imagination is formed by their belief context so that they are able to see other dimensions of reality and understand their place in the scheme of things. I would have given away my doctorate in theology for a moment of experiencing their profound sense of mystery and dread. If those who are proud of their unbelief question the scavengers' faith, I can only paraphrase Carl Gustav Jung who asked, Did you ever have a religious experience? They will answer in the negative naturally. I can only say to the militant atheists, "I'm sorry. The scavengers have."

The Resurrection of Christ has resulted in centuries-long reflection on what it means to be a human being. This reflection included questions about the relation of the self to the body, occasioned explorations into human identity, and resulted in the return towards a more holistic understanding of the human person. Pope Benedict XVI, in his homily at the Easter Vigil, April 15, 2006, said that the Resurrection of Christ is something more, something different: "If we may borrow the language of the theory of evolution, it is the greatest 'mutation,' absolutely the most critical leap into a totally new dimension that there has ever been in the long history of life and its development: a leap into a completely new order which does concern us and concerns the whole of history." The Resurrection is a qualitative leap in the history of "evolution" and of life, according to him, "towards a new future life, towards a new world which, starting from Christ, already continuously permeates this world of ours, transforms it and draws it to itself." The Resurrection inaugurates a new form of life, a new dimension of creation. As the poet wrote, "Our measure is not dust, enough to fill a small cup, our measure is Christ, unbroken, everlasting." This is the credo of the scavengers, which goes against the materialist view of reality that understands the universe as being dead, and even if there is life in it, will one day end up in a state of absolute lifelessness.

The parish of the Risen Christ is at the very heart of the universe when scavengers celebrate their own resurrection and the coming of the new heavens and the new earth during their parish fiesta. The Resurrection is God's promise that justice will triumph, a promise the scavengers reenact in their daily celebration of the Eucharist. Attention was often called during homilies and catechetical instruction to the connection between Jesus' presence in the Eucharist (1 Cor. 12:23-26) and his presence in the hungry people of the world (Matt. 25:35). In the breaking of the bread, that staple lacking to the wretched of the earth, the life of the resurrected one becomes present reality. This assures believers that death will not triumph in the end. Sin and injustice will in the end be abolished. Belief in the Resurrection and Eucharist binds together the love of God and political action, the spiritual, and the material. Through the Eucharist, the Risen Jesus becomes the dynamic power at the heart of the universe. The whole of creation, the entire universe, will share in the fulfillment of all things in Christ at the end of time.

Resurrection faith is an alternative to atheism and agnosticism. The irreducibly unique elements in the Trinitarian schema of salvation where Christ dies and rises again is a paradigm for action to relieve the misery of, and set free, the one billion human beings living below the poverty threshold and the renewing of the face of the earth. Belief in the Resurrection grounds the principles of human dignity, freedom, and human rights in a democratic society, and the concomitant struggle for peace and justice. It calls us to look towards the future to find meaning and purpose in the universe based on the divine promise that continually calls it to become more than itself. Faith in the Risen Christ must be actualized more perfectly in new democratic and economic contexts in such a way as to command the respect even of unbelievers.

WHAT KIND OF GOD DO YOU BELIEVE IN?

If they think they ha' slain our Goodly Fere
They are fools eternally,
I ha' seen him eat of the honey-comb
Sin' they nailed him to the tree.
        —Ezra Pound, "The Ballad of the Goodly Fere"

I have always been fascinated by the deep religiosity of the scavengers and their joy in the midst of squalor. Jesus relied on simple, uneducated people like them who only knew how to submit to him and through them made wonderful things happen. In the garbage dump, all abstractions disappear. Among the scavengers, the Gospel becomes flesh and blood and life. And I become both shepherd and witness.

In the memorable words of Albert Einstein, "The most beautiful and profound emotion we can experience is the sensation of the mystical. It is the source of all true science. He to whom this emotion is a stranger, who can no longer wonder and stand rapt in awe, is as good as dead. To know that what is impenetrable to us really exists, manifesting itself as the highest wisdom, and the most radiant beauty which our dull faculties can only comprehend in their primitive forms—this knowledge, this feeling is at the center of true religion." Einstein wrote that the deeply emotional conviction of the presence of a superior reasoning power, which is revealed in the incomprehensible universe, forms his idea of God. Einstein identified God with the impersonal laws of nature: "I believe in Spinoza's God, who reveals himself in the orderly harmony of what exists." For Spinoza, God is the universe taken as a whole. This identification of God with the universe is called pantheism.

The scavengers on Smokey Mountain believe in a personal, loving, and compassionate God who concerns himself with the destiny and actions of human beings.[6] The scavengers worship a God active in the universe in a personal sense, the transcendent mystery that is the origin, the ground, and the goal of everything that is. This means we can and do have a real relationship with ultimate reality, both immanent and transcendent, who opens up the future. In this relationship, we also realize our personhood. "What is God, and what am I?" are one and the same question. In religious experience, we "touch" the divine in our own innermost self because we are created in the image and likeness of God. The cosmic sense of communion in religious experience is the experiential ground for belief in a personal God and for the sense of personal identity. This ultimate reference point of the experience of communion must be personal, since human beings are persons capable of relationship. This is the experiential basis for belief in a personal God.

The problem of reconciling religious experience and faith with modern science is encountered not only in religious experience, but also in issues such as the origin of the universe, the basis of morality, and the existence of God. Finding common ground in exploring these issues becomes more difficult when the scientists are also unbelievers who want to destroy religion. There has been a spate of books lately denouncing religion, with undisguised hostility and vitriolic hatred, calling it a curse to humankind.[7] Most of the authors are scientists. Their shrill denunciations using arguments from science, often going beyond the boundaries of the scientific method, verge on antireligious hysteria. Combative, militant atheists look down on religion as collective hallucination or idiotic superstition.[8] I accept their criticisms with forbearance and compassion, realizing that the accusations are not completely groundless. In his commentary on article 21 of *Gaudium et Spes*, Pope Benedict XVI wrote that the article should have recognized the church's failure in the social field in the nineteenth century. It should have been admitted that "we owe it to the atheists' attack that we have become properly aware once more of our own duties."[9]

Karl Rahner suggested that one should test one's own faith and spirituality in intellectual solidarity with those who have excluded God from their horizon. There is a cognitive part of me that is atheist, a part that can be at home in a world characterized by the absence of the divine. I have to deliberately confront this part if I am to restore the integrity and vitality of my faith day by day, if I am to realize that God is not an object among others, that God is beyond my reach. The cognitive dimension is only a part of the God debate. The existential dimension encompasses a wider realm in the life of real human beings like the scavengers on Smokey Mountain—it is here that our humanity is defined more fully. The God debate should also talk about global poverty, global terrorism, and global warming. We inhabit the same biosphere, and we all have the same right to inhabit it, whether scavenger on Smokey Mountain, billionaire in Wall Street, or atheist in the laboratory. We all have the same duty to defend it and allow it to flourish. I would like to see what the implications of atheism would be for worldwide poverty, environmental degradation, and widespread terrorism. I would also like to see how unbelief can give hope to a planet in peril.

The intense religious experience of the scavengers is confronted by the unbelief of the new atheists. The scavengers believe in an eternal God out of whose creative power all things emerge and into which all things return. The notion of divine revelation in the Christian tradition is closely connected with the notion of a personal God who is both the creator of the universe and constantly sustains it in existence. Since he is by nature outside the physical boundaries of the universe, we can only talk about him in metaphors and analogies; otherwise we can say nothing about God at all. Thus, theology cannot fulfill the demand of atheists that the God experienced in mystical union and ritual worship, by definition transcendent, be presented for investigation like any other object in the world. According to C. S. Lewis, this is equivalent to asking the architect to be the fireplace or a piece of furniture in the house he has designed. The theological definition of the God Christians believe in is more subtle and robust than the God being attacked by the new atheists.

Reasoned faith has something to say about providing a stable definition of what human becoming is, where it leads to, and what is its ultimate meaning. Many believers have taken up the challenge of the militant atheists and have articulated their theological positions in the intellectual dimension. Using the latest findings in astrophysics, philosophy, and basic logic, Robert Spitzer, in carefully reasoned and well-documented arguments, puts forth evidence capable of grounding reasonable and responsible belief in a superintelligent, transcendent, creative power as the origin of the universe. There are rational foundations, he writes, for the existence of a unique, unconditioned, unrestricted, absolutely simple, superintelligent continuous Creator of all else that is, the causative power transcending universal time and space.[10] John C. Lennox, who teaches mathematics and philosophy of science at Oxford, says that the rational intelligibility of the universe points to the existence of a mind if one considers the most recent science from physics and biology.[11]

The problem is not between science and faith but between naturalism and theism. And positions taken for or against naturalism or theism are structured by one's worldview, which is shaped by culture, experience, and reflection. This is the reason why very few people are convinced by reasoning alone that God exists. People are very seldom persuaded by logic to change their views because these views are shaped by their preconceived and subconscious assumptions. The scavengers believe in a God they want to worship, pray to, and devote their life to serving, a God in whom all things live and move and have their being, a God who gives them life, a God they encounter in religious experience. The God the scavengers believe in possesses all the perfection of being that evokes humility, trust, adoration, reverence, and commitment. We discover the personal God when we go to the very depth and center of our being. We have to turn to the depths of our humanity if we are to encounter ultimate reality. We encounter God as our innermost self and at the same time as the Wholly Other. St. Augustine said that God is *intimior intimo meo* (closer to me than I am to myself).

There are no disembodied souls calling for rational proofs for God's existence; the faith communities on Smokey Mountain consist of flesh and blood human beings with their ideals and jealousies, their dreams and pettiness, their conflicts and intimacy, their confrontations and forgiveness. The God debate should be conducted with flesh and blood human beings too, even if all this debate is completely unintelligible to the scavengers. Instead of the modern question "Is there a God?" I found out that the question the scavengers asked was "Where can we find God?" The point of departure for the God question and the worldview behind it is different in the garbage dump. Their very being and their joyousness fling a challenge to unbelief that are totally unexpected. As John Horgan in his *Rational Mysticism* pointed out, "Just as believers in a beneficent deity should be haunted by the problem of natural evil, so agnostics, atheists, pessimists and nihilists should be haunted by the problem of friendship, love, beauty, truth, humor, compassion, and fun. Never forget the problem of fun."

To view the world in purely physical terms is inadequate

to explain the religious experience of the people of Smokey Mountain. It does not do justice to the way they understand their humanity. For the scavengers, religious experiences are crucial for their explanation of what being human means and their understanding of personhood. They invest these experiences with ultimate meaning and value. It is their way of finding meaning in their ravaged and cruel environment. They told me they experience a cosmic sense of communion with everything in the world, an experience of contact with something beyond the self, and an overwhelming sense of a conscious presence that pervades the universe. This way of looking at and experiencing the world shape their communal life. In the rites and narratives of religious faith, the scavengers come to apprehend a way of seeing and responding to the reality they experience as a community. They have no idea of a privatized spirituality removed from communal activities.

In the past we remember the genocides, the crusades, and the depredation of other cultures inflamed by religious zeal and in our times through a religious frenzy attaching itself to religious ideals. Jacob Needleman reminds believers of the bitter egoism with all its violence and inhumanity played out on a massive scale—on the scale of whole nations and peoples, whole historical epochs—because of a crippled relationship to the idea of whatever is called God. He likewise reminds unbelievers of how much grief and sorrow has arisen because of a set of mind and the disillusioned heart that leads a person to turn away entirely from the possible influence, in one's life and behavior, of what is immeasurably higher both above and within ourselves.[12] Believers and unbelievers should therefore discuss what kind of God they mean because it has a profound bearing on how they conduct their personal lives and how they organize their community. Albert Einstein is credited with the quote that science without religion is lame, religion without science is blind. Do ethics and spirituality lie at the very core of what is good about our being human? Understanding the religious experience of the scavengers may provide new insights into our nature, to new rules of engaging in prophetic dialogue, and to new horizons of global collaboration.

EAST IS EAST AND WEST IS WEST

*Oh, East is East, and West is West, and never the twain
    shall meet,
Till Earth and Sky stand presently at God's great
    Judgment Seat;
But there is neither East nor West, Border, nor Breed,
    nor Birth,
When two strong men stand face to face, tho' they come
    from the ends of the earth!*
    —Rudyard Kipling, "The Ballad of East and West"

The intense religiosity of the scavengers comes face to face with the nihilism of militant atheism. What can I, as a Filipino theologian, say about all this debate regarding the existence of God? Sometimes, as the smoke from the dump site whirled around the room and I read the debates between atheists and religionists framed in a Western view of the world, I always felt like T. S. Eliot's patient etherized upon a table while the women come and go, talking of Michelangelo ("The Love Song of J. Alfred Prufrock"). From my vantage point, the God debates are clearly structured by the philosophical and metaphysical assumptions inherent in the Western view of reality. I would have wanted the debates to be like the streets in the poem "that follow like a tedious argument of insidious intent" to lead me to an overwhelming question—"Is the universe kind to the poor and the oppressed?"

Ludwig Wittgenstein, echoing Nietzsche, wrote that "if we spoke a different language, we would perceive a somewhat different reality." The limits of our language are the limits of our world. Since no language is fixed, unalterable, and complete, it is impossible for us to "place ourselves outside the particularities of language to arrive at a truth, a way of understanding and responding to the world that applies to everyone at all times."[13] One of the most difficult problems I encountered in the garbage dump was how to explain to the scavengers theological ideas I learned from the West and bridge the language barrier between Western theology and their religiosity. When I was teaching at the Catholic Theological Union in Chicago, a few female students carried small bells to class and rang them whenever the lecturer engaged in noninclusive, sexist language. This problem does not exist in Filipino languages, which do not have words for daughter or son, niece or nephew. They have only the equivalent of "child," and this has to be specified as female or male. There are many other gender-neutral words in Filipino languages like *asawa* (husband or wife), *magulang* (father or mother), *kapatid* (brother or sister), *biyenan* (father-in-law or mother-in-law), *manugang* (son- or daughter-in-law), *bayani* (hero or heroine). There are other theological problems in the West that are structured by their languages, especially the problems of speaking about God. Many of these problems do not exist in Filipino languages.

Our language shapes the way we think about space, time, colors, and objects. When I started to learn Italian, German, and French (required for the study of theology in Rome, apart from Latin and Greek), I had to learn new ways of thinking—grammatical gender and the pluperfect subjunctive do not exist in our languages. Studies have found that language affects how people understand events, reason about causality, keep track of the number of objects, conceive material substance, perceive and experience emotion, reason about other people's minds, choose to take risks, and even on the way they choose their careers and their spouses.[14] The languages we speak shape the way we look at the world, structure the way we think and the way we live our lives. Language entraps us in a set of cultural assumptions like a train following the railroad tracks. As linguistics professor George Lakoff explains, "Language always comes with what is called 'framing.' Every word is defined relative to a conceptual framework."

Indo-European languages are strongly noun oriented and lend themselves to a way of looking at the world in terms of objects, categories, and fixed boundaries rather than of processes and transformations. Because of semantic drift, our mental constructions and our languages have outrun our intuitive and sense perceptions. The new physics with its emphasis on complexity, nonlinearity, and self-organization sees nature with no fixed forms; it is an open system characterized by flux and constant transformation, with limitless dimensionality and countless possible combinations. Superposition and entanglement seem to tell us that human languages cannot provide an adequate description of reality.

Sometimes the descriptions of religious phenomena that some scientists offer with unfettered self-assurance seem to me comically, or perhaps dangerously, oversimplified because of their reductionist method and the language they use. There are still many in the West who think of language as one-to-one correspondence (the representation paradigm) with objects in the world, thus often identifying the definition with what is defined. Religious fundamentalists and scientific materialists are mired in this kind of understanding. Kant already dealt a death blow to this view when he declared that we can only deal with phenomena. He said that the noumena, the *Ding-an-sich*, the thing in itself, is beyond knowledge and articulation. He claimed that we can never know reality because in the very act of knowing, human reason structures the world according to the fundamental laws of its own functioning, or as Wittgenstein said, we make to ourselves pictures of facts. Quantum indeterminacy confirms that the act of observing changes the reality we are investigating. Kant however claimed that our moral reasoning presumes (but cannot prove) standards of right and wrong vested in an ultimate moral judge who has the power to reward and punish.

The universe is real and independent of our observations. However, explanations of the universe are produced by human observers and are therefore relative to their capacities, education and training, languages, assumptions, and worldview. It is not the universe or its properties but the languages in whose terms we know them that are socially constructed. Our prior beliefs, concepts, and training influence the character of our perceptual states and the way we pose questions and answer them. They shape our representation and description of the world. Peoples and cultures have different worldviews and levels of consciousness and express these in their own languages. These differences cause a lot of misunderstanding in the world today, especially since many in the West deny interior transcendence and the various levels of consciousness.

There is need for prophetic dialogue so that reality can be seen from many points of view, especially after Heisenberg's principle of indeterminacy, or Kurt Goedel's incompleteness theorem in mathematics. Goedel's theorem has proven that within any deductive system, there are truths that cannot be proved. Even within simple, formal systems like mathematics, one can make statements that could never be either proved or disproved within the terms of that system. Thus, there are mathematical truths that can never be proven empirically. Goedel's theorem suggests that uncertainty is inherent in the nature of logic. In this light, I believe that militant atheists and religious fundamentalists have a shallow appreciation of the dangers of too much certainty.

The understanding of the world, of time and history in the West is based on the visual patterning of experience. In my dissertation, I sought to show that it is the visual patterning of experience that primarily shapes the definitions, notions, and categories of Western thought and languages. Plato judged seeing as the sharpest among the senses by which we can apprehend reality. Vision creates sharp boundaries, a radical distancing and opposition between the seer and what is seen. It delineates and divides. One who patterns his or her experience visually becomes aware of the world as the sum of visible objects and ends up maintaining representation as the ideal form of knowledge.

The visual patterning of experience with its sharp boundaries demands logical consistency, the absence of contradiction, complete objectivity, and absolutely certain knowledge. This way of looking at the world predisposes one to need certainty, power, and control. And so the Newtonian distinction between observer and the observed exercised a strong hold on the ethos, methodology, values, and the vast technology that was unleashed by Western science. Mechanistic images gave rise to a mechanistic way of looking at the world. Reductionist, objectivist, and determinist views made people see themselves as separate, isolated atoms connected only by force or influence. Behavior was thought to be determined only by biology and conditioning, leaving no scope for human initiative and responsibility. Nature became value-neutral, an object to be studied, conquered, and used. It is easy for this way of looking at things to fall prey to the idolatry of absolute certainty and to treat complex, emergent phenomena as if they were simple.

The desire to calculate, control, and subdue nature was easily carried out by a disengaged, amoral, autonomous self in this view. The insistence of the autonomy of the self from nature blocked the way towards wholeness and unity. Western thought has not overcome the radical split it made between spirit and matter since the time of Plato. This split has permeated Western philosophy, theology, spirituality, and science. Thus, the assumption of scientific research, according to John Haught, is that the universe is essentially dead, and the reductionist method proceeds through the progressive expurgation of the vital features of an essentially lifeless and mindless universe. And so, "the idea of an essentially lifeless and mindless realm of matter has come to serve as the philosophical foundation of modern scientific thought."[15] Life and mind are now the unintelligible exceptions that have to be explained in terms of what is lifeless and mindless.

Western views often oscillate between absolute certainty and complete skepticism regarding the truth. There is perpetual opposition between faith and reason, particular and universal, man and woman, individual and society, tribe and state, which is seldom reconciled. Westerners have a low tolerance for cognitive dissonance and usually deal with it by doing away with one of the conflicting ideas. If they cannot reconcile subjectivity and objectivity, they do away with subjectivity—only the sensory, empirical, material world exists. If they cannot reconcile the idea of the scientist as participant or observer, they do away with the participant mode, the self-referential dimension, thus failing to take into account the human being doing the experiments. Cognitive scientists today see vision as a proper subject for understanding the brain's link to our conscious experience and for speculating on the nature of the mind. The visual patterning of experience is still in place.

The visual patterning of experience leads to either/or thinking. Either/or thinking is a trap—it cannot cope with paradox and ambiguity. It is a mind-set filled with boundaries and leads to a dualistic worldview that sees nature as dead and passive, a vast cosmic machine. Haught wrote that this is the manifestation of a

will to control which "seeks by fiat to force all possible explanations into a single manageable level where the obsessive need for
immediate clarity rules out rich understanding."[16] This view can
no longer hold because we now know that fluctuation, randomness, and indeterminacy characterize the fundamental structuring of the cosmos. We live in a world of creative emergence. God
did not create a tightly controlled mechanistic cosmos that results
in robotic behavior. God created human beings to be free. God
plays dice with the universe—divine creativity employs chance
and indeterminacy for his ultimate purpose of a universe bringing forth beings who are free to choose. Self-transcendence, the
continual creative advance into the new, is built into the fabric
of the universe. For example, the capacity for slight error is the
real miracle of the DNA; it was designed from the beginning to
make small mistakes. Creativity, not chance and randomness,
builds the cosmos—there is directionality in its evolution. In this
context, both/and thinking that quantum physics makes both
possible and necessary is required for understanding reality as
a whole. Both/and thinking characterizes to a large extent the
thinking of the scavengers in the garbage dump.

The science of certainty and the religion of certainty are
engaged in a battle to the death in Western culture, both fueled
by the need for absolute certitude, objectivity, and predictability.
Both can learn from the adaptiveness of the scavengers' way of
looking at the world. The God debate will take a very different
turn when conducted in the garbage dump where there is little
of the Western intolerance of uncertainty, subjectivity, and cognitive dissonance. The scavengers are at home with contradictions and use a certain way of reasoning that stresses matters
of degree and large shades of gray between black and white.
The adaptiveness of the scavengers allows them to live even as
the smallest whatever in the universe, the quarks, are seen as
packets of potentiality in a fuzzy world where boundaries have
an elusive nature.

The scavengers, like most Filipinos, pattern their experience
aurally, since theirs is still mostly an oral culture. Where Westerners tend to isolate and dissect, the scavengers contemplate
an ordered whole and intuit a depth behind spatial depth that
grounds the simultaneity of all things that are successive in time.

The scavengers see time and eternity not in terms of exclusiveness but of interpenetration. This aural patterning of experience can more easily perceive what poet Rainer Maria Rilke called the depth dimension of our inwardness and its social dimension. In this view, religion is not a private matter but relates essentially to human sociality. Faith needs the conscious experience of one's own relatedness to others. It needs both the social context and lived experience. A solipsistic way of looking at the world will hardly discover God in this evolving universe. A purely privatized religion is a contradiction in terms in both/and thinking.

The scavengers believe in the *loob*, the inner being of our humanity, our subjectivity, our capacity for emotion, thought, understanding, and love. An either/or way of thinking cannot say much about the inwardness and interiority, the insideness and withinness of things. It finds it difficult to deal with issues like subjectivity, uniqueness, or what Gerard Manley Hopkins called the inscape and instress in his poems, which are resistant to complete objectification. As a method of inquiry that abstracts from qualities, vitality, and subjective feelings, science is simply not programmed to penetrate the mystery of life, according to Haught. Also, science cannot do this because it assumes that the universe will end in a final, irreversible disintegration—absolute death and nothingness is the destiny of everything real. This would trivialize and paralyze human ethical aspirations. Everything is depersonalized and objectified, subservient to an exclusively materialistic view of the world. Human action is rendered meaningless from the start, and hope is suffocated at the moment of its birth.

The people of Smokey Mountain have the ability to relate things that analytically and rationally do not belong together. The God question cannot be answered by the mind alone, according to them. We have to ask it with our whole being. And that is why there are no atheists among the scavengers. They have a strong desire to spend time with God and celebrate his glory. Their worship leaves room for mystery as they celebrate the God who transcends all limitations. They are capable of holding opposites and reconciling contradictory elements in their minds, like God's immanence and transcendence, faith and reason, spirit and matter, facts and values, contradictions that would trigger cognitive dissonance among people who pattern their experience visually. The religious experience of the scavengers orients their being towards a transcendent reality. This orientation grounds the intensity of their religious festivals and their joy in life. It provides them with a sense of who they are and what their place is in the scheme of things. The scavengers would think that the wave-particle duality in quantum physics is not a problem at all if it is explained in a way intelligible to them. If they can sustain their both/and thinking in the face of globalization, they might help transform the world in worshipful awe and intimacy.

The pendulum in the West constantly swings between narcissism and nihilism in the either/or way of patterning experience that splinters and fragments the whole. If their instruments cannot measure it, then empiricists reject everything in the inner dimension where nothing can be objectified. The solipsists say only their interior experiences are real and doubt whether other human beings exist. While rationalists believe that reality can be known by the mind alone, empiricists claim that the only basis of knowledge is sensory experience. There is always the predisposition in the visual patterning of experience to constrict reality and place it on Procrustes' bed so that all contradictions disappear. The visual patterning of experience is predisposed to believe that there is only one truth about the human condition, that it holds true for all people at all times, and those who do not subscribe to it are in grave error and, for some, even worthy of death.

Studies have shown that there are fundamentally different thinking processes in the West and in the East—the one analytical, the other more holistic, which might correspond to the visual and aural patterning of experience, to either/or and both/and thinking. Asians, according to a study by Richard Nisbett of the University of Michigan, perceive situations as fluid and integrated, and view a situation as a set of interrelated elements. The thinking style of Westerners tends to focus on one aspect of the situation, on what seems to be the most important factor in a situation. The Western thought pattern favors the rules of formal logic. In one experiment, two groups of subjects from Asian countries and from America were asked to describe an animation of fish swimming underwater. The Asians overwhelmingly describe the background—"there is a pond"—and could no longer recognize the fish from the first experiment when they were shown against a new background. The Americans almost always started with a description of the biggest, fastest-moving fish and quickly recognized it even against a new background. Nisbett theorized that East Asians exist in complex social networks where attention to context is needed to function effectively. They therefore see themselves as a small part of the immensity of the universe. Westerners stress independence and self-determination because they live in less constraining social worlds and hence see the world as something that can be understood and dominated.

Nisbett's studies of the differences between Asian and Western thought patterns showed that Asians are more oriented towards group relations and obligations. The Asian mind-set tends to be more holistic. It pays attention to entire fields and is oriented towards a contextual view of the world. It makes little use of categories and formal logic, sees events as complex and determined by many factors. Asians emphasize change, recognize contradiction, and the need for multiple perspectives, often searching for the "Middle Way" between opposing propositions and making space for difference. The Western thought pattern has a tunnel-vision perceptual style, focusing on particular objects in isolation from their context. If one knows the rules governing objects, one can control the behavior of those objects. Westerners are more analytic, paying attention primarily to the object and the categories to which it belongs. They are prone to use rules, including formal logic, to explain and predict the object's behavior. The problem-solving techniques they employ are mostly rule based.[17]

There is evidence of a genetic basis for behavioral differences between racial and ethnic groups. Cultures shape minds and brains. Brain research suggests that Eastern culture tends to inculcate interdependence (characterizing society in terms of relational obligations), and Western cultures emphasize independence (stressing personal agency and will) as frames of reference for seeing the world and one's place in it. East Asians are raised to believe that we are all connected and that the needs of the group are more important than the needs of the individual. Western Europeans and North Americans are taught to prioritize their own goals, feelings, and achievements. Social rewards and punishments follow accordingly.[18]

Like that of Asians, the worldview of the scavengers, structured by their culture, might be more adapted for life if the universe is an eternal dance of cosmic energy in unbroken harmony and wholeness. Their aural patterning of experience perceives the whole. Their mind-set focuses on the gestalt—it is more intuitive than rationalistic-discursive. If relationship is all there is to reality, then relationship is the ground for understanding the world, the basis for all definitions, and the basis for understanding the kind of God one believes in. From my experience of working with the youth, and judging from the results of studies on the neuroplasticity of the brain, I have reason to believe that the members of the Internet generation with their ability for multitasking and parallel processing, will favor the both/and thinking prevalent in the East.

Christian faith is meant to be open to discussion, to question, to reinterpretation and inculturation. Jesus, the Christ, the alpha and the omega, is the same, yesterday, today, forever, but our statements about who he is and what he did for us are always fragmentary and provisional because we are fragmentary and provisional beings—we see through a glass darkly. Knowledge emerges out of the interactions of mind, language, and world. Wendell Berry wrote that "mind = brain + body + world + local dwelling place + community + history."[19] Our view of the world is shaped not only by the perceptual processes of our brain, but also through our relationship to ourselves, to others, and to the world, together with cultural and social influences, education, and spiritual inclinations. Thus, it is difficult to find God if you think with the prefrontal lobe alone.

The new ways of thinking call into question many of my basic assumptions as a Filipino about what it means to be a human being in an evolving world. I have waded through much of scientific literature and its sometimes arcane jargon. So far, I have not found an intellectually satisfying explanation of where the universe really came from, how life and consciousness came to arise from mindless matter, or how energy fields and quantum fluctuations could give rise to conscious experience. There is an abundance of answers and a surfeit of certainty and conviction, but the answers are always framed in Western categories.

The insights on the different mind-sets from cross-cultural studies and brain research can lead us to examine our own habits of mind and beliefs. Do we often primarily employ either/or thinking or do we use both/and thinking? The universe exists independent of our human and social constructs: it is polyvalent and multidimensional. Reality has many dimensions and is filled with surplus meaning. It has to be viewed from various perspectives. As moral beings we have to see it from many points of view in order to gain wisdom. In light of global emergencies, we should move away from the conviction that there is only one correct way to understand something or one right way to do it. We should encourage participation because the universe welcomes diversity since it is characterized by a multiplicity of meanings and values. We should engage in introspection and investigate our preconceived notions about reality, time, history, and humanity, and the influence of the individual person's experiences and background on prior beliefs and commitment.

The results of studies regarding differing worldviews should frame the context of the God debates and bring them to bear on giving hope to this planet in peril. Prophetic dialogue should focus on questions about life, humanity, consciousness, on ideas of truth and evidence, and on the limits of human knowing in light of differing contexts and languages. The universe is complex and dynamic, therefore fuzzy logic and fractal probabilities might best describe both the universe and our approximate understanding of it. Wisdom comes from a mysterious presence transcending sense perception. This wisdom is to be learned personally in relationships—healthy, faithful, and passionate relationships. The scavengers' faith in a loving God and their religious festivities shape their values and guide their behavior. These values convey a wisdom that is open to continuous dialogue and mysterious presence. Thus, the scavengers believe that what happened in Calvary is useful to us only when we live it, make it part of our life; otherwise, life will be devoid of satisfying personal and social meaning.

Anyone suggesting that the law of gravity be worshipped will be laughed by the scavengers out of the garbage dump. Carl Sagan already noted this difficulty some time ago, but Carolyn C. Porco still imagines a congregation of the Church of Latter-Day Scientists raising their voices "in tribute to gravity, the force that binds us all to the earth and the earth to the sun and the sun to the Milky Way." Left with a residue of unfulfilled longing in a godless cosmos and the intimation of an intolerable emptiness, she laments the fact that scientists in their spiritual quest to feel connected through an understanding of the natural world lack ceremony and ritual, the initiation of baptism, and the brotherhood of communal worship.[20]

Both science and religion formulate a certain way of looking at the world, and both evoke and sustain moods and motivations that are consonant with that particular way of looking at the world. A sense of transcendence is basic to the human response to the grandeur of the cosmos. Thus, Joel Garreau suggests the creation of some new rituals, a liturgy of life everlasting when a person receives his or her first cellular age reversal workup. This tells me that many scientists possess some sort of spiritual response to the vastness of the universe; they are thirsting for transcendence, longing for the infinite, remaining awestruck as they behold its immensity and duration, filled with wonder by the fact that anything exists at all, even if their responses are mostly extensions of pantheistic mysticism.

Faith however does not focus the human spiritual impulse on the physical universe but locates the source of spirituality in a realm beyond it. Faith holds that a supremely perfect Creator is the only proper object of unlimited devotion, the horizon that propels us forward as we work to build the earth. This ever-receding horizon cannot be framed within cognitive boundaries. The denial of the underlying spiritual reality in the cosmos eliminates the credibility of worship and denies that there is any moral order in reality. If the universe will end in darkness in a never-ending void, I cannot see why anyone should be doing science at all and why it is worth seeking the truth.

I believe that the mystery of religious consciousness, even plain consciousness and its attendant creativity (possibly quantum in origin), would be the clue to the mystery of the universe. Will the new science be able to bring objective study to bear on subjective experience? So far, cognitive science is still mostly in thrall to mechanistic paradigms and treats human beings as objects of study. It assumes that the human mind works like a computer and has therefore concentrated its studies on the physiological basis of cognition. It mostly excludes emotion, the ability to pay attention, memory, consciousness, and creativity, which are of utmost importance to human beings. There is much study being done on the brain, but it is mostly centered on neuronal activity, the effect of drugs on brain capabilities, and the mechanics of perception.

Einstein already remarked that the fact that the universe is intelligible grounded his sense of infinite mystery. If you let wonder fill your being, it will take you out of yourself into the stunning mystery of a world that facts alone cannot explain. William Byers claims that the science of wonder is perfectly compatible with the religion of wonder—they are basically the same thing. The religion of wonder is centered on a God of love, compassion, and justice. It will be a religion that leads to spiritual wisdom and will be part of the solution to global emergencies.

WHAT DOES IT MEAN TO BE A HUMAN BEING?

Whatever faith may be, and whatever answers it may give, and to whomsoever it gives them, every such answer gives to the finite existence of man an infinite meaning, a meaning not destroyed by sufferings, deprivations, or death.
—Leo Tolstoy

Is God really a delusion and religion the opium of the masses? What difference does the profession of faith in a Supreme Being make in our life and in our world in the face of the global threats we confront today? Does religion intensify, as the militant atheists allege, the very forces that keep the scavengers poor—ignorance, fatalism, fear? Can the scavengers' deep religiosity bring back to Christianity the spirit of contemplative consciousness that has been lost in ordinary piety? Can Catholic social doctrine encourage the poor to acquire expertise, enter the circle of exchange, and develop their skills in order to make the best use of their capacities and resources, as Pope John Paul II wrote, in order to build global shalom?[21] If different cultures see reality from different perspectives, how can we understand one another and work for a common objective?

Tina Beattie claims that the very parameters of the current God debate need to be called into question.[22] These parameters are too narrow, reflecting the mind-set of a relatively small group of white intellectual males who have hijacked the debate as an ahistorical conundrum to fit their own militant allegiance to Western rationality and individualism. As an Asian, I would heartily agree with her and would like to expand the parameters of the God debate to the whole of life, to the wider questions about religious experience, history and terrorism, peace and justice in a postmodern world, garbage dumps and climate change, all of which impinge deeply on human life. Questions about evidence, proof, and rationality should not be framed along the lines of the Western mind-set alone. We have to look for empirical evidence that white male Westerners who never knew hunger and whose lives were never threatened are at the peak of the evolutionary scale; otherwise, they should stop talking with contemptuous arrogance as if the other races and cultures possess but little knowledge and civilization, barbarians unworthy of dialogue and engagement, grossly ignorant like those peoples in the past who were colonized, enslaved, and decimated in the name of an empire where the sun never sets. If unenlightened religious fundamentalists and militant atheists are unable to hear the sound of the left hand clapping, they still have a long way to travel towards a level of consciousness that can attain a more profound insight into what the universe really is like and what kind of creative designer can bring it into existence and guide it to its ultimate fulfillment.

I would venture to suggest then in light of the different levels of consciousness and perspectives that the God debate, while continuing to discuss cosmic and subatomic issues, should also discuss first, the human desire for more; second, the movement towards wholeness; and third, the metaphysical implications of the relatedness of everything; and lastly, the issues surrounding the creative mind and the ability to discover the new. Values would also be a good issue to deal with in the God debate because the biological imperative demands that we become fully human in order to grasp the humanity of the "other." Against the dictatorship of relativism, reality exists independent of our human and social constructs, and it should dictate values that would make life and consciousness evolve more fully. Even science is predicated on a whole set of beliefs influenced by context and culture. We have to ground the God debate then in how we understand our humanity and what values we should espouse so that our humanity can flourish.

The God debate should also ask which stance before an evolving cosmos makes people happy. Additionally, whether one believes in God or not, views of the world should be judged, according to Thomas Berry, "primarily by the extent to which they inhibit, ignore or foster a mutually enhancing human-earth relationship." He said that human ethics is derived from the ecological imperative, and so the human community is subordinate to the ecological community. We have to agree on sustainability indicators so that we can collaborate on doable environmental projects. We also have to discuss how we arrive at the truth. Worship and celebration, for example, contain within themselves a distinctive mode of knowing through participation in a divine reality that the scavengers experience intimately. This knowledge orders the scavengers' priorities and shapes the character of their relationships. They suffer from poverty and material deprivation, but they are rich in belongingness and family and community. This gives their lives a primordial experience of human identity. They show childlike trust in the power of God to give meaning to the chaos in their lives despite the lack of material possessions.[23] And that is why they always smile and laugh. I never laughed as much as I did when I was with the scavengers. They do not want to live in rich subdivisions if given the chance because as they said, "We might not be able to laugh as much as we want."

The story of Smokey Mountain is a celebration of a people's will to survive and the innate capacity to dream of a better tomorrow as they journey between random possibilities and ordered structures in partnership with others. This ability to dream and transform reality and work together in community to achieve their dreams sets human beings apart from other animals and gives them hope. While Smokey Mountain served as a nightmarish symbol of a desperate nation, shown again and again on television channels in many countries and featured in newspapers and magazines countless times, the garbage dump is also a monument to human inventiveness and creativity rooted in faith. Human beings are vessels of clay containing miracles of grace and redemption. If we make the effort, we can arrive at mutual understanding and collaboration as residents of the same planet.

In the global world, East can meet West, and both can be enriched by the encounter. The visual patterning of experience can be enlarged by the aural structuring of the world, and either/or thinking can be enriched by the both/and mind-set. We all have much to learn from each other. We should structure the dialogue then with the overarching question of what it means to be a human being. This is the first overriding question that scavengers would like to ask. The scavengers know the sweet joy that comes only through being emptied and a life built around other human beings and faith in the Almighty. And they fought for their rights, took their destiny into their own hands to shape the future they want in light of their faith. In the midst of squalor, they created an environment most conducive to joy in worship. They told me they have nothing else except God's love and mercy and forgiveness and grace. And that is why life is a perpetual celebration for the scavengers of Smokey Mountain.

We cannot go on with a society in which individuals shape their own meaning and goals, totally unconcerned with the good of the community and the planet. We have to discuss moral obligations and ethical norms in light of the kind of world we would like to hand on to future generations. The scavengers say that religious experience and the commitment to a Supreme Being are an essential part of being human. It is the ground for their moral obligations and ethical norms. The militant atheists say this is a delusion. What kind of understanding then of our being human can give hope to a planet in peril?

Christians, in the face of secularization and militant atheism, have to prove by their actions that this pledge of fulfillment in the triune God who created the world, redeemed the human race, and sanctified us to bring us to share God's own triune life and plenitude is the ultimate hope for this planet in peril. It is also one of the best arguments for the existence of God, the rightness of religious experience, and the most firm basis for hope. They have to work together with those who have different beliefs and those who do not believe. Brain research shows that we have a bias for optimism. Human beings are evolved to hope, to believe that things will become better than they are at present. We have to come together in mutuality and respect, with confidence in the possibility of global cooperation and responsibility in common hope for a sustainable future. Together we shall overcome global poverty, global terrorism, global warming.

TOWARDS A WORLD GLOWING WITH HARMONY AND UNDERSTANDING

We have to learn to live together as brothers and sisters, or we will perish together as fools.
—Dr. Martin Luther King

On May 21, 2011, Pope Benedict XVI spoke with the astronauts in the space shuttle Endeavor and the International Space Station. He blessed them all and told them, "You are representatives spearheading humanity's exploration of new spaces and possibilities for our future."

We all are journeying towards the future on spaceship earth. The global emergencies we face have deep spiritual and moral implications for the future. The people of Smokey Mountain therefore call on each one of us to look at the planet's problems in a systemic way, in terms of relationships, patterns, and dynamic processes. We have to see the problems in light of the interconnectedness of everything in the cosmos. We have to refocus our values on relationship, community, and ethics in the face of the ecological and social crises facing the world today as we fulfill the biological imperative and forge a world glowing with harmony and understanding. We have to share our experiences and reflections with care and compassion, with genuine openness to the truth and the freedom to seek it no matter where the evidence leads.

We need to be sensitive to human suffering and collaborate in promoting the paradigm shift that is urgently needed, as it is now a question of the survival of human civilization as we know it. We also have to look ahead and see the problems in light of intergenerational responsibility—we are accountable to future generations. We must expand our consciousness and hasten the process of interconnecting to recapture the flow of creativity that can save the biosphere. We must avoid worldviews built on the language of the past and engage in crafting new language and thinking to confront the global emergencies.

These questions are an invitation to look at the problems of the planet as a whole, as interconnected, and as part of our evolutionary journey into the future in an ever-expanding universe. David Ramsay Steele wrote that atheism is like pure water, but it is a negative. It cannot tell us how to conduct our personal lives or organize our social order.[24] Personal conduct and social organization are very good topics to begin the global dialogue. We would like to add a third issue: how to build a sustainable future for the whole planet. We would like to conduct the dialogue on these issues then with faith in the Trinity in its personal, relational, and dynamic aspects as points of departure: how the scavengers think personal life should be conducted in light of their faith in the one and triune God, what kind of social order they wanted to organize in light of the primacy of relationships, and what projects they promoted in order to help assure coming generations of a sustainable future.

Our suggestion is to conduct the global dialogue in light of the new science, which shows that the characteristics of the cosmos are as follows:

Unity: The world is literally a uni-verse imbued with uniform order. It is a unified whole. The scavengers call it *sansinukob, santinakpan, sandaigdigan,* always with the prefix that means "one." The Filipino sensibility, which constantly seeks the spirit of complementarity and harmony, might lead to the rethinking of the global vision and the transformation of dehumanizing structures.

Interconnectedness: The universe is a web of relationships in a ceaseless flow of energy. It is an infinite variety of patterns that melt into one another, an endless interplay of quantum fields oscillating in rhythmic movements. Everything is connected to everything else—*ang lahat ng bagay ay magkaugnay,* as the scavengers would say.

Dynamism: The universe is in a state of continual motion, both on the cosmic scale, with galaxies moving away from each other, and on the subatomic scale, with elementary particles as bundles of energy and sets of relationships that continually reach outward to other things, four-dimensional entities in the space-time configuration. Change, growth, flow, development, process, and evolution characterize the cosmos, which moves in dynamic balance between intermingling and orderliness, between different levels and types of consciousness.

This global conversation conducted in light of the unity, interconnectedness, and dynamism of everything that is should focus on what makes us human.[25] Experiencing ourselves as infinite possibilities, we long for a vision of truth, beauty, and goodness that will complete us. These issues can be the starting point for a global conversation, for prophetic dialogue. In light of Christian hope, theology's task is to clarify these issues in the face of the radical openness of the universe to new possibilities and to clarify the task of building a new reality that corresponds better to God's promised future. In doing this, theologians can learn from the scavengers how to create a way of life that is more celebratory and festive, life in its fullness, life that is full of hope. Theology can learn from the scavengers to focus on celebration, play, and humor as the necessary companions of the struggle for a new world if this struggle is not itself to be overwhelmed by the spirit of the rigidity and closedness of the scientific materialist view of the end of the universe. This is the best explanation of how belief in God is intuitively plausible.

How can the global dialogue be allowed to flourish between those who believe and those who do not in light of their profound differences? St. Augustine of Hippo already established the framework for this global conversation between believers and unbelievers: *in necesariis, unitas; in dubiis, libertas; in omnibus, caritas*—in necessary things, unity; in dubious things, liberty; in all things, charity.[26] This framework can help in mediating misunderstanding, settling conflicting claims, and guiding us to peaceful coexistence. Each culture can contribute something to the accumulation of human wisdom and can therefore learn from each other.

Aristotle wrote that the human and humanizing political task is to reflect on how we should order our life together. As the three Magi in W. H. Auden's "A Christmas Oratorio" declared, "To discover how to be human now is the reason we follow this star."[27] The question of how to become human and how to humanize the world takes on a more urgent tone today, when we, children of Mother Earth, are all truly connected but still very much apart.

The journey of the people of God from the garden to the heavenly city will require each one to join in the adventure with the God-before-us, the God-with-us, and the God-within-us in a lifetime process of becoming human, reaching out and breaking free. The corresponding values are integrity, solidarity, and creativity. We would like to ground these values in the very being of the Triune God, as guideposts in the difficult path by which grace conforms human beings to Father, Son, and Spirit.[28] These values are intended to guide believers in asking the fundamental questions: What kind of people should we be? How can we live together? What is worth aspiring for? These three values are also in response to the three fundamental questions the scavengers are asking: What does it mean to be a human being? How can we treat each other as brothers and sisters? How can we create a sustainable future in a universe of ceaselessly complex, emergent, and adaptive systems? These values also correspond to the new paradigm in science that moves towards wholeness, thinks in terms of systems and networks, and is dynamic and processive. This trinitarian standpoint is the Christian contribution to the global conversation that makes believers take complexity, indeterminacy, and unpredictability as the primary consideration in looking at an emergent universe and finding out where cosmic history is leading up to.

If all of us can agree on a common destiny for the human race and work to achieve it, there will be lasting hope for this planet in peril.

NOTES

[1]The International Social Survey Program done in thirty countries in 1998 showed that 79 percent of Filipinos chose a positive response to "I know God exists and have no doubt about it." This was second only to Chile, which had

81 percent. A study done by the NCOR research group of the University of Chicago that collated data gathered in 30 countries since 1991 found that 94 percent of the people of the Philippines said they had always believed in God, followed by Chile wit 88%, and the United States with 81 percent. The report written by Tom Smith, "Belief About God Across Time and Countries," was released on April 12, 2012. "While I have doubts, I feel that I do believe in God" was chosen by 13 percent; 3 percent believe in God some of the time, but not in others; another 3 percent do not believe in a personal God but in a higher power of some kind; 1 percent do not know whether there is a God or not, and there is no way to find out; and 1 percent do not believe in God. A similar survey done by the Social Weather Station in the Philippines in 2008 found no significant difference in the percentages of the responses.

²John Mbiti wrote that in Africa, traditional religions are not primarily for the individual but for his community. To be human is to belong to the whole community, and to do so involves participation in the beliefs, ceremonies, rituals, and festivals of that community. The root of this is the African understanding of what it means to be a human being: "I am because we are; and since we are, therefore I am." Quoted in Robert B. Fisher, *West African Religious Traditions: Focus on the Akan of Ghana* (New York: Orbis Books, 1998), 64.

³See Dionisio Miranda, "What Will You Have Me Do For You?" in *Catholic Theological Ethics in the World Church*, ed. James Keenan (Manila: Ateneo de Manila University Press, 2008), 179. Miranda claims that because many insist on replicating Western discourses on Asian soil, theological ethics is often seen as "an esoteric debate among an exclusive club, intelligible if at all only to Christian audiences, meaningless to the vast majority, unremarkable in its results, and mediocre in its effective witness." It has become so identified with the negative and judgmental but rarely with the inspirational and constructive.

⁴I am grateful to Dr. Alejandro Roces, who often visited me on Smokey Mountain to reflect on folk religiosity and share jokes, for the description of the celebration of fiesta in the Philippines included in these pages.

⁵See Anne Hunt's discussion of the Trinity and the death and rising of Christ in *The Trinity and the Paschal Mystery: A Development in Recent Catholic Theology* (Collegeville, MN: Michael Glazier, 1997).

⁶See Max Jammer, *Einstein and Religion* (Princeton, NJ: Princeton University Press, 1999). Many scientists believe in Einstein's God. See Corey S. Powell, *God in the Equation: How Einstein Became the Prophet of the New Religious Era* (New York: Free Press, 2002). Powell wrote that spirituality is an integral component of the way humans process information about the world and proposes a religion of rational hope, a new faith he calls sci-religion that captures both the mystical and the empirical. A 1998 survey of the University of Georgia showed that 93 percent of scientists in the United States are either atheists or agnostics. A recent survey done by Gallup Poll showed that 92 percent of Americans believe in a personal God, compared to 96 percent when Gallup first conducted the survey in 1944. According to a 1998 survey published in *Nature* magazine, only 7 percent of the members of the National Academy of the Sciences professed belief in a "personal God."

⁷Chris Hedges claims that the new atheism has become a surrogate reli-

gion, and its proponents "embrace a belief system as intolerant, chauvinistic and bigoted as that of religious fundamentalists." See Chris Hedges, *When Atheism Becomes Religion: America's New Fundamentalists* (New York: Free Press, 2008), 1.

[8]The roster includes Richard Dawkins, *The God Delusion* (Boston: Houghton Mifflin Co., 2006); Sam Harris, *The End of Faith: Religion, Terror and the Future of Reason (New York: W.W. Norton, 2005);* Victor J. Stenger, *The New Atheism: Taking a Stand for Science and Reason* (Amherst, NY: Prometheus Books, 2009); Daniel Dennett's *Breaking the Spell: Religion as a Natural Phenomenon* (New York: Viking, 2006); and Christopher Hitchen, *God Is Not Great: How Religion Poisons Everything* (New York: Twelve Books, 2007). David Marshall, in *The Truth behind the New Atheism* (Eugene, OR: Harvest House, 2007), engages the new atheists and responds to their challenges. See also John F. Haught, *God and the New Atheism: A Critical Response to Dawkins, Harris and Hitchens* (Louisville, KY: Westminster/John Knox Press, 2007); Scott Hahn and Benjamin Wilker, *Answering the New Atheism: Dismantling Dawkins' Case Against God* (Steubenville, OH: Emmaus Road, 2008); Keith Ward, *Why There Almost Certainly Is a God: Doubting Dawkins* (Oxford: Lion Press, 2009); Alistair McGrath and Joanna Cullicutt-McGrath, *The Dawkins Delusion: Atheist Fundamentalism and the Denial of the Divine* (Downers Grove, IL: InterVarsity Press, 2007).

[9]See Herbert Vorgrimmler, ed., *Commentary on the Documents of Vatican II*, vol. 5 (London: Burns and Oates, 1969), 156. Blessed John Paul II has this to say about the relationship of science and theology: "Science can purify religion from error and superstition, and religion can purify science from idolatry and false absolutes." See "Science and Faith," address at the University of Pisa, September 24, 1989.

[10]Robert Spitzer, *New Proofs for the Existence of God: Contributions of Contemporary Physics and Philosophy* (Grand Rapids: Eerdmans, 2010).

[11]John C. Lennox, *God's Undertaker: Has Science Buried God?* (Oxford: Lion Press, 2009).

[12]Jacob Needleman, *What Is God?* (New York: Penguin Books, 2011), 139.

[13]Jonathan Sacks, *The Dignity of Difference: How to Avoid the Clash of Civilizations* (New York: Continuum, 2003), 54.

[14]Studies show that people who speak different languages do think differently and that even flukes of grammar can profoundly affect how we see the world. Language, central to our experience of being human, helps construct our mental lives. It is not only a tool for expressing thought, but actually shapes thought. See Lera Boroditsky, "How Does Our Language Shape the Way We Think? in *What's Next?: Dispatches on the Future of Science*, ed. Max Brockman (New York: Vintage Books, 2009), 116-19.

[15]John F. Haught, *Christianity and Science: Towards a Theology of Nature* (Maryknoll, NY: Orbis Books, 2007), 136. See also John F. Haught, *Science and Religion: From Conflict to Conversation* (New York: Paulist Press, 1995); John F. Haught, *Is Nature Enough: Meaning and Truth in the Age of Science* (Cambridge: Cambridge University Press, 2006).

[16]Haught, *Is Nature Enough*, 146.

[17]See Richard Nisbett, *The Geography of Thought: How Asians and*

Westerners Think Differently . . . and Why (New York: Free Press, 2003). See also Bruce E. Wexler, *Brain and Culture: Neurobiology, Ideology and Social Change* (Cambridge, MA: MIT Press, 2008). Niall Ferguson claims that what propelled the West to a position of predominance were competition, science, property, modern science, consumption and work ethic. See Niall Ferguson, *Civilization: The West and the Rest* (London: Allen Lane, 2011).

[18]The research was based on the brain's serotonin system, which is related to socioemotional sensitivity. The brains of the East Asians predispose them toward interdependence, establishing this as a cultural value. See Matthew D. Lieberman, "What Makes Big Ideas Sticky? in *What's Next?: Dispatches on the Future of Science*, ed. Max Brockman (New York: Vintage Book, 2009), 90-103.

[19]Wendell Berry, *Life Is a Miracle: An Essay against Modern Superstition* (New York: Counterpoint, 2000), 48.

[20]See Carolyn C. Porco, "The Greatest Story Ever Told," in *What Is Your Dangerous Idea?: Today's Leading Thinkers on the Unthinkable*, ed. John Brockman (New York: Harper Perennial, 2007), 153-55.

[21]*Centissimus Annus*, 34. For a systematic compilation of Catholic Social Teaching, see Pontifical Council for Justice and Peace, *Compendium of the Social Doctrine of the Church* (Rome: Libreria Editrice Vaticana, 2004).

[22]Tina Beattie, *The New Atheists: The Twilight of Reason and the War on Religion* (Maryknoll, NY: Orbis Books, 2008). She claims that the debate is dominated by the opinions of a small clique of white English-speaking men who fail to address the most significant humanitarian questions of our time and the role religion plays in generating and sustaining hope, meaning and creativity, "without which we would be less than the humans we are" (ibid., 10).

[23]Bill McKibben, in *Deep Economy: The Wealth of Communities and the Durable Future* (New York: Henry Holt and Company, 2007), wrote that research has shown that greater wealth does not always equate with happiness. Economic growth is producing more inequality than prosperity, more insecurity than progress. The rates of alcoholism, suicide, and depression have gone up in wealthy countries.

[24]David Ramsay Steele, *Atheism Explained: From Folly to Philosophy* (Chicago: Open Court, 2008). Steele also claims that deep down, neither does theism.

[25]See Keith Ward, *Religion and Human Nature* (Oxford: Clarendon Press, 1998), for a discussion of human nature in light of different religious traditions.

[26]I am advocating a global conversation along the lines of Juanita Brown and David Isaacs with the World Cafe Community, *The World Cafe: Shaping Our Futures through Conversations That Matter* (San Francisco: Berrett-Koehler Publications, 2005). The process being advocated has seven core design principles: set the context; create hospitable space; explore questions that matter; encourage everyone's contribution; cross-pollinate and connect diverse perspectives; listen together for patterns, insights, and deeper questions; and harvest and share collective discoveries.

[27]Ishikawa Takuboku was a poet from Japan who died of tuberculosis

when he was just twenty-six years old. He gave us his formula for being a poet. "First of all, a poet must be a human being," he wrote. "Second, he must be a human being. Third, he must be a human being." This injunction holds not only for poets, but for all members of the human race. Ernst Stadler's command to those who are cut off from the world, alienated from who they are deeply, is also relevant here: "*Mensch, werde wesentlich!* (Man, become substantial!). This last line of Stadler's poem, "The Saying," has been translated by Stephen Berg thus: "STOP BEING A GHOST!" See Edward Hirsch, *Poet's Choice* (New York: Harvest Book, 2006), for articles about these two poets.

[28]Integrity, solidarity, and creativity as core values also correspond to what M. John Farrelly said: "Our search is not primarily an intellectual search but a search we make as person, as communities, and indeed as one human community moving through history." See M. John Farrelly, *The Trinity: Rediscovering the Central Christian Mystery* (Lanham, MD: Rowman & Littlefield, 2005), xii.

Chapter 4

GOD AS LORD OF HISTORY

LET MY PEOPLE GO!

Together we can build an integral human development beneficial for all peoples, present and future, a development inspired by the values of charity in truth. It is essential that the current model of global development be transformed through a greater, and shared, acceptance of responsibility for creation: this is demanded not only by environmental factors, but also by the scandal of human misery.
—Pope Benedict XVI, August 26, 2009

Young people wearing white headbands carried the image of their patron, the Risen Christ, on their shoulders. They were joined by hundreds of women carrying religious images and men with white headbands carrying the image of the Christ child. Others brandished placards while praying the Rosary and singing hymns. Marshals directing traffic in the crowded streets led the way for the throng of scavengers marching to demand from the government their rights to decent housing and livelihood. Traffic was at a standstill and the din of blaring horns was deafening, punctuated now and then by crisp curses from the drivers of the stranded vehicles. Acrid fumes from huge trucks hauling container vans, their engines idling, filled the air. Bystanders egged the throng on with words of inspiration or made fun of them with biting comments. Uniformed police officers watched in the sidelines for troublemakers. The prayer rally/freedom march went on in silence.

The people of Smokey Mountain were mounting a demonstration to express their demands to the government to close the dump site and build houses for their families.

As I watched from afar (I was often left behind to take care of the small children), it was difficult for me to imagine that they would arrive at this juncture—the scavengers fighting for their rights themselves in a nonviolent and disciplined way. On similar occasions, when they were joined by their allies among the urban poor organizations from near-by parishes, the number of people swelled to more than fifty thousand people marching in the streets. In the end, the government closed the dump site and built houses for five thousand scavenger families. The victory of the people on Smokey Mountain proved that when power rests with the community to decide how to gain control and manage their own resources to meet their needs, life flourishes. The sense of dignity of the people is enhanced. They are given hope.

It was one of the proudest moments in the history of the dump site when then-President Fidel V. Ramos announced in 1992 after one of these rallies that the scavengers' request for the closing of the garbage dump and the construction of housing was approved. I can still see the faces of the scavengers flushed with victory. But it took years of community organizing to build up a movement like this, years of dedicated, committed effort to transform consciousness and understanding. That is the way the world changes. There are no quick solutions to social transformation. Shared vision and right values need a long time to take root. But the people eventually won. That is what the church could be if its stories speak directly to people's hearts.

The same struggle for global justice is materializing today in thousands of demonstrations and power struggles using social networking sites, laptops, and cellphones in communities all over the world to pressure venal leaders to resign or to implement radical reforms. I would like to share here my joy and my passion with all young people who intend to join this struggle for justice, peace, and integrity of creation in other parts of the planet. They often asked me what more they can do to help the deprived and the oppressed. I want to tell the people occupying Wall Street and those doing the same in hundreds of other cities a few stories about how sustainability, social transformation, and integral human development can be fostered as long-term objectives by people of faith even if they live in a garbage dump. I would like to share the story of how the scavengers, impelled by their faith in the triune God, succeeded in organizing themselves and pressuring the government to close the dump site and build houses for twenty-five thousand people. As Margaret J. Wheatley said, "There is no power for change greater than a community discovering what it cares about."

The people of Smokey Mountain proved how a community united by shared vision and shared values successfully resisted bureaucratic power and reversed unfavorable government decisions. Networking with other communities enhanced the power to bring about long-term systemic change. They struggled to become a subversive community challenging government corruption and the values of the free market. Theology helped by assisting actual human communities forge a vision of freedom and equality, animated by the undying hope that points to justice in this world and to its fullness at the end of history. The small faith communities on Smokey Mountain attempted to reflect the values rooted in the Trinity in their activities, because the triune God is revealed when people who were once enslaved and oppressed are set free to enter into the shalom of the Kingdom. Christians have to prove that they encounter the Father in Jesus through the Spirit by seeing the triune God in every human being they meet and transforming the world in light of the values of the Kingdom.

The story of the Trinity is the way Christians answer questions of origin and destiny, questions of identity and purpose, questions of meaning and morality, and questions of ultimacy and finality. It is the way Christians approach the power and mystery behind all reality and all life. It is the way they justify their existence and their rationale for why they are important. It is the central idea that more profoundly reveals the foundations of Christian faith. In light of this Trinitarian faith, the whole approach to community organizing on Smokey Mountain was based on process and evolution. We had to continuously craft a new vision of human nature and the future, drawing on both theological and scientific resources to relate the scientific idea of the universe and of history with the theological idea of creation and ultimate fulfillment in the context of faith in the Trinity. We chose an understanding of history that evoked a sense of belonging to the universe without compromising the truth of revelation, an understanding of creation that sees the universe become conscious of itself in the human spirit. We therefore had to press Trinitarian language into yielding further speculative insight that can explain how life should be lived and what kind of society we should build in the dump site.

The signals of transcendence can be discerned, and the supernatural is available to us in the common situations and moments of everyday life, including life in garbage dumps if we know where to search.[1] There is a beyond in the midst of the hustle and bustle of daily life if we view it with the eye of contemplation. There is a ground of being that is the origin, the source of ultimate meaning for our lives, and the basis for hope in the future from the vantage point of higher levels of consciousness. For Christians, the Trinity grounds the interconnectedness of everything that is—three differentiated social persons in one God, the Lord of history, moving simultaneously in divine choreography of service in total self-giving love. We therefore had to look at Trinity-inspired responses in order to more creatively respond to the emerging challenges and opportunities in the dump site. At the core of Christian faith is the conviction that the universe remains forever open to the future because the name of this future is "Father, Son, and Spirit." This core is the context of the scavengers' asking the primary question of what needed to be done to transform the dump site.

The people of Smokey Mountain tried to live up to a faith that involves "fighting for justice, standing up for the voiceless and the weak, reaching out in acts of kindness and compassion for the stranger and the outcast, living a life of simplicity, cultivating empathy and defying the powerful."[2] It is critical for a community not only to be involved but to assume responsibility for transformative action. Faith in the Trinity is a commitment to care for the Other and for the earth, and therefore it can be a spirituality of resistance, a spirituality born of struggle against the world's evils. Through faith in the triune God, the people of Smokey Mountain found the courage to combat injustice and at the same time enlarge the circle of their compassion. They strove to work for the development of interior consciousness and networked with other groups as they fought for equality and called on individual scavengers to assume more responsibility for themselves. They integrated the growth of consciousness with the development of the political and economic well-being of the community. Personal holiness went hand in hand with social transformation when asking the question "What must I do to make a difference?"

There was a very strong typhoon that fateful Sunday in August 1978, when the sisters of Mother Teresa of Calcutta, the Missionaries of Charity, accompanied me to Smokey Mountain a few days after I came back from Rome. The streets were heavily flooded. One of the nuns, Sr. Tobit, who was the novice mistress, fell into an open sewer as we alighted from the jeepney. Her white sari turned dark from the brackish waters. It hardly fazed her or the other nuns.[3] They kept on praying the Rosary as we entered the dump site, and the unbearable smell assaulted my nostrils. I had no idea where it would lead. I had an inkling that I was launching into deep and uncharted waters. And yet I knew that my whole life had been leading up to this moment. From then on, my life changed forever—I discovered how I could go on living. There was a way out of my mind, out of myself. I felt like I was being born again!

My primary intention was simply to be with the scavengers in a concrete gesture of solidarity. I suddenly came face to face with people I never knew existed in actuality, scavengers who were born in misery, lived in squalor, and died in obscurity. I saw how intense, how intimate, and how absorbing the scavengers' lives were. Every little shanty that the sisters visited concealed real people with very interesting life stories. I celebrated the Eucharist regularly in a small chapel I found out was dedicated to the Risen Christ. We also conducted feeding programs for the undernourished children and invited medical teams to treat the sick in the dump site. Soon the people had to enlarge their chapel to accommodate those who joined the worship services.

I invited the seminarians to do apostolic work in solidarity with the scourged Christ suffering in the garbage dump. Seminarians from Christ the King Mission Seminary in Quezon City and Divine Word Seminary in Tagaytay were assigned to the dump site for their apostolic work during weekends. Summer camps were also conducted for six weeks during vacation time where catechetical work and community organizing were stressed. I instructed the seminarians to spend time with the people, listening to their stories, and then to look for theological issues that we can discuss in class. The seminarians found out the scavengers ranked their needs this way: survival, solidarity, security, sustainability, and spiritual growth.

Immersion among the poorest of the poor became an integral part of the spiritual formation of future missionaries. They were trained to engage in apostolic activities to strengthen relationships among the people and deepen solidarity in line with faith in the Trinity. The seminarians helped the people to reflect on the Word of God in order to learn how they can connect their faith to the work they were engaged in—mostly scavenging in the dump site. To win their trust, the seminarians had to articulate the vision of the Kingdom of God and make it tangible and easily communicated so that the poor will see its benefits and then commit to it. I explained to the seminarians that to engage in political or economic action, in order to improve the situation of the poor, is part of working out one's salvation. We wanted to build ecclesial communities living out Kingdom values that truly incarnate faith in the triune God among the poor, a faith that would set them free.

Evangelization is not just a matter of Gospel transmittal. Merely to focus on doctrinal propositions, pastoral methods, and know-how will lead a missionary to lose touch with the very roots and goals of proclaiming the good news in prophetic dialogue. Preaching and worship should engage the whole person, both missionary and scavenger, so that through an integral, interactive, and creative spirituality, everyone can reach their full potential. Being a community of faith means a community that allows everyone to be aware of their inner truth and be embraced by the outer truth at the heart of reality. Evangelization is not a one-sided affair. The poor have a lot of things to teach missionaries about God and the world. Many of these missionaries later said their lives were profoundly transformed by their experience in the dump site.

Several SVD missionaries later joined me in the dump site. They conducted house visitations and ate and slept with the scavengers in their shanties. They were appalled by the ruined environment and the wasted lives. I saw several of them weep silently or stifle sobs when they saw the poverty of the people. I also saw several of them retch as they came to the dump site. Many of the missionaries, especially the younger ones, used to a middle-class environment, were unprepared to deal with the myriad hopes that begged for reassurance, the many terrors that pleaded for consolation, and the rats that ate through their backpacks to get to the sandwiches inside. They told me later that the experience helped them understand and deal with the whole life and dynamic of living with the poor in other countries they were sent to, especially in Africa and Latin America. It is the same daily battle to survive and endure in poor communities everywhere on the planet. The experience helped the missionaries realize that identification with the wretched of the earth is identification with the Crucified God.

The seminarians helped the people identify the values they wanted in their community: *pagpapakatao* (becoming a human being), *pakikipagsandiwaan* (reaching out to others), and *pagkamakasaysayan* (to adapt to changes in history). The seminarians also helped the scavengers discover the most pressing and urgent needs that they would like addressed. They guided them to direct their anger and resentment into positive action to effect changes in their neighborhood. The seminarians in turn were asked to reflect on their difficulties and frustrations when the lofty ideals and theories they learned in the seminary encountered the realities of human conflict in the dump site. In their work for sustainable social transformation, they faced the difficulties of developing relationships of interdependence, responsibility, and mutual respect. And so they were mentored on how to be agents of transformation while continually being transformed themselves. We also tried to harmonize the core teachings of community organizing with the evolutionary worldview to bring about this new world.

The priests, seminarians, nuns, and lay volunteers organized, mobilized, and sustained the scavengers' communities in the neighborhoods. The Gospel was read in light of the poverty and misery, drawing lessons about transformation from the understanding of the triune God as community that the scavengers could use to take control of their lives and build cohesive communities of hope. The basic idea was to learn compassion—*cum* + *patere* in Latin, to suffer with. The seminarians were asked to accompany the scavengers in the garbage heaps and to go around the city in pushcarts looking for pieces of plastic and cartons in the trash heaps. They had to try to understand the scavengers' condition, fathom their motives, their dreams, their needs, "their hopes and their joys, their griefs and their anxieties" (*Gaudium et Spes, 1*), to see the world through a scavenger's eyes, to think like a scavenger, to *be* a scavenger.

Our goals made us see the world in a way that others with different goals would not. The seminarians were required to ask the scavengers what they thought they needed, what was important to them, how their social systems functioned. The seminarians were guided to search for the Trinity's liberative power, which creates new forms of communion with the poor, which then opens the possibilities of new ways of encountering the triune God. They had to make the scavengers understand that their well-being was linked to that of their neighbors. They were asked to look for feelings of powerlessness, frustration, and pain among the people to prod them to work towards bigger goals. In this way, the scavengers found new ways, new understanding, new possibilities, new inspiration, and new hope on how to organize themselves to secure their rights and build a better future for themselves. The organizing had to be based on the principles of altruism and trust, on tolerance of diversity, on sharing and caring, and on values based on Trinitarian belief.

THE PREFERENTIAL OPTION FOR THE POOR

*The Church's mission is to identify itself with the poor;
therein it will find its salvation.*
—Archbishop Oscar Romero

The prevailing understanding of how to solve poverty is through trickle-down economics: letting unregulated market forces, guided by the invisible hand, allocate resources and determine economic priorities to drive economic growth. Since the poor have little opportunity to access financial resources to set their own economic agenda, they are left to deal with the human and environmental costs of globalization without creating enough wealth to achieve material sufficiency. The only way to empower the poor in this context was to "rebuild local economies and communities from the bottom up."[4] Pope Benedict XVI has taught that love for widows and orphans, prisoners, and the sick and needy of every kind, is as essential to the church as the ministry of the sacraments and preaching of the Gospel (*Deus Caritas Est, 22*). This preferential option for the poor and vulnerable includes all who are marginalized by the global economy on the whole planet—unborn children, persons with disabilities, the elderly and terminally ill, and victims of injustice and oppression. This option addresses the whole person, including the social, political, and economic dimensions of humanity. Faith communities must imitate nature and life, which is a "fundamentally cooperative, locally rooted, self-organizing enterprise in which each individual organism is continuously balancing individual and group interests," and organize themselves as a democratic, market-based, community-serving alternative to socialism and neoliberalism.

The Constitutions of the Society of the Divine Word enjoin its members to show a preferential option for the poor (c. 103) who have a privileged place in the Gospel (c. 112), because poverty as lived by Christ demands solidarity with the poor and the oppressed (c. 209). Asian bishops have identified option for the poor as the basic principle of doing mission in Asia.[5] A major theme of the prophetic tradition of Israel is the conviction that real belief in God entails solidarity with the poor to ease their undeserved suffering by establishing *sedaqah* (justice) and *mishpat* (judgment). The God of Abraham, Isaac, and Jacob wants righteousness to flow like a river (Amos 5:24). The SVD constitutions are very clear on the causes of the injustice that brings about the lack of feeling for one's inner being. The struggle is not only against famine, ignorance, and the denial of human rights, but especially against the sinfulness of the human heart that is the root of these evils, not only personal evil but also structural evil.

The poverty of the scavengers is the result of the way Philippine society is organized. It is organized in favor of an elite who monopolize economic and political power. This systemic social injustice is rooted in, and continually breeds, unbridled greed, a materialistic way of life, and a culture of death. Integrity, collaboration, and a new, creative language of the faith community should instead characterize the way Philippine society should be organized. Death-dealing forces that condemn millions to remain on the margins of life through famine, chronic disease, illiteracy, and poverty (*Evangelii Nuntiandi, 30*) have to be overcome. More humane living conditions must be created by communities of faith in collaboration with the Trinity's salvific work here and now, since "action on behalf of justice is a constitutive dimension of preaching the Gospel" (*Justice in the World, 6*). Faith is not only a matter of personal ethical decisions, but also of social ethics dealing with issues like poverty, environment, human trafficking, and other systemic forms of injustice.

The poor on Smokey Mountain were trained to conduct Bible sharing focused on topics relevant to the poverty of their community. They were reminded to forge the future themselves. Isaiah 65 served to remind the scavengers that "You were not meant to live like this." They then became more engaged and started embarking on a series of small struggles that led to greater involvement and commitment. Their optimism and self-confidence grew with each small victory, which they celebrated with the usual spaghetti with watery sauce and bread liberally smeared with mayonnaise. Being admitted to the sacrosanct offices of government officials to discuss their demands was already cause for celebration and finding something to laugh about afterwards. But it was crucial for the leaders to decide which battles were worth fighting and which to leave for another day. To create a cohesive community, the message was constantly drummed into their brains: "One for all and all for one—we live and die together!" sealed with a handshake taken from the Roman legions of yore. Unity was critical to success and even survival. We had to see to it that the hotheads would not gain the upper hand (they were manufacturing homemade shotguns and sharpening their machetes for the eventual matchup with the military) and keep the leftist-leaning from riding on the crest of the people's struggle so that we can be true to our pledge of nonviolent struggle for justice.

We had to be very sensitive to cultural values among the poor. We had to root our vision in the values of Filipino culture. We inculturated our organizing principles into Filipino culture to focus on solutions to poverty, violence, and the degradation of the environment. Confucius already said that it is impossible to know people without knowing the force of words. Filipinos have a proverb about words cutting like a sharpened bolo. The scavengers were sensitive to a fault. A few words misunderstood will cause them to shy away or even take revenge. We had to conduct conflict resolution workshops to deal with anger before it got out of hand, bring back isolated factions, engage dissidents, and avoid needless power struggles among the leaders. We had to deal with disagreements, unresolved issues, bullying behavior, and passive aggression by treating everyone with respect and involving them in the decision-making process.

The converging dynamic of *kalayaan* (freedom) and *sambayanan* (community), which shaped the lives of the ancient Filipinos, moved us forward to a new future for all humanity and for Mother Earth. The integration of all parts of the *loob* (inner self) and rebirth in the *sambayanan* (community) in identifying and connecting with others in solidarity is the passage from darkness into the light. Light was understood in terms of *kalayaan*, of enlightenment, prosperity, and true brotherhood, which can be accomplished through *awa* (mercy) and *damay* (compassion) for human beings, animals, and inanimate objects.

The journey towards *kalayaan* includes not only concern for the liberation of all persons, but also the struggle for economic equilibrium, political participation, and self-transcendence. The vision of the triune God in whom alone all truth can be found is the cornerstone of the justice and the freedom our forefathers fought for against colonial masters. If we are to veer away from the path that leads to extinction, Filipinos have to relearn the values of their forefathers, which were framed by their faith in God. This sense of history was communicated to the scavengers through songs, poems, drama, and role-playing.

In the context of Filipino culture and Trinitarian faith, the Divine Word missionaries started to organize the community and build Basic Ecclesial Communities (BECs) in the garbage dump. BECs are small groups of people in a neighborhood, patterned after the divine community, who come together on a regular basis to foster their spiritual, personal, and apostolic growth. The Gospel makes sense of our profoundly relational character in light of faith in the Trinity so we work to strengthen human communities around us as well as the Christian community, the church.[6] We had to create faith communities that move with change—flexible and adaptive communities that empower rather than stifle. We had to strike the balance between the personal need for freedom and autonomy and the community's need for order and control. The strategies decided on were increasing people participation; focusing on the Bible and scriptural values; strengthening the integration of faith and life; deepening commitment to work for social change; and providing a new vision, new hope, and new meaning to the scavengers.

The BECs are designed to serve the common good and promote the dignity of the human person created in the image of the holy and triune God. The Second Plenary Council of the Philippines in 1991 provided a holistic vision of the BECs—a community of disciples living in communion, participating in the mission of Christ as a priestly (worshipping), kingly (serving), and prophetic (evangelizing) community. The BEC is a way of life—a communitarian way of living the Christian life where there is communion (a sense of belonging, participation, and sharing); where they come together regularly to reflect on the Word of God and to celebrate their faith in the liturgy; and where they work together for social transformation—for integral human development, justice, peace, and the integrity of creation.

The BECs were organized into cells of twelve to fifteen families each and were headed by a *punong-alagad* (servant-leader).[7] In accordance with the principle of subsidiarity, decision making was pushed down to the level of these cells, so that all concerned could contribute their utmost. The principle of subsidiarity from Catholic social doctrine means that decisions that can be made at the lower level must be referred to a higher level of authority only if the lower level cannot deal with the problem adequately. Thus, the BEC cells were structured to distribute responsibility, accountability, and the authority to make decisions. Examples were given to explain this idea: the cells in our bodies that communicate with each other, or bees, working together in a hive, that regulate one another. The principle of subsidiarity required that the members be taught the BEC organizational structure as the blueprint for a spiritually motivated organization. They also needed to be equipped with cognitive skills to participate in the conversation and dialogue, and then we had to trust that they would make the right decisions and implement them effectively. This in turn required the constant effort to integrate spiritual principles, values, and insights with community organizing. Christian social teaching was used to explore the social dimensions of faith. These principles were our guide in fostering a genuine integration of faith and action in the BECs and sustaining the engagement of the members. The challenge was how to put these principles into coherent patterns of reflection and action.

WITNESSES TO THE WORD

We are dust from our birth but in that dust is wrought
  a place for visions, a hope
That reaches beyond the stars, conjures and pauses the
  seas, dust covers our own
proud, torn destinies.

—Elizabeth Jennings

More than 95 percent of the people on Smokey Mountain were baptized Catholics. The fundamental questions then were as follows: How can the scavengers begin to form stronger faith communities of commitment and mission in light of their baptism? How can faith motivate them to participate in the task of helping themselves? What can be done about the wasted human potential, the untapped creativity, and the unmotivated talent of the scavengers? How can pastoral work help move them beyond relief and social services to empowering themselves to work for their own liberation? How can they use their own unique gifts, talents, and interests to live out joyously their call to be a chosen race, a royal priesthood? How can a community of hope be empowered to live out their baptismal calling to proclaim, to serve, and to build relationships?

The answer to all these questions is that the Church must take root in the very heart of the community. Life in community is the primordial form in which the triune God prepares human beings to participate in the divine life. In their Bible sharing, the poor were led to listen to each other before the triune God. I found out that the scavengers interpret the Bible allegorically. I tried to explain the Bible verses using hermeneutics and redaction criticism until I realized that their interpretation was often more psychologically astute than mine. They were better able to grasp the integrative and transformative dimension of Scriptures. They read the Bible and they heard God speaking to them in every verse. I realized they were looking, not for meaning, but for presence. And so we tried to derive the form, activities, and apostolic thrust of the ministry in the dump site from the political, economic, social, and political context of the scavengers—"And the Word was made flesh, and dwelt among us" (John 1:14).

Trinitarian faith created new visions of freedom and possibility for the community on Smokey Mountain. It gave the scavengers new ways to think about themselves and their own hope in a universe of constant flux and unpredictability, to make the garbage dump "a place for visions and a hope beyond the stars." The Trinity became a metaphor for self-organizing communities so that people could learn how to maintain the balance between the one and the many, between unity and diversity. Through community, through unity in diversity, we were helped to discover our deepest and truest selves, the fullness of who we are. That very same Word, the Logos that became flesh in Jesus the Christ, is at work in the community and in the cosmos, helping us discover our humanity, our yearning for relationship, community, meaning, dignity, and love. As witnesses to the Word, we had to establish communities of faith that value and make use of the totality of who we are as human beings. We had to fill our yearning for wholeness, our longing for a sense of belonging and move towards the future in communion, secure for all our frailty because we believe that the triune God creates both the call and the response.

The Trinitarian *perichoresis* is a metaphor for the fullness of life in a cosmos where existence is movement and relationship. *Perichoresis* comes from the Greek *peri* (around) and *chorein* (to dance), a dancing around each other. It is the term used by the early church fathers to mean that each divine person contains the others at the center of being. The BECs were then understood as moving harmoniously with the environment, gracefully moving through time and space in disorder and indeterminacy. These communities were intended to become a dynamic, networked dance of creative relationships in which the members join in playful combinations of their talents and skills, and thus transcend the illusion of separateness by building networks of contacts, influence, and leverage.

Faith in the Trinity is faith in the *perichoresis*, a dancing together of the three divine persons that invites interpretation, contemplation, and a sense of wonder. This faith leads to the fullness of life in a universe moving towards fulfillment and completion. The new science shows that self-organizing structures are able to maintain their overall form and identity only when they allow greater degrees of individual freedom, when they are able to maintain the balance between control and autonomy. We continually tried to learn how to arrive at this balance. Watching the Children of Mother Earth rehearse their dances gave us insights into how to balance movement and harmony within the community. We asked ourselves what dance and choreography in the swirl of movement and melody, in light of the *perichoresis* (dancing together) in the Trinity, can teach us about power and movement, of how the dynamic combination of bodily move-ment and group cohesions, the interpenetration of chaos and order, of stability and change, can add to group unity.

The first hurdle we had to overcome was the lack of trust among the members. They came from different regions of the Philippines and were reluctant to be open and vulnerable to strangers. They considered anyone who did not live in their immediate vicinity an alien. We first had to explain the positive aspects of beneficial partnerships and symbiotic relationships. The cooperative aspect of the web of life was explained as the source of significant innovations in the evolution of the world. The web of life started with the coming together of different kinds of bacteria to form the first eukaryotic cells, cells with a nucleus that opened the door for multicellular life. We used this metaphor to explain the advantages of solidarity and co-operation, of consensus-based decision making and reconcilia-tion across tribal loyalties and narrow family ties. Covenantal language was used to "create a bond of trust through the word given, the word received, the word honored in mutual fidelity."[8]

Community organizing is the practice of continual active discernment. We had to continually reflect on Filipino cultural values to find out which can further or hinder the organization of communities. We had to experiment with new ways of think-ing to create healthy, productive, and sustainable communities because our affections and loyalties pervasively shape our learn-ing. Sometimes we had to challenge prevailing cultural standards like the narrow view of who is one's neighbor. Sympathy is the core human value, and communities have to be organized so that the human predilection for compassion and mutual sup-port will be fulfilled. We therefore stressed joint activities and community projects that stimulated the creative yet sympathetic engagement of the scavengers.

Community organizations enable the management of greater flows of energy and information and increase the number of options and choices that in turn increase accountability and responsibility. The fundamental questions always were what does it mean to discover Father, Son, and Spirit in the garbage dump, and how does one know when it happens? To ask the question, "What sense do slums and garbage dumps make?" is the same as asking, "What meaning does my life have?" The question about the Trinity is implied in the question about an unjust and war-torn society, about environmental degradation, and about ourselves.

THE BUILDING OF COMMUNITY IN THE GARBAGE DUMP

Hope is the orientation of the spirit; an orientation of the heart; it transcends the world that is immediately experienced, and is anchored somewhere beyond its horizons. . . . It is this hope, above all, which gives us the strength to live and continually try new things, even in conditions that seem as hopeless as ours do, here and now.

—Vaclav Havel

The Trinitarian worldview was used to structure the scavengers' experiences, define their circumstances, and actualize their possibilities. Trinitarian faith was utilized to shape their understanding of themselves, to give them hope that change is possible. The scavengers were taught that without discovering the triune God, men and women will never fathom the depths of their humanity as a web of relationships that is the source of meaning and security. Their capacity to do good was founded on their recognition of who they are—made unto the image and likeness of the triune God. Thus, we tapped into their own resources and underused talents by encouraging creativity and responsibility. We celebrated small successes, like the reconciling of families who have feuded for a long time. The church was brought down from the chapel into the shanties of the scavengers to provide them with the understanding of God as community and as Lord of history. A premium was placed on relationships and a perception of themselves as bonded together in solidarity and communion. We had to give the people enough hope and confidence to take the first steps to set themselves free.

The elaboration of a social-ethical commitment from faith in the Trinity was the start of theological coherence, the merging once more of the spiritual and material aspects of life in the lives of the scavengers. The unifying force of the Trinitarian faith was a source of energy to face the challenges of transforming the garbage dump. It helped build a community where each person was granted respect in a climate of openness and trust, a community where everyone was set free to become all that they can be. Unity in diversity is the melding of self-interests; communion is the sharing of the same faith, values, ideals, and destiny. Strong communities are an essential foundation for authentic peace, so the BECs were built on mutual trust and communion to allow the members to share the risks and create resilience in the face of trials and tribulations. Building communities of trust was essential to help the scavengers recover the inner resources that good community organizing needs. Trust can only be built on integrity and compassion. It is a requirement for empowerment and is at the heart of community organizing.[9] We fostered a kind of leadership that stressed compassionate pastoral responsibility and clear decision-making processes. In this way, increased leadership possibilities began to surface.

I was struck by the fact that a disproportionate number of women were elected leaders of the BECs. Perhaps it is because they are more persistent and patient in organizing the families in the neighborhood. The preponderance of women leaders ensured that female values effectively balanced male excesses. In a cultural setting that was connective, intuitive, and responsive at its core, it would have been suicidal to gut female influence.[10] Women leaders were good listeners, they asked questions of others instead of assuming that they knew everything. They responded sensitively to a different point of view and were more flexible. Because of their nurturing nature, they sought to support, enable, and care instead of seeking to control and dominate. In a flattened world, which is moving away from the world of hierarchy, women can better function relationally, intuitively, systematically, and contextually.

The men on Smokey Mountain were usually more oriented

towards action, towards the abstract, towards independence. Women were more oriented towards relationships, nurturance, and responsibility. I had to be aware of the different orientations and the type of consciousness of men and women in order to maintain harmony in the community. Studies done on the essential difference of how men and women think suggest that, on the average, more men are systematizers and more women are empathizers.[11] However, I got a big laugh when I mentioned to the women that more men are systematizers. They said the men were totally unsystematic and disorganized (*kalat*) during the celebration of the last parish feast. They had to come in and take charge.

The voices of women have to be heard so that communities can bring more life and light to this planet in peril. Although it goes against the grain of my temperament, I had to admit that peace and justice can only be won through the spirit of humility and repentance of our own complicity in the violence raging across the world today. As a man, I had to purge myself of the hidden aggression, the manipulative strategies, the will to power, and the desire to overpower all opposition that are the root of all violence. I had to reflect long and hard on how these attitudes might color my understanding of God. The women on Smokey Mountain taught me about the power of power-lessness. Sometimes a man can live his entire life without ever knowing for sure if he is a coward or not. I am sure I am one. The women of the dump made sure I knew. During our rallies and demonstrations against the government, they told me to watch over their children. They knew that in my cowardice and fear, I could have started something that would result in trouble and bloodshed. The women stood their ground when in harm's way, clutching their religious images and praying the Rosary. As they continually reminded me, water can carve canyons in hard rock drop by drop.

For several years while I was in the university, I played judo and karate. Judo teaches one how to use an opponent's strength against him instead of meeting brute force with brute force. It is the art of using an opponent's strength to defeat him. Our leaders spent a lot of time thinking how to turn an opponent's strength into a constraining weakness so that we will achieve the objectives of the community—like how to get clean water into the households, how to succeed in closing the dump site and building homes for the scavengers. We had to discuss who or what our opponents were in the first place. We had to think differently because we wanted the rules to be changed. After we determined the barriers to our objectives, we thought about how we can turn our weaknesses into strength to overcome these barriers. The process of communal discernment was often brought into play—the process of reflecting and discussing to reach deep insight and exercise good judgment. But we always focused on the people's own strengths—their faith, their humor, their ingenuity, and their numbers—to move them from problem solving to dreaming of new possibilities. Once they bought into the dream, there was an explosion of curiosity, effort, and new ways of approaching problems. Increased collaboration and creativity brought about more happiness among the members.

Dr. Robert Linthicum of World Vision International's Office of Urban Advance helped in mentoring community organizers on Smokey Mountain to engage in strategic planning. His team conducted workshops on Smokey Mountain for key community leaders and seminarians about the principles and objectives of community organizing. World Vision also funded a grant to train the leaders of the community so that they themselves could empower their members. We had to constantly improve teamwork and minimize political infighting and factionalism in order to build communities that practice self-government and foster a forward-looking spirit. Everyone had to understand the community's vision and be convinced that it was worthwhile and doable, if everyone was going to contribute to the success of the community's mission.

Dynamic, highly skilled, and highly motivated teams were the secret of our community organizing efforts. The leaders were never paid and worked with the community by choice, often at great sacrifice. The principles of community organizing on Smokey Mountain always stressed the participatory process: the scavengers themselves had to articulate a common vision, describe what actions should be taken to realize the vision, pinpoint who shall be responsible, decide within which time frame tasks should be accomplished, and define with what resources these actions should be undertaken. Communion grounded in faith in the triune God was always the ideal put forward. The values of integrity, solidarity, and creativity were inculcated through retreats and recollections, songs, poems, and plays. We went on with our community organizing work by muddling through, looking for patterns, flow, shape, and direction over time. Later on, we structured our efforts through the 5 P's: *Pananaw, Pagkilala, Pangangasiwa, Pagkilos,* and *Pangangailangan.* This can roughly be translated into: Visioning, Invitation, Governance, Operations, and Resources (VIGOR). The VIGOR format was also used in the social analysis of economic, political, and cultural structures that had a bearing on the community to establish interdependent teams characterized by reciprocal cooperation.

Visioning is the forging of a common dream, the bonding within a larger framework of shared intention, which clarifies the purpose and direction of the community. The personal and communal search for meaning and the cohesive sense of purpose empower the community. This required a lot of group discussions and assemblies to find out what the community would like to happen in the future and align the self-interest of the individual with the well-being of the organization. This also included the discussion of sentiments (*damdamin*) and ideas (*isip*) that shape the vision (*adhika*) in order to expand the sense of self and the sense of belonging and kinship and express them in the same language (*wika*). We believed that the organization should be shaped by dreams and visions, not primarily through rules and structures. Antoine de St. Exupery suggested that if we want to build a ship, we should not immediately encourage people to gather wood, divide the work, and give orders. We should first teach them to yearn for the vast and endless sea. So we crafted a compelling image of what the scavengers' future would look like and showed them how their interests could be realized by enlisting to fulfill the common vision. We focused on the dream of having the dump site closed and houses built for their families to energize the scavengers to fight for their rights.

A shared vision as a source of the community's vitality is crucial for social cohesion in order for groups and associations to bond into a mutually enhancing, synergistic whole. Shared vision grows out of the individual vision of each member. We understood vision as an energy field, a force of connections suffusing the entire organization that influences the behavior of every member and creating positive energy. Seeing the faith community as the Body of Christ in terms of energy fields, we viewed believers as waves of energy, spreading out to the world, growing in potential, empowered by the vision of the triune God as community. In light of Trinitarian faith, the Body of Christ was understood as a living organism. The community is more fundamental and purposeful than the members. It can achieve goals that are quite different from the original aim.

Once a common vision had been identified and embraced, *Invitation* was the identification of all potential stakeholders and asking them to join and form a community structured by mutual commitment and collaboration. This also included the identification and invitation of natural leaders to help create a community of process and relationships. Looking at the community as a living system required different leadership expectations and analytic processes. People support what they have helped build.

Governance was the decision-making process on how to order the organization and define tasks. This included the drafting of a constitution and bylaws submitted to the Securities and Exchange Commission for registration. This was required for government recognition of the organization as a legal entity. Training was then given on relational and communication skills; on organizational processes; and on integrative, collaborative, and creative decision making to maintain form without rigid structures.

Our organizational methodology saw the community as made up of connecting energy fields in an ongoing dynamic process. Disequilibrium was understood to be necessary for continued growth and for the giving of form to what is unfolding. The communities were designed to adapt to change. This was very difficult to achieve because of the orientation to the past common to Filipino thinking.

Operations were the activities that the community undertook in light of the defined goals to attain the vision within a community that had the properties of living systems. The seminarians found out that the best way to make everyone a stakeholder was to hand over the process of building to those who will implement it, structured by cooperation and energy exchanges.

Resources involve the identification and gathering of money and materials to fund the activities undertaken. Fund-raising activities helped realize the vision, without forgetting that the greatest resource is the people themselves.

We found out that it was difficult to maintain interest when there were no more issues and problems to face. As one of our leaders said shortly after the government approved their demands and the houses built for them, "It is boring now when we have no more opponents to contend with." The community flourished in a context between too much order, where they were bored, and too little of it, where they were confused. We were forced to focus attention on emergent, creative, and holistic social processes and sought a dynamic balance between the two. We had to accept that given forms of order are transient and that organizations evolve through a continual strategy of taking risks.

THE YOUTH AS HOPE FOR THE FUTURE

Youth lives on hope, old age on remembrance.
—French Proverb

Young people aged thirteen to twenty-four were divided into their own *sambahayan,* patterned after the organizational structure of the elders. The presidents of the *Kabataang Sambayanang Kristiyano* composed the Youth Council and were represented in the Pastoral Council by three members. Social relations were enhanced by faith in the triune God and good will to others and to Mother Earth. There was a Youth Mass with drums and electric guitars every Saturday afternoon. The liturgy celebrated the beauty and pain of the world, the connectedness to Mother Earth, and the struggle for social justice. There were life in the

Spirit seminars and Growth in the Spirit seminars organized by charismatic groups. We conducted seminars on the Scriptures to guide their growth in the spiritual life. There were regular formation and leadership training, and conscientization programs.

We organized the youth cooperative with more than two hundred members. Others just helped out in the cooperatives of the elders. They fashioned little baskets and decorative articles from used paper and dried plants. They organized garage sales to earn their allowances. They took care of the seedlings in the seedling nursery and helped in reforestation efforts. They were also active in the advocacy for the dredging of the two rivers on both sides of Smokey Mountain, which were full of garbage and already biologically dead. The youth groups reached out to other youth groups in Manila such as the Archdiocesan Youth Council. They gave support to other depressed areas where the BECs were also organized when there were mass actions against arbitrary demolitions. The youth also participated in rallies and demonstrations. They often marched to protest against drugs and vigorously supported the political advocacy of their elders regarding the development for Smokey Mountain. They were also involved in raising funds to build the church by collecting used clothing and shoes, used appliances, and other material that could be recycled. They sold these to raise money for their activities.

The *Sandulaan,* the performing arts group of the youth, which performed in plays and interpretative mime, was a potent force in cultural remolding and formation. They performed on television and on stage. They acted out the Gospel on selected Sundays. They also performed during cultural nights and organized dance parties to foster mutuality and intimacy. They attended seminars on zero waste management and were informed about the ravages wrought on the environment on Smokey Mountain. They propagated the ideas they learned through their plays and skits. The youth also established linkages with young people from Japan, Germany, and Austria who have visited them. They exchanged letters and cloth paintings. The Children of Mother Earth, who perform dances and rituals of indigenous peoples, are all members of the youth group.

Social networking technology has unleashed the true power of togetherness among young people, including those on Smokey Mountain. This togetherness and connection is often more important for them than food—they prefer to buy prepaid cards for their cellphones and the Internet. They maintain multiple and intersecting groups of friends. The McCann survey showed that young people all over the world define themselves primarily by their ability to connect, to share, and to broadcast. In China and India, according to the survey, two-thirds of young people admit that their friends have more influence over their decisions than their family does. If your picture is not uploaded or if you are not tagged, you don't exist. With a mass audience, most of them suffer from social status anxiety. They have hundreds of deletable friends, but they also crave authenticity and genuineness from their friends. Fake friends are called "plastic" among the young people on Smokey Mountain.

In their global context, the *Kabataang Sambayanang Kristiyano* has made a perceptible impact in nurturing the spiritual life of its members, improving the quality of life with regard to education, health care and provision of facilities, minimizing drug addiction, and supporting their elders in the struggle for peace and freedom. Collaboration is hardwired in their brains.[12] The McCann study also showed that young people all over the world pride themselves in working in a group or team. Thus, the young people were encouraged to look forward, take an interest in issues beyond their immediate environment, believe in their ability to shape the future, recognize individual responsibility and personal accountability, and become aware of their dignity as human beings. They slowly took over the leadership of the community as the earlier leaders retired or drifted away. The youth are the hope of Smokey Mountain. The youth are the hope of the planet.

A PEOPLE TRANSFORMED

A man who possesses a veneration of life will not simply say his prayers. He will throw himself into the battle to

preserve life, if for no other reason than that he is himself
an extension of the life around him.
                                   —Albert Schweitzer

Extreme poverty, the long years of passivity, and silence resulted in the stifling of creativity, the lack of critical consciousness among the scavengers, the continuation of the dependency syndrome, and the wallowing in apathy and resignation. But after years of struggle for peace and justice, the people were transformed.

Slowly, imperceptibly, the scavengers moved towards a critical consciousness and improved the mechanism for people's participation. As they came together in mutual help and social involvement, as they articulated their needs and took a transformative stance toward reality, they became more and more agents of their own progress, better able to shape their destiny and create their own history. After the transfer to the permanent housing in the former dump site, the BECs continued their work on the three levels of the BECs: spiritual, developmental, and liberational. We have empirical evidence to show that religion, at least in the garbage dump, among the poorest of the poor, is not "a moral sickness" as Victor Stenger alleged or "irrational, unreal, and immoral," as the novelist Martin Amis wrote.[13] Religion on Smokey Mountain is not "the sigh of the oppressed creature, the heart of a heartless world, and the soul of soulless conditions," as Karl Marx declared. It is definitely not an opium for the scavengers. It set them free to craft their own destiny through education and livelihood programs that have gone beyond the garbage dump, programs like the e trading network, which seeks to connect the urban and rural poor to trade directly using information and communications technology.

To dream is the birthright of every human being. The dream of the people of Smokey Mountain is to continue to become a rich and diverse settlement where the needs of daily life are met for the mutual benefit of each person and the whole community. It is basically a dream of living on the planet with respect for all beings and ecosystems. Diversity implies the responsibility of each participant to contribute to the duties and pleasures of communal living: respect for the community of life, ecological integrity, social and economic justice, democracy, nonviolence, and peace. It is now possible to create new forms of worldwide collective and democratic power by linking these communities globally and giving billions of poor people a democratic voice in fashioning their collective destiny. This will shift the world's balance of power. The dream is about a restored relationship to nature and coming together as one in a common effort to give hope to this planet in peril.

The Smokey Mountain vision offers an alternative to commercial globalization and environmental exploitation, addressing community needs instead of foreign interests. It manifests the inner craving for a more balanced spiritual life, a loving place for children to grow up in, and a lifestyle that does not force parents to leave their children all day as a price for being a member of a consumer society. It aims to reverse the speedy disintegration of supportive sociocultural structures and the upsurge of destructive environmental practices on the planet. It involves the search for a common foundation for human freedom and solidarity so that people can organize communities that will enhance the noblest that they are and the best that they can become.

The community organizations on Smokey Mountain have become part of the emergent global civil society, a self-organizing, planetary-scale social organism that functions as the common conscience of the human race. When community members discover true meaning in cultivating the gift of service in a creative cosmos, a global revolution will be born. It will not be like other revolutions in the past because it will not require armaments to succeed. It cannot be successfully resisted by killer squads, fighter planes, and cruise missiles. It will originate with empowered communities and their networks. What is most profound about the protest movements blossoming today is not their demands, but rather the nascent infrastructure of a common humanity beyond race, creed, or nationality.

A network of interdependent communities like that on Smokey Mountain turned global will provide much-needed hope to this planet in peril.

NOTES

[1]Peter Berger, *A Rumor of Angels* (New York: Doubleday, 1969). Langdon Gilkey also tried to show that there is an ultimate dimension to our ordinary secular experience in *Naming the Whirlwind: The Renewal of God-Language* (New York: Bobbs-Merrill, 1969).

[2]Chris Hedges, *When Atheism Becomes Religion* (New York, Free Press, 2009), 5-6.

[3]Collette Livermore left home in Sydney at age eighteen to join the Missionaries of Charity and was given the name Sister Tobit. She left after eleven years in the convent, became a medical doctor to serve the poor in the outbacks of Australia and in East Timor. She wrote her story in Collette Livermore, *Hope Endures: An Australian Sister's Story of Leaving Mother Teresa, Losing Faith, and Her On-going Search for Meaning* (North Sydney, NSW: Random House Australia, 2008).

[4]David C. Korten, *The Great Turning: From Empire to Earth Community* (San Francisco: Berrett-Koehler Publishers, 2006).

[5]"BISA 1: Final Reflections of the First Asian Bishops' Institute for Social Action," in *For All the Peoples of Asia: Federation of Asian Bishops' Conferences' Documents from 1970-1991*, vol. 1, ed. Gaudencio Rosales and Catalino Arevalo (Quezon City: Claretian Publications, 1992), 199-202.

[6]Timothy Keller, *The Reason for God: Belief in an Age of Skepticism* (New York: Riverhead Books, 2008), 235.

[7]Owen Phelps understands servant-leadership as including the roles of both shepherd and steward. See *The Catholic Vision for Leading Like Jesus* (Huntington: Our Sunday Visitor, 2009). See also Ken Blanchard and Phil Hodges, *Lead Like Jesus: Lessons from the Greatest Leadership Role Model of All Time* (Nashville: W Publishing Group, 2005).

[8]Jonathan Sacks, *The Dignity of Difference: How to Avoid the Clash of Civilizations* (London: Continuum, 2002), 202.

[9]In the context of corruption in the Philippines, Aloysius Cartagenas stresses the importance of teaching Filipinos the concept of the common good and understanding citizenship as an expression of discipleship and a path to holiness. Basic Ecclesial Communities, according to him, must function as "democratic communities that search for and envision the common good" and must serve as fora where the voices of the poor can be heard. See Aloysius Cartagenas, "The State of the Nation and Its Implications to the Church's Social Praxis," *Talad*, 2001, p. 123.

[10]Sally Morgenthaler, "Leadership in a Flattened World: Grassroots Culture and the Demise of the CEO Model," in *An Emergent Manifesto of Hope,* ed. Doug Pagitt and Tony Jones (Grand Rapids: Baker Books, 2007), 187.

[11]Empathy is keeping in mind the thoughts and feelings of other people and being sensitive to another person's thought and feelings. See Simon Baron-Cohen, "A Political System Based on Empathy," in *What Is Your Dangerous Idea? Today's Leading Thinkers on the Unthinkable,* ed. John Brockman (New York: Harper Perennial, 2007), 204-6.

[12]See Don Tapscott, *Growing Up Digital: The Rise of the Net Generation* (New York: McGraw-Hill, 1997); Don Tapscott, *Grown-Up Digital: How the Net Generation Is Changing Your World* (New York: McGraw-Hill, 2009).

[13]I am used to considering multistage samplings, margins of error, and coefficients of correlation, and it never fails to take my breath away when scientists and other writers make pronouncements with unabashed certainty about large populations with utter disregard for percentages and representativeness.

Chapter 5

GOD AS CONSUMING FIRE

THE DYNAMIC AND EVOLVING UNIVERSE

In the beginning, God created the heavens and the earth.
—Genesis 1:1

Human beings are essentially story-telling creatures, desperately seeking meaning to give themselves a sense of their place in the scheme of things. Stories are the way people make sense of their world. A Filipino creation story recounts how the first man and woman emerged simultaneously from separate sections of a piece of bamboo floating in a river. Hearing knocking sounds from the bamboo, a large bird pecked at it. The bamboo broke open and out came *Malakas* (the Strong) and *Maganda* (the Beautiful). Upon seeing the woman, the man cried *"Ba!"* the root word of *babae*, woman. Upon seeing the man, the woman cried *"La!"* the root word of *lalake*, man. Looking around and beholding the grandeur of the world, both cried *"Ha!"* the root word for God, *Bathala*. The symbols for the feminine and masculine principles, *ba* and *la*, are joined in the myth by *ha*, the symbol for God. In the collective consciousness of the Filipino, one cannot speak of human beings except in the context of God and nature. One cannot speak of the world except in the context of God as ultimate horizon and human beings as self-conscious observers. One cannot speak about God except in the context of the world and of human beings.

The story about the world has moved from the mythic to

the scientific, from a static to a more dynamic one (*Gaudium et Spes, 5*).[1] We now have to view the universe and human history in terms of billions of years. We are told today that the universe began 13.7 billion years ago in a primordial cosmic explosion called the Big Bang. In that singularity, physical reality moved from chaos to cosmos in the most absolute silence one can imagine. We live in an expanding universe, with galaxies hurtling away from us at close to the speed of light at the edge (estimated to be a million billion billion kilometers away from earth). Our solar system orbits around the center of the Milky Way (our own galaxy with 100 billion stars) once every 200 million years at a speed of 800,000 kilometers per hour. There are 100 billion other galaxies in the immensity of space of our observable universe (80 billion light years across). The values for the laws governing the cosmic order are fine tuned to an extraordinary degree so life and consciousness came to be. We owe our existence to an extremely improbable chain of events in a vast, emergent cosmos.

We are told that human beings are part of an evolutionary movement on this planet that started more than four billion years ago.[2] Our destiny is intimately linked with the future of delicately balanced life-systems in the biosphere. We live on a vulnerable planet under threat from all sides even as it floats in splendor like a pale blue marble in the vastness of the cosmos. Life and the mind of human beings are a fundamental part of the nature of the universe. The evolving universe produced conscious beings, a universe in which their personal decisions and choices affect the future, even as they have been on earth only about 100,000 to 150,000 years, an absolutely short time in cosmic duration. Human beings are, according to Alexander Pope, "Sole judge of truth, in endless error hurl'd: The glory, jest, and riddle of the world!"

These new ways of understanding the world call into question many of our fundamental assumptions of who we are, what it means to be a human being, and what kind of God to believe in. As rational beings, we have to come to terms with this new understanding of the world because, as St. Augustine already argued, rationality is a requirement for belief. How can Christian believers, in light of this new understanding of an evolutionary cosmos, fulfill the injunction of St. Peter: "Always be prepared to give an answer to everyone who asks you to give the reason for the hope that you have" (1 Pet. 3:15)? What does it mean to have faith after Charles Darwin, Albert Einstein, Sigmund Freud, Max Planck, and Werner von Heisenberg? If things are evolving and if human consciousness is evolving along with the galaxies and supernovae in space, where can faith in the triune God find a standpoint from which to understand the whole evolutionary process?

The new worldview corresponds more and more to the scavengers' view of the world. They are at home in ambiguity and uncertainty in a universe characterized by indeterminacy. They understand their humanity in terms of relationships. On the other hand, the new understanding also goes against their views on fundamental issues, like issues of free will and life after death. I had to scamper back to my notes in theology to research and review the doctrine of the Trinity with fresh eyes. I had to look at myself with fresh eyes, too, in order to unite experience and reflection. Then I looked back at the religiosity of the scavengers, the community organizing methods we used, the livelihood and educational programs we ran, and our advocacy for the environment in light of relationships and connections of the new physics.

These new ways of thinking called into question many of my own basic assumptions about the universe, my humanity, and my final destiny. Because of our colonial history, Filipinos are educated in the Western system. I was told in high school to memorize *Invictus* by William Ernest Henley: "I am the master of my fate, I am the captain of my soul." I sang with Simon and Garfunkel while studying in the university, "I am a rock . . . I have my books and my poetry to protect me." I was supposed to square up to the "slings and arrows of outrageous fortune," head bloodied but unbowed. I was told that man is a naked ape and that "nature is red in tooth and claw" (Alfred Lord Tennyson, *In Memoriam*). Life is a never-ending warfare (the Hobbesian war of all against all) because *homo homini lupus* (man is wolf to man, according to Plautus in *Asinaria*). I was taught in philosophy about the disembodied, self-contained, ahistorical, and isolated monad, and about the solitary atom. I was taught in theology that the human being is an *individua substantia ratio-nalis naturae* (individual substance of a rational nature). It was hammered into me that every question is a problem to be solved objectively—inner truth is a romantic fantasy, and subjectivity should not come into the act of knowing. I was convinced that a thing cannot be and not not be at the same time, and parallel lines can never meet no matter how far extended.

The new science offers a whole new way of thinking about ourselves and our relationships, about the meaning of being human, and our place in this fuzzy universe.[3] Subatomic physics is fully as strange and fuzzy as the cosmos. Elementary particles are now thought to derive from immaterial wave packets or strings that vibrate. These packets or strings act more like members of an interactive and interdependent community that reach out to other objects. The image of reality has moved from fragmentation and competition to wholeness and collaboration. Reality is now understood to be an evanescent dance between potentiality and actuality, between facts and possibilities yet to be. Biologists tell us now about the web of life and the evolutionary dance of communal celebration. The human mind is no longer a ghost in the machine but an endlessly innovative participant in the creation of the world. Truth is now understood to be integrative, interactive, and dynamic. The rest of the world has yet to come to terms with this new understanding of the world from science. It should make everyone pause when one is tempted to insist that the version of history one happens to think is true is the only true one.

Modern science suggests that contradictory explanations of reality can both be simultaneously true. Quantum physicists tell us now that any two points in space are both separate and not separate. Nothing exists independent of its relationships, whether looking at galaxies, subatomic particles, or human affairs—relationships are all there is to reality. Reality is now understood as being made up of occurrences and relationships rather than of atoms and particles. Time and space are no longer understood as fixed, absolute qualities. There was no time and space before the universe came to be—St. Augustine already wrote about this sixteen hundred years ago. St. Augustine also elaborated the idea of God's continuous creation, saying that the universe was brought into being in a less than fully formed state but was graced with the capacity to transform itself from unformed matter into a truly marvelous interaction of structures and life forms and levels of consciousness. Thus, an evolving universe was never a threat to faith. Believers can reconcile their faith with scientific facts.

These new understandings are transforming our prior ideas about matter, energy, space, time, and causality. It is very difficult to come to terms with the central concepts of the new science— wave-particle duality, indeterminacy, nonlinearity, and acausality. It requires giving up deeply held philosophical assumptions and familiar categories of analysis and adopting a completely new way of understanding physical reality. The quantum way of thinking, however, also provides a rich repository of images, metaphors, and allusions with exciting applications for theology as we, with our incessant curiosity, continually ask where the universe came from and how life and consciousness arose. Since faith sees the cosmos as an epiphany, theology should help contemplative wisdom gleaned from living in an evolving universe to lead to social transformation as the anticipation of the fullness of life at the end of the world. Since both science and religion exercise profound sociocultural influences, both have to reconcile their current knowledge of the universe with the way the political, economic, and social institutions are organized. We have to make the dialogue between science and theology intentional, explicit, and transparent as much as possible, intelligible and relevant to the lives of the people.

Since I believe that the universe is an encounter with the holy, that it is the primal revelation of the divine, I had to reflect on the scavengers' story in light of the findings of quantum physics and molecular biology. All the while, laughing with the scavengers during their celebrations and weeping with them when their children died, I had to keep in mind the sacred understanding of cosmic history. I studied differential and integral calculus in the university, and I had to keep asking, for instance, where the laws of mathematics and physics come from, with all their beauty and elegance. The words of Paul Davies, a theoretical physicist and cosmologist, kept ringing in my ears: "Why a set of laws that drive the searing, featureless gases coughed out of the Big

Bang toward life and consciousness and intelligence and cultural activities such as religion, art, mathematics and science?"[4] How does one understand faith in light of the wave-particle duality of quantum physics? What does human freedom mean in a universe ruled by the calculus of probability? How can one discover the divine dimension in a universe structured by the law of entropy?

While I worked in the dump site, I was teaching a full load at the seminary: Introduction to Theology, Creation, Christology, the Trinity and special courses on various theological topics. Science presents new realms of challenge and promise for theology's tasks and its place in the world. One cannot teach the doctrine of creation without coming face to face with the Big Bang Theory and the implications of an expanding universe since we have to live our life of communion with ultimate reality through a sacramental, creation-centered spirituality. One cannot teach theological anthropology without dealing with the findings of evolutionary biology and neuroscience. One cannot teach eschatology without dealing with the question of whether ours is an open or a closed universe. Christian faith holds that there is no opposition between nature and grace or between truths discovered by reason and those revealed by God. Theology is a method of inquiry that assumes reason is a divine gift and can be used to make faith and the human condition intelligible and relevant in the face of the recent findings of science. Ralph Waldo Emerson aptly put it: "The religion that is afraid of science dishonors God and commits suicide."

I therefore had to take scientific findings seriously and engage in theological investigation while remaining immersed in the lives of the scavengers on Smokey Mountain. I had to confront the question of whether it is possible to conceive of the holy and triune God as working within the fundamental indeterminacy of quantum theory without in any sense usurping physical laws. I had to discuss the doctrine of the Trinity, the Incarnation, and the understanding of grace in light of quantum physics so that theological students can be updated on the latest challenges posed by scientific discoveries; and through the dialogue between faith and science, the scavengers can be given reasons to hope. I had to grapple with the social and theological implications of the "singularity" in cosmology and in artificial intelligence experiments.[5] Religion, like science, makes claims about the truth, and theologians need to argue for the reasonableness of those claims. But I will leave the direct dialogue with science to theologians who are trained scientists, like John Polkinghorne, Arthur Peacocke, Alistair McGrath, Francis Collins, Kenneth Miller, Ian Barbour, and others.[6] They can write from both the inside and the outside of the scientific culture and adapt the position of both participant and observer, of actor and spectator.[7]

Science works well in explaining physical reality but does not do so well as a guide to moral decision making and responding to the human quest for meaning. Noam Chomsky wrote, "As soon as questions of will or decision or reason or choice of action arise, human science is at a loss." The best hope for the biosphere is when people embrace voluntary simplicity in their lifestyles. How can science make people do this voluntarily? How can most of the research on military capability be shifted towards renewable energy based on wind, solar, and biomass technologies? Will our future be a bleak existence in which out-of-control genetics, robotics, information technology, and nanotechnology consume every resource on the planet? Or will we have a future in which a small minority of white supremacists from the West with control of resources and armaments use these fabulous technologies against others to enslave them once again?

Dialogue between religion and science becomes difficult when some scientists declare that science gives us the whole explanation about everything in the universe. They maintain that science alone can lead us to the deepest and most fundamental level of the being of the cosmos. It is not faith that is in conflict with science, but this kind of scientific materialism that holds that reality consists of matter alone, that material reality is all there is, and that life and consciousness are ultimately reducible to chemistry and physics. In the words of Bertrand Russell, "Blind to good and evil, reckless of destruction, omnipotent matter rolls on its relentless way." This view holds that the universe is destined for final exhaustion due to entropy and will eventually perish—and thus, sheer nothingness is the final fate of the universe.

In light of quarks and leptons in quantum physics, in light of complexity and chaos theories, it would be very interesting to discuss with materialists the meaning of "matter," which today has become an utterly ambiguous and controversial concept. In quantum physics, matter is conceived, no longer as particles, but as patterns of dynamic energy. Elementary particles are in a constant state of flux and transformation of energy. New evidence from quantum theory points to nonmaterialistic (information-like) dimensions of physical reality. And there are the discoveries of neutrino masses, dark energy, antimatter, and dark matter. Dark matter is what scientists call the mysterious "missing" mass that they know must be out there but cannot see and measure. It comprises 96 percent of the universe, and its nature and origin is one of the great unsolved mysteries of physics.

The new understanding of what it means to be a human being in an interconnected, dynamic cosmos is going to radically influence our future. Anything new and powerful is always scary. Many are afraid that the tools of genetic engineering might fall into the wrong hands, for example. The dangers are real and serious. Science and mechanization have taught us how to produce things, for instance, but not how to harmonize production with the needs of the biosphere and the ecosystem. We are weighed down by material things that we cannot pay proper attention to, and then we throw them away. They end up in garbage dumps like Smokey Mountain or in the world's oceans.

I have tried to conduct this conversation as an interplay between scientific and theological questions, not as argued but as lived in a garbage dump. The elegance and beauty of scientific laws strengthen my faith in an intelligent, omnipotent Creator, but I believe that science cannot tell scavengers what kind of society they should build because of its reductionist methods. This should come from our spiritual, artistic, and ethical values. However, science helps us gain a better appreciation of the wonder of being human, according to Pope John Paul II in his address to the Pontifical Academy of the Sciences on November 11, 2002. He said science can purify religion from error and superstition; religion can in turn purify science from idolatry and false absolutes. Science and religion, the Pope continued, "can draw the other into a wider world, a world in which both can flourish. We need each other to be what we must be, what we are called to be." Science can provide us with a greater understanding of our place in the universe and show connections between our history and the history of the cosmos.

I believe that science is a sacred mission and that scientific knowledge brings the burden of responsibility. The idea of community is crucial to the scientific enterprise. Scientists are a community operating on objective methods, but they also belong to the human race. They should take a global view and hold the interests of the world community to be paramount. They should participate in the human search for a global ethos to decide the basic goals for living together on the same planet. If they will try to find out how they might help in attaining these goals, how to mitigate the risks and exploit opportunities of new discoveries, science and technology will help greatly in providing hope for this planet in peril.

DOING THEOLOGY IN THE GARBAGE DUMP

Now I become myself. It's taken
Time, many years and places;
I have been dissolved and shaken,
Worn other people's faces.
    —May Sarton, "Now I Become Myself"

I taught theological students in the seminary while working in the garbage dump. At the start, I was bothered by the fear of encountering the students as alien "others" just like my encounter with the scavengers. I used to hide behind the table when I began to teach. I barricaded myself behind my credentials of a doctorate from the Pontifical Gregorian University where two-thirds of the popes studied theology. Parker Palmer says this fear comes from the need for security: "the security of controlling the classroom agenda, of avoiding serious challenges to one's authority, of evading the embarrassment of getting lost in territory where one does not know the way home." [8]

Many of the students were present bodily, but their minds were elsewhere. Theology for them was a pointless exercise that had nothing to do with their lives. I know, because they were just like me when I was at the other side of the podium. We just wanted to be ordained priests at once so that we could serve the poor. We listened without being engaged, we memorized the notes mechanically, studied enough to pass the examinations, and burned our theology notes the day we graduated. Our personal experiences were never brought to bear on the subject matter to gain new insights. We were awash in the absolute certainty that what we study is true because it is revealed by God. We never asked what revelation and truth would mean in a historically and culturally bound theology, in a universe that is continually evolving, in a planet besieged with intractable problems.

It took time before I was able to invite the seminarians and their insights into dialogue in the classroom and negotiate the narrow path between discipline and freedom. I brought the seminarians to the dump site so that the destitution and the both/and mindset of the scavengers could confront and disturb their complacency. I wanted them to learn about the contemplative character of integral theology, of theology "as an activity that draws together biblical reflection, spiritual direction, liturgical clarity, doctrinal precision, aesthetic considerations, and disciplined ethical discernment and engagement."[9] I wanted them to unite the intellectual dimension of the faith with the experiential and introduce scientific and cosmic elements into a new theological synthesis. I told the seminarians that by living among the poor, they had to consider their immersion as an ascetic discipline, like fasting and mortification, so that they could move to higher levels of understanding in doing theology.

Theology at its best should be logical and reality based. It should be able to stand up to scientific investigation by defining its own modes and methods, its data-gathering techniques and rules of evidence, of validity and reliability as it investigates the self, community, and nature in light of the contemplative dimension. I asked the seminarians to use science as a tool for promoting a better understanding of religious truth. I told them to create research instruments and conduct face-to-face interviews regarding what the scavengers really believe about who Christ is and what he did for humanity. They then went to interview farmers and fishermen, prisoners in death row, and prostitutes in the red-light districts. They found out the big gap between what they study in seminary classrooms and what the people actually believe. The essential theological terms were not translated from the Spanish during colonial times into the local languages for fear of syncretism. Theology even today is taught mostly in English in the seminaries. Therefore, there has been very little reflection done in the local languages, around 87 of them, since the Spaniards left the country.

The seminarians found out that 23 percent of those interviewed thought that *Santissima Trinidad* (Most Blessed Trinity) was the name of a woman. They had to discover new theological terms afterwards to express theological concepts intelligible to the scavengers and relevant to their lives—*santatlo* for "trinity," for instance (from *isa*, one, and *tatlo*, three). We still have to think about the meaning in Filipino of "begotten," "consubstantial," or "procession," not to speak of *ousia* (nature) and *hypostasis* (person) from the conciliar pronouncements regarding Christ and Trinitarian faith in the early centuries of the church.[10] I had the seminarians do their final examinations in the dump site, as children with bloated stomachs excreted intestinal parasites in the gutters outside the chapel, as ex-convicts with gang tattoos all over their bodies sharpened their icepicks and jungle bolos in the alleys along the trash heaps. They had to whisk away the buzz flies as they answered questions about what the Trinity should mean for these people.

The church will not make a significant dent in the poverty of more than one billion people earning one dollar a day unless seminarians, pastors, priests, nuns, bishops, and lay leaders will leave the comfort of their air-conditioned rooms, share the misery of the poor, and be touched and wounded by their pain. Only in this preferential option for the poor will they be able to explain church doctrines in language the poor can understand and can then help set them free. In the early history of the church, it was not so much the partnership with Constantine that turned the Roman empire Christian. It was the sacrifices of Christians who picked up female infants exposed to die and of believers who took care of the sick at the risk of death during epidemics that converted the majority of people during that period.[11]

And so, in teaching theology while living among the poor,

I try to articulate my position as a Filipino Catholic priest, a member of a global religious congregation, without apology as I live among the *basureros* and face the challenges of quantum physics. I make no claim for universal significance except for those engaged in the same language game as I am, those who accept the same existential foundations of faith that I embrace. I am more concerned with the coherence of faith with social justice and the moral claims of the scavengers. I also hold that theology has to be held to the same intellectual standards as any other discipline in the attempt to face honestly the conflicts that it has to confront when it dialogues with a world of cultural diversity and religious pluralism. I believe that theology has a special responsibility to ensure that its insights into matters of meaning and teleology should be made available widely, not just to a narrow class of insiders.

Is my journey to find the truth an impossible pilgrimage, a vainglorious quest, a grievous delusion to seek for the irreducible otherness of the Wholly Other in a universe where even if you had all the information about a physical system, you can only predict its future behavior probabilistically? All I know is that I have to hold on to what I think and feel is true. Relieving the scavengers of their misery has been a dream like an inner fire deep within me, a fire stoked by my experience of inner emptiness. This dream has become a quiet flame that I cannot disregard nor forget for long—this is my truth. This fire blossomed forth in the garbage dump to consume my self-absorption and my cowardice. It set me free from trying to lead and justify a self-satisfied materialistic lifestyle securely wrapped around a cocoon of mindless activities. This is the experience I tried to share with the seminarians as we searched for answers to life's pressing questions on Smokey Mountain.

As a theologian seeking to come to terms with scientific discoveries, I aim to participate in the dialogue from the point of view of the people on Smokey Mountain. There is a tremendous amount of hunger for redemption and transcendence among the scavengers. If only they can find the words to describe their experience of God, they will be better theologians than I will ever be. The scavengers experience God in an immediate, intuitive way. They are filled with a sense of immediacy and transcendence that is second nature to them. The poor commune with the infinite; they are lost in the presence of God when they pray. They experience the beyond in the daily events of their miserable existence. I have learned something about theological integrity from the poor who take for granted that God is part of life, just like one's limbs and one's memory.

Searching for God in solidarity with the scavengers, participating in the way of the cross in a community of faithful, hopeful and loving relationships, I experienced the opening up of my inner self to mystery. I was filled by the grace of a deep unquenchable yearning of the spirit that enabled me to hope against all odds. I experienced this yearning in the face of the bewilderment I share with science regarding the fuzziness of the cosmos: "What we have been learning in our time is that we really do not know this place or how it works, and we comprehend ourselves least of all. And the more we learn, the more we are—or ought to be—dumbfounded."[12]

These are the conversions that I underwent, conversions that shape the way I conduct my personal life:

1. From the objectifying syndrome of thinking with the mind alone, abandoning truth in favor of facts, dispassionately observing things and people by means of empirical measurement and logical analysis, I moved towards integral thinking and doing. I believe thinking is no longer just the use of cold reason alone, devoid of imagination, inquiring with deadly logic into a graceless universe. I believe that truth is the conformity of life to reality, a life filled with splendor and beauty. Scientists believe in the ultimate rationality of the cosmos. I postulate a personal God to make sense of the ultimate rationality of the cosmos. Pope Benedict XVI remarked that if the human mind can manage to understand nature through mathematics, it means that the objective structure of the universe and the intellectual structure of the human being coincide. The scientific worldview actually sets Christian faith in a context that seems to bring out richer depths of meaning, which have always been implicit

in them. And Christian beliefs provide a way in which the universe disclosed by science can be plausibly seen to have meaning and purpose.[13]

2. From the alienating syndrome that situated me as the center of the universe, I moved towards reaching out to the "other" in dynamic interaction in the mutually responsible and transforming relationships in the garbage dump. These relationships are interwoven within the whole fabric of reality. I intend to understand the meaning of "humanity," "consciousness," and "reason" from this experience of interpersonal communion among scavengers on Smokey Mountain. I have discovered that the presence of God is most deeply felt when the mind has stopped frantically grasping for definite formulations, endlessly labeling, categorizing, and polarizing. One should instead engage in personal relationships with other human beings and embrace the cosmos in integrity, solidarity, and creativity to encounter the God who is consuming fire.

3. From a static way of being, I moved towards becoming all that I can be in a dynamic movement of balance between wholeness and becoming. Becoming human in integrity means creatively moving towards God, the Other, and the whole of creation. I believe that the God hypothesis is the best explanation of the world in an evolutionary worldview. My search for the triune God is the desire of my whole self to relate to the Wholly Other, who, according to Martin Buber, is also the Wholly Same. I have abandoned the quest for ultimate certitude and precise definitions since ours is a universe ruled by indeterminacy and as the Wholly Other, God can never be adequately described by words.

I am committed to belief in God, because it is the most morally demanding, psychologically enriching, intellectually satisfying and imaginatively fruitful hypothesis about the ultimate nature of reality known to me.[14] I have reached the conclusion that in the quantum world, there is no reason why believers should feel insecure about their faith. Christian theology, inspired by faith and structured by reason, is the coherent account of the belief that the universe was created by a God who is a community of persons who have loved each other for all eternity.[15] Love requires freedom; the power to choose evil over good; the power to discern hope, and faith, and inspiration. Contrary to Einstein's wish, this God plays dice with the universe, fashioning it through the power of the Spirit in such a way that life would originate and evolve on its own and come up with beings endowed with free will. From so simple a beginning at the start of creation, "endless forms most wonderful and most beautiful have been, and are being evolved," according to Charles Darwin.

This is what theologians have been saying all along.

SEEING WITH THE EYE OF CONTEMPLATION

When you are no longer at the mercy of your obsessions and you feel the love of God burning ever more deeply in your heart, when you come to the stage when the thought of death no longer fills you with dread—for you look on it merely as a dream of the night or, more to the point, as a welcome liberation—then you have indeed found the pledge of your salvation. On that day, you will be filled with ineffable joy for you carry the Kingdom of God within you.
—Theognostos the Priest

Daniel Goleman cites a report published in the *Proceedings of the National Academy of Sciences* in 2004 described a research project to measure the brainwaves of Tibetan monks during meditation. There were monks whose high amplitude gamma-wave activity (expanded awareness, alertness, insight) was 100 percent above the baseline.[16] Two monks who had meditated for 44,000 and 55,000 hours, respectively, had gamma levels that leapt to 600 percent and 800 percent above the baseline. The study suggested that meditation alters the structure and functioning of the brain. Prayer and meditation have measurable effects on both states of consciousness and physiological processes and have become an area of experimental research. Results demonstrated significantly increased blood flow to the inferior frontal and dorsolateral prefrontal cortical regions while the subjects engaged in intense meditation. The results of the disciplined work of inner empiricism, however, are often rejected as emotional, mystical, irrational, and primitive by many scientists. At any rate, they are beginning to be aware of the struggle necessary to attain genuine inner knowledge and the discipline of interior experience, how thousands of hours spent in meditation enabled the monks to reach higher forms of consciousness.

Subjective experience is a difficult problem in the study of the mind because it cannot be explained in terms of mechanisms. Religious experience is basic and universal to human beings, but we only have fragmentary knowledge of the brain, of consciousness, or of subjectivity. There are principles that apply to religious experiences that even science does not yet understand. Perhaps the brains of the monks with the intense amplification of neural activity during meditation and the brains of scavengers during religious celebrations can tell us something more than brain scans about consciousness and memory, how and where cognitive activity happens, and how the brain decides what is good, true, and beautiful. It would be interesting to find out scientifically whether the scavengers experience a different form of reality after years of intense spiritual experiences, especially during Holy Week celebrations, since they relate with God as a "Thou," not an "It." For the scavengers, faith in this "Thou" is empowering, consistent, compelling, and perfectly rational, but they told me that their experience is inexpressible and indescribable, and that it is impossible to convey what it is like to one who has never experienced it.

A human being cannot escape the need to order the world and make sense of experience. Our brains are evolved for order. The mind can engage with the totality of the cosmos and discover the numinousness in it. The brain's compulsion to order is one reason why I believe in a creative designer who willed that life and consciousness be built into the cosmos. Apart from the order in an indeterminate cosmos and the anthropic principle (we live in a universe that seems to favor life and consciousness because a large number of fundamental physical constants that would allow life to arise lie within an extremely narrow range),[17] I also choose to believe because of my primordial religious experience of the irreducible mystery in the death and rising of Jesus the

Christ. Because of the fundamental indeterminacy of reality, I find no reason why I should not follow my heart and leap into the darkness of the cloud of unknowing.

In the garbage dump, I have experienced the devout and cleansing initiation into ritual and mystery, the healing and transforming sense of awe and dread before the transcendent, and of being bathed in the numinous power of the *mysterium tremendum et fascinans* (terrifying and fascinating mystery). While engaged in Bible sharing with members of the Basic Ecclesial Communities and listening to the way the poor understand the Word of God, the atmosphere in the room often became charged with earth-shaking possibilities, gently ushering me into a graced dimension of the universe. While celebrating the Eucharist with the scavengers, I often experienced a flooding radiance, a vitality and aliveness of mind and body in clarity and focus. These deep emotional states that I experienced are real and true. Atheists might question whether they have a real congruence with a Necessary Being, but the feelings are real and true. They are no simple fantasy, inert daydreaming, or vain imagining. The direct experiences of interior illumination, the stunning, mind-numbing experiences of inner light, of boundless freedom and limitless existence are just as real to me as my experience of rocks and trees.

On Smokey Mountain, I was often moved, in the words of Rudolf Otto, by "a feeling that at times come sweeping like a gentle tide, pervading the mind with a tranquil mode of deepest worship." I often felt enveloped in the peace that passes human understanding, a peace transcending the separation of self and the universe as I became wholly immersed in the vulnerability of the scavengers' lives. I often rested, in the words of St. John of the Cross, in the naked, stark elemental awareness that God is as he is and I am as I am. The moments of experiencing the mystery that is at once fascinating and terrifying, moments when one is set free from the burden of conscious living, are also moments of feeling its absence all the more keenly. The emptiness and desolation that comes afterwards makes the longing for these moments even more painful as I remain, in the words of C. S. Lewis, "stirred by a longing for the longing that had just ceased." Experiences like these have been proven to be biologically, observably, and scientifically real by research on the brain.

Being overwhelmed by the God who is consuming fire is a terrible experience. It shakes the core of our becoming and topples the false gods we carve from our own masks. The way of surrender, however, the relinquishing of control can lead to moments, according to Emily Dickinson, when God

> *. . . stuns you by degrees,*
> *Prepares your brittle nature*
> *For the ethereal blow . . .*
> *Then nearer, then so slow*
> *Your breath has time to straighten,*
> *Your brain to bubble cool,*
> *Deals one imperial thunderbolt*
> *That scalps your naked soul . . .*

Where do these internal emotional states come from? Why do they color the way we see things, the way we experience the world? In my experience, these internal mental states go far beyond what I apprehend through physical experience. I believe that my faith can remain authentically spiritual and rooted in the foundational experiences of my particular religious tradition while being fully aware of its evolutionary origins, social functions, psychological dynamics, and economic implications. It is because of these experiences that I believe religious experience is a deep and meaningful feature of the cosmos.

I believe that the spiritual experiences of many people in the garbage dump are even deeper than mine, only they do not have the words to express them. The scavengers and I believe that we are communing with God in and through the divine Word, and we live for God by the power of the Spirit. I can easily grant that people who do not have the same experiences can deny God's existence and consider their unbelief perfectly rational and justified. But I also hold that my faith is rational because I have grounds for my belief, the same experiential grounds for believing that there are rocks and trees outside the window. My consciousness is the personalization of my brain and my neural connections were set up as a result of my personal experience and what I have learned since I was born. I have internalized structures of plausibility from my upbringing and theological training. My personality differs from those of unbelievers because of these circumstances, but we are all human just the same.

It is from the contemplative dimension of consciousness that I engage in dialogue with the poor. Essential parts of religious experience are contemplative and liturgical practices for coming to know and participate in the power of the transcendent, for disciplining the mind, and for conforming the will. One cannot have a religious experience out of the blue. One has to work for it. And one has to look at it from a specific point of view. Interior states of consciousness cannot be seen in the same way as galaxies are seen through a radio telescope or mitochondria in a microscope, and so I have a hard time analyzing this religious experience because subjectivity is central to the religious consciousness. How can I explain my faith to others who do not believe and even to those who do? What language shall I use?

Mystics who tried to describe the unity of consciousness transcending both subjectivity and objectivity were forced to speak in paradox and contradiction. They asked that we simply accept our own understanding and experience of the unity of consciousness even as they could never be objectified or conceptualized. However, experience is also mediated socially. We make sense of our inner ideas and emotions by relating with others. Every experience is an interpreted experience; it cannot be separated from its own distinctive web of communal meaning. And so, a spirit seeking to grow in contemplative knowledge should be rooted in the community. It is dangerous to go into solitude, according to Thomas Merton, merely because one likes to be alone. It is dangerous to be obsessed with the study of the self alone, focusing on one's own subjectivity. One does not go to the triune God alone. That is why I have allowed the scavengers to define who I am, what I am made of, in the face of communal experiences of the transcendent. The scavengers make me feel at home with myself. It is among them that I have discovered who I really am. With them, it is easier for me to believe in a beyond.

The garbage dump is a blessed, sacred place, if one has eyes to see. There is something soothing about the familiar, even if it is as ugly as the garbage dump, because it has become my home.

As Zen beginners are always taught, "Look beneath your feet."

I ONCE WAS LOST AND NOW AM FOUND

We shall not cease from our exploration
And the end of all our exploring
Will be to arrive where we have started
And know the place for the first time.
                    —T. S. Eliot, "Four Quartets"

Since I was a child, I had the example of what deep religious faith meant from my parents. I first learned of God as a person as I watched my mother pray before the Blessed Sacrament in church. From the gleam in her eyes, I discerned that she was not just talking to herself—she was talking to someone vital, powerful, yet insubstantial. Now my deepest proof (you cannot really "prove" God's existence) after my sojourn in the dump is from the insight of Nietzsche: "All joy wills eternity, wills deep, deep eternity," even as I wallow in a darkened emotional state of active receptivity and the world shines forth with an immaculate inner light—I am one with all there is.[18] In the *Magic Furnace*, Marcus Chown described this cosmic oneness even in the physical sense: "In order that we might live, stars in their billions, tens of billions, hundreds of billions even, have died. The iron in our blood, the calcium in our bones, the oxygen that fills our lungs each time we take a breath—all were cooked in the furnaces of the stars which expired long before the Earth was born."[19] We are composed of stardust, recycled waste from the death of countless stars. The universe is one big garbage dump that recycles everything, and we are one with it.

Ensconced in this sense of cosmic oneness, I have learned how to read the Bible, no longer seeking meaning but presence, no longer overly concerned with correct interpretation but with the oceanic feeling that the triune God dwells among us. The scavengers shared with me their insight that sometimes God does not answer your prayers because your heart is not ready for the answer. Or God simply says, "No!" You just have to wait. And anyway, you do not pray just to ask for things, they said. You pray because you worship in the spirit God as a fountain of power and joy, according to them. Thus, it is a gift just to be in God's presence when I feel the dissolving of bodily boundaries, the sensuous being-at-one with, and grounding in, the cosmos. I experience the breaking free from mundane connections in a titanic feeling of unity with the totality, of communion with all creation, in the words of Evelyn Underhill, in "one piercing act of loving comprehension."

In moments when I felt most alive on Smokey Mountain, I experienced neural firestorms of joy and exultation, a sense of gratitude beyond words, a joyous communing with the object of my life's quest. And it generated nice feelings in the *nucleus accumbens* in my brain to hear the Lord say to me, "I know that you have little strength, yet you have kept my word and have not denied my name" (Rev. 3:8). And so, it is the scavengers who minister to my soul now, teaching me how to wait, allowing me to discover the rich variety of ways in which the triune God makes his presence known to us in nature and in history, in the nebulae and black holes, in the freeing of captives, and in securing justice for the poor and the destitute.[20] It is their point of view I consciously take when I teach in the seminary and try to come to terms with the latest findings in astrophysics and evolutionary biology. Their suffering, their hope, and their experience of mystery become points of departure for my theology.

It was not all joy in the garbage dump, however. The peak spiritual experiences were few and far between. It was a very difficult responsibility to make decisions that no matter how you decided, some people would get upset. It was a never-ending conflict between struggle (personal and social) and contemplation. I had to do constant battle with the resident gorgons in my own house—pride, anger, sloth, avarice, lust, gluttony, and envy are still alive and well in my soul.

It was hard to figure out how to allocate meager resources to where they would do the most good in the dump site. When help did not arrive and there was no money to pay the teachers in our kindergarten, or when the roof leaked, or I had to bring someone to the hospital, I tossed restlessly in bed. I shared their pain and insecurity. I was their priest and I had to drink the cup of bitterness for them. I was called to dread and worry for them: "In my flesh I fill up what is lacking in the suffering of Christ" (Col. 1:24). Sympathy, according to Sophie Scholl, who fought the Nazis in a nonviolent way, is often difficult and soon becomes hollow, if one feels no pain oneself. But after all these years, I know I can never be completely one of the poor, even with my vow of poverty. As a member of a religious community, if I am stripped of everything, I just walk to our nearest rectory and I will have everything again. I can fast for days, secure in the knowledge that anytime I want to, I can eat to my heart's content. I can never totally feel what it means not knowing what to eat for the next meal, how to pay the hospital bills, or whether there will be enough money to bury me when I die.

Being with the scavengers in their struggle against poverty and oppression, I stopped clinging to things and worrying about the future. I tried only to live in the present fully and faithfully. Like St. Teresa of Avila, I thanked God for the things I did not possess. I no longer do for the scavengers what they can do for themselves. I have moved beyond feeding programs for the children, bringing the sick to the hospital, and helping bury the dead to the mobilization of the community for self-help and struggle for houses they can call their own. The scavengers have moved from hovels to condominiums in medium-rise buildings. At present, they are into strategic management and systems development for entrepreneurial training. They are linking self-managed networks of the people on Smokey Mountain with thousands of farmers and fishermen in the rural areas through the Internet.

Even if I had very little, I preferred the pain and the grief and the torment and the desperate dreams I experienced in the garbage dump to the feeling I had in Rome of being tired of myself, impervious to caring, no curiosity, no enthusiasm, not a shred of hope at all. The garbage dump shook me out of my narcissistic self-definition, my narrow-mindedness, my cowardice especially. I was forced to make space for another way of seeing the world and acting within it to free myself from callousness and self-absorption. The scavengers taught me that suffering is an evil that will always be there because of the evil that is in myself. I had to sacramentalize my experience in light of the cross, situate the suffering of the scavengers within the ambit of a redemptive future in order to restore myself to what is deepest within me. Life is more precious to me now, more compelling, something to be clung to and relished, and my responsibilities for it all the more urgent.

After years of mourning for children who died before their time, I have come to know life as a gift, especially since I did not expect to survive long in the dump site—I was sure to die by a bullet or an infectious disease. I have seen too many people in the trash heaps snatched away in a heartbeat with feelings left unspoken and dreams unrealized. Fear of being killed never abandoned me; I took it with me whenever I was in the dump site. I was forced to cherish the fear, to nurture it, embedding it in every cell of my body as I walked the tightrope of survival. I have been afraid so long that terror had become a friend, always at my side, never leaving me, keeping me vigilant, the bolts of electricity firing in bursts from the dopamine in my neurons whenever I sensed that danger was near. It helped me to pray and to foster mindfulness and gratefulness to have death always at my side. Surprisingly though, despite the fear, I am at peace. Unlike Unamuno who said that the effort to comprehend death caused him the most tormenting dizziness, the constant presence of death reminds me of the triune God who lives forever. Living in the garbage dump has taken me to the edge of the fear of death, taught me how to surrender to it, and finally be freed from it—"O Death, where is your victory? O Death, where is your sting?" (1 Cor. 15:55).

I had to confront my fears with joyful hope.

Unlike me, the scavengers are not afraid of death; they live each day with pain and dying. The poor on Smokey Mountain are adapted to the unforeseen and accustomed to the unexpected. They fear pain and death less than I do, and having been taught by life the uncertainty of things, they are always ready to take a risk—*Bahala na*! ("come what may" or the phrase can also mean "in the hands of God"). They are used to typhoons and earthquakes and fires. They are on friendly terms with fate and face tragedies, even death, with calm assurance. Resignation and fatalism are writ large in their understanding of the world.[21]

Acceptance of anything that happens is an important facet of their religious experience. They look at the world with the eye of contemplation so they do not lose their trust in God even in the face of death. The scavengers are only afraid that after they die, they will not be reunited with their loved ones.

The scavengers taught me, as I joined them in a journey of faith and service, that it is in accepting our own brokenness with others that we will discover peace and experience a clear-headed sense of bliss. We have to be open enough, empty enough to trust and receive the grace of the triune God amidst the poor. The poor can become a privileged place of meeting the Wholly Other whom we can discover only with courage and inner freedom. Being with the poor is also a spiritual experience. It is the same God we discover in our hearts that we discover among the poor in purity of heart, inward transparency, and authenticity. The search for the good, the true, and the beautiful is the search for God, whether one searches for God consciously or not. Human beings endowed with freedom are capable of participating in the evolution of the universe and of vindicating all that is good, true, and beautiful. Where God in his hiddenness can be disclosed, there is the glimmer of hope that the light has come.

I came to realize that one of the spiritual disciplines in order to move to higher realms of consciousness—just like reading Scriptures, fasting, praying, and worshipping in the liturgical action of the church—should be physical contact with the poor. Growing into the history of the triune God among the poor is growing into a living obedience to the Crucified Christ. This can teach us the discipline of relatedness and communion, and make us understand the underlying interconnection of everything in the cosmos. Living with the poor might give a certain urgency to the questions that touch on the meaning of life and might allow us to learn how to wait on God in openness and trust, in the deep-seeing consciousness that understands with compassion.

The scavengers led me into places beyond that part of me that wants to be safe and secure. They taught me how to create a sacred space where I can wait for the triune God. They taught me that doing justice, loving mercy, and walking humbly before the holy and triune God (Mic. 6:8) is most important when doing theology. Being with the poor should be an essential ingredient of our spiritual life so that we can finally detach ourselves from our false, illusory self. If we are never in their presence, if we never break bread with them, and if we never hear their stories, there is something essential that is lost. If we always avoid them, if we are always afraid of them, something vital is really missing in our spiritual life. It might be difficult then to be carried by the triune God into our own mystery and freedom without humility, without taking off, as C. S. Lewis put it, "a lot of silly, ugly, fancy-dress in which we have all got ourselves up and are strutting about like the little idiots we are."

The journey into the triune God and the search for ultimate truth should translate into the journey to the hovels of squatters, into the dungeons of death-row inmates, into hiding places for battered women and prostitutes in red-light districts. Everyone needs to be in solidarity with the poor of the world because they are most often the sinned against. The triune God is hidden among them, so prophetic dialogue with the poor can be a transformation of the heart, a receiving of blessing, a relieving of pain, a strengthening of hope. It is coming into my own, into my own way to the triune God.

I do not need God as a crutch to ease the pain of existence, as Richard Dawkins accused believers in *A Devil's Chaplain*, to "suck at the pacifier of faith in immortality" in order to dwell with the scavengers on Smokey Mountain for thirty years. I lived in the garbage dump so that I could find myself. I did it so that I could arrive at higher dimensions of consciousness. I could not have done otherwise. I made my choice; I stood my ground. This is the highest expression of my personal freedom. That is all I can ask of myself in this life—to be true to what I am, to be true to the immediate experience of the triune God through my conscience. If I am only for myself, as Rabbi Hillel once said, then what am I?

The poor can become revelation and disclosure to those who look at life with the eye of contemplation. The scavengers became "good news" to me, for they bore witness to the love and power of God who takes the side of the poor. With them, I was able to derive faith from doubt and hope out of paradox. With them I have experienced immense joy, often without rhyme or reason, keeling over in laughter, glorying in just being with them while the dump continued to burn.[22] The garbage dump brought me back to life. I can now say to God with Mary Jo Leddy, "It is enough. I have enough. I am enough. Life is enough. With all my heart, I thank you."

I laugh, therefore the universe is.

REMEMBRANCES OF THINGS TO COME

A seeker ran through the streets shouting over and over again, "We must put God in our lives. We must put God in our lives." "A poor soul," an Elder smiled wanly. "If only we realized the truth: God is always in our lives. The spiritual task is simply to recognize that."
        —Anthony de Mello, *Sadhana*

Prophetic dialogue with the poor has something to do with the sense of awe that lets God awaken capabilities we are afraid to contemplate. The scavengers have taught me much about joy and peace, love and compassion, and prayer—things I would never have learned in libraries and websites—and a lot about grief and violence and fatalism and resignation too, and the cross as a reminder of God's presence at the heart of all human suffering. The gleam of the scavengers' eyes, the contours of their countenance, and the sound of their names have consoled me immeasurably. I have been wounded by their words, which stung like a bullwhip. I have listened to their songs, which have the saltwater taste of tears in them. I learned not just about the pain and struggle of a wounded people, but also about their gifts and graces. When one is in the realm of the mystery, every explanation seems gratuitous. One must live life forward in learned ignorance and radical uncertainty through the cloud of unknowing. The secret is in not being paralyzed by the ignorance and the unknowing and to keep on going beyond the limits of the imagination and the understanding, to keep on pushing against all boundaries and control.

I have basked in the sunlight of being so absorbed in God as to forget the pain of being alone while I prayed with old women scavengers the Mysteries of Light of the Rosary. The place seemed to light up with the glow of gratitude and wonder. In moments like these, I hear the gentle yet insistent call, not only to suffer with the poor, or work with the poor, but to be really poor. Being really poor means to rest my hope in the triune God alone. It also means to hold out my hand and allow the poor to wrap my belt around me and lead me where I do not want to go (cf. John 21:19). It means sharing the most significant moments of their lives. It means being shouted down by the scavengers if my plans do not correspond to their dreams. Praying with the scavengers, I asked only to be changed in ways I cannot imagine as pieces of the darkness that has haunted my journey finally slip away into the vastness of space.

When I am with the scavengers, the big black hole in my chest disappears. I stop trying to control the future and let God shape my life. I have spent too much time trying to control everything in my life, but I found out it is futile. It is a hollow pursuit. There is not much we can do before an earthquake or a tsunami or when terrorists crash airplanes into our skyscrapers, and especially when our own death comes. We have to arrive at a level of consciousness where everything becomes a sacred object, numinous, to be handled with awe and reverence, a level of consciousness where we feel a presence closer to us than our breath, closer than our thoughts, closer even than our consciousness of who we are. We have to reach a spiritual state with "the soul in prayer, no matter the position of the body." We have to pray ourselves into new ways of thinking and behaving if the world is to be given hope and transformed by grace. The Spirit who has always been at work in us is in full control, drawing us into a future beyond all imagining.

The lives of the poor have fed my imagination. I have shed with them tears of horror, of terror, of fury; tears of compassion; tears that fell on the desert of self-absorbed obsession; tears that created an oasis of empathy, creativity, and courage in my soul. If I had left and run away from the garbage dump, there is no doubt in my mind that I would have destroyed myself completely. I stayed with the scavengers to remain alive. I needed their faith to protect me against myself because our destiny, mine and that of the scavengers, is beyond our togetherness. We are called not merely to union but communion with the triune God. In this communion, we discover the interconnectedness of all things, and we grow in compassion and gratitude.

Prophetic dialogue with the poor must be coupled with reflection and a centeredness that comes from prayer and meditation. Prayer has to become an everyday experience lived with gratitude and wonder. In prayer, I try to attain moments of silent, sacred attentiveness. This I do by constantly practicing the art of being fully present, like a candle whose flame remains still in a windless room. Ancient Hindu disciplines call this "stopping the whirlpools of the mind." Buddhists call it "calming the monkey skittering about." Mostly, however, my prayer is still full of inner contradictions, frustrations, restlessness, drowsiness, distractions, depression, and boredom. It is characterized by irregularity, lack of depth, and perfunctoriness, despite St. Paul's counsel to pray constantly (1 Thess. 5:17). There are moments when I wrestle with God the whole night (Gen. 32:25) saying, "I will not let you go until you give the parish cooperative a machine that can turn food waste into organic fertilizer." I spend hours arguing with God about why the children are dying in the garbage dumps. But there is little use in debating with the master of the universe. He just directs your gaze to the mangled body of his Son in the garbage dump outside Jerusalem. Jesus did not offer doctrines to be subjected to objective scientific proof. He told his disciples to take up their cross and follow him.

I try to arrive at mindfulness and heartfulness in prayer and bring these to bear on all aspects of my life. My formula for prayer is very simple: I just sit and wait. This is hard work—to arrive at the fiercest attention possible. It involves focusing the mind on what one is doing, doing everything with one's whole self. It is a back-breaking struggle to engage in intense and sustained practice just to be still, simply to be present, attentive and aware, putting aside ideas, thoughts, judgments. The spiritual life, according to Thomas Merton, is first of all a matter of keeping awake. Sometimes as I sit and watch my thoughts come and go, I see fearsome dinosaurs, incubi, troglodytes, and all kinds of monsters similar to the ones I saw while peering at the fire in the garbage dump. So most of the time, I just sit still, not minding the monsters at all, count my breath and pray a version of the Jesus prayer, praying unceasingly the "Glory be to the Father and to the Son and to the Holy Spirit" as a mantra to create an inner stillness, even as I remain among scavengers who have been silenced, whose voices have been stilled. I sit in the lotus position and try to reach the lucid silence of the heart the Desert Fathers sought. With detached impartiality, I try to arrive at that pure center of awareness where I am no longer plagued with attachment to my body, my desires, my feelings, my anxieties, my thoughts.

The God who is consuming fire fascinates and frightens me by his silence, which can be a form of intimacy and distance. Standing still and indwelling the vast expanse of awareness, this silence and distance disclose dormant dimensions of my prophetic dialogue with the poor. It helps me discover points of congruence between my method of prayer and who I am. If we are open enough, perceptive and persistent enough, to connect with others and the world, we can become greater than ourselves. And so I plod on in my pilgrimage in that ravishing and ravaged territory between the two eternities, filled with mingled guilt, humiliation, and the resolve to carry on with prophetic dialogue with the poor and the despised. I plod on with passion and devotion, even when I continue to be afraid, amidst the atmosphere of mindless violence and the proximity of death. But because of the Incarnation, nothing human can be alien to us, even fear and dying.

Now praying is just being there and pondering on the unveiling: "Be still and know that I am God" (Ps. 46:11). Words seem almost as though unavailing against a presence and luminosity that is just so simply there. This presence burns a space in my inner self so that the Spirit of the Christ can transform me into his image and likeness. When one is pervaded by the sense of belonging to the universe, one can withstand the temptation to cynicism, anger, and discouragement as one engages in the lonely battle to demolish the empires of those who exploit the weak and the downtrodden. We have to indwell the truth given to us as a gift. Truth is integral, communal, and dynamic. Truth can only be disclosed in personal relationships—not only through sense perceptions and logical connections. Life in its wholeness is not merely sensation and reason but the body, spirit, empathy, intuition, fantasy, and faith. A person's capacity for truth increases in direct proportion to the capacity for conscious and reflective relationship.

In this way, prayer bears fruit in social transformation.

A SILENCE ON FIRE

I will try, like them to be my own silence. And this is difficult. The whole world is secretly on fire. The stones burn, even the stones they burn me. How can a man be still or listen to all things burning? How can he dare to sit with them when all their silence is on fire?

—Thomas Merton

After thirty years of living in a ravaged environment, I burn with a love for the earth whose principles are so fine tuned and its future so abundant that it absolutely demands the existence of God. Robert Penn Warren gave advice on how to live in the world: "We must try/ To love so well the world that we may believe, in the end, in God" (*Masts at Dawn*). Only by living completely immersed in the world can one learn to leap into the darkness of faith. My awe of the universe becomes more profound the more I understand it from the description of science and from the pictures of the Hubble telescope and articles from scientific magazines. Science has given me tremendous opportunities for worship and gratitude. Science has deepened my appreciation of the scope of divine purpose and providence because of its discoveries in the realm of the immense and the infinitesimal, of its explanations of complexity and emergence.

After years of seeing sparrows drop like stones when they passed through the smoke of the dump site, I feel indescribable joy whenever I see birds nesting in the mango tree beside my parents' house every time I visited them before they passed away. Filled with a profound sense of awe at the mystery of existence and an unalloyed delight in everything that is, I understand completely what Edna St. Vincent Millay felt when she exclaimed, "O world, I cannot hold thee close enough!" I am grateful to the triune God for every moment, for every perception. I have been filled with wonder at the immensity of the cosmos and the abundance of the earth while grieving because of the hard-heartedness of human beings. I was given a renewed appreciation of the world and its splendor, its immensity and beauty, its perils and cruelty, by the people in the garbage dump.

The life of the spirit is both serenity and struggle as we plunge burning into the agony and the ecstasy, the griefs and the joys of the people of the world in self-effacing devotion and service to the poor. When we consume the bread and wine at the Eucharistic celebration, we are reminded that we are also supposed to be consumed by God who will test us by fire to separate the gold from the dross. We are supposed to be consumed by the Divine Word, who came to set the world on fire, who was consumed by zeal for the Father's house and who baptized with fire and the Spirit. We are supposed to be consumed by the Spirit who came down on the apostles in tongues of fire and who will renew the face of the earth. Fire evokes the sense of power and energy, the same power during the first Pentecost that energized the mission of the early church. "We are called," wrote Henri Nouwen, "we are blessed, we are broken, and we are fed to the world." By eating from this bread, we become bread for everyone else; we become one with the Christ of the burnt men and women.

Encountering the God who is consuming fire, I have allowed the suffering of the scavengers to enter into the depth of my heart and be turned to compassion. A strange, blissful calm finally settled upon me. "This is a garbage dump," I said to myself, feeling an incredible lightness of being, "this is where I ought to be." Although I have accomplished little, I hope that I have traveled far in my journey into solitude, into higher realms of consciousness. I take consolation in the prayer of St. Bernard of Clairvaux: "No one would know how to seek You unless he had first found You; so that You want us to find You in order to seek You and to seek You in order to find You."[23] My prayer remains, as St. Augustine put it, *sanare oculum cordis*, to heal the eye of the heart that I might behold God's terrible and haunting beauty. Fantasy, imagination, intuition, humility, awe, and reverence now play a bigger role in my ceaseless quest for the ultimate. I know now that the story of my life should no longer be a story of conquest but of discovery. I must continue the search for the God who is unknown in his ultimate essence—beyond words and concepts, beyond mathematical equations, beyond all forms of objectification. As Meister Eckhart suggested, "Seek God so as never to find him."

The journey into solitude is participation in the community of the triune God, developing compassion for everyone and discovering the interconnectedness of everything that is. In solitude, I discover moments of meaning and interconnectedness, moments of elusive joy that flash momentarily and disappears. The suffering and the solitude in the garbage dump led me, as Saul Bellow wrote in *Herzog*, to "a more extended form of life, a striving for true wakefulness, and an antidote to illusion." My stay in the garbage dump has opened paths through which a deeper understanding of faith and church can be imagined through pain and failure, humiliation and alienation. I have found solitude while seeking the Divine Word that silences the arrogant and the fool.

The work is never done but it is enough to live in the gratuitousness of the gift. One grand illusion is to think that one has finally arrived just because there are glimpses of grace, moments of ecstasy and epiphany, moments of inspiration and elation when everything finally makes sense and the pieces of the jigsaw finally fit. Any attempt to communicate this experience in words is already to become a traitor. So as long as we are pilgrims, truth will never be adequately expressed, doubts will never be completely overcome, nor guilt fully removed, the pain washed away, fears stilled, self-pity surrendered, and the enemy expelled. But I have come to terms with my imperfections through a spirituality in which mind and heart collaborate in the quest for the ultimate.

I had to share the scavengers' pain with an attitude of pure receptivity and inner emptiness so that I could travel farther into higher dimensions of consciousness. I am grateful to the scavengers for the experience of pain and struggle with them that makes it less difficult for me to spurn any temptation to self-reliance and easier to empower others to share their gifts with one another. I am humbled by their joyful endurance in the midst of the squalor of their surroundings and their dignity in their suffering; I admire their resourcefulness with the little they have and their joy in the midst of misery. It has taught me of the seemingly limitless capacity for wisdom and compassion that exists in every human being. I have learned that the bravest, the most loyal and loving people in the world seldom have heroic physical attributes or the auras of very holy people. Their faces can be those of scavengers in a garbage dump.

We can know ourselves only by embracing commitment, only by relating to others. And so, I and my brokenness have finally made a truce. I do not deny the brokenness and the vulnerability but I no longer choose to dwell in them in deadly solipsism and morbid self-absorption. In the state the world is in now, battered and embattled, defeating my self-absorption is a salvific necessity. I have found out exactly who I was meant to be. I am a priest, it is everything that I am—without it I disappear. This is the way I have chosen to conduct my personal life—to be consumed by zeal for peace and justice. The dark night I experienced made me turn to the poor, and my stay in a garbage dump made me turn toward the earth. I therefore had to connect spirituality with social justice and ecology. The three are intimately related. If the mystical tradition, which survives now mainly in monasteries, is brought back to the parishes and homes, and if this is linked to social justice and care for creation, there will be hope for this planet in peril.

In the search for peace and justice, brokenness and anger and doubt can be places of surrender and transformation and discovery. My search for the triune God is made clear by what Simone Weil wrote: "It is necessary to have had a revelation of reality through joy, in order to find reality through suffering." The burning garbage that I saw reflected in the eyes of the scavengers revealed to me the hidden but real presence of God, the God whose response to my sins was not to strike me down for being a sinner but to give me a blessing. I wake up and dance in the clarity of perfect contradiction—I am a sinner and I am loved by a God who asks no questions about my worthiness to be his priest—no analysis, no argument, no description, no definition. It is enough to simply be. And so I try to live up to the vow of Teilhard de Chardin, the Jesuit scientist and theologian: "As far as my strength will allow me, because I am a priest, I would henceforth be the first to become aware of what the world loves, pursues, suffers. I would be the first to see, to sympathize, to toil—the first in self-fulfillment, the first in self-denial—I would be more widely human and more nobly terrestrial in my ambitions than any of the world's servants."

I am happy to be in a universe where I can work continually on becoming free, even as my experience of God could be described in terms of restlessness and exile, of disquiet and homesickness. My inward pilgrimage is the desire to fill an emptiness that the world cannot fill. Simone Weil wrote about prisoners in solitary confinement separated by a stone wall through which they can only communicate using taps and scratches. She said that it is the same with us and God—every separation is a connection. In my quest for the God who is consuming fire, I am behind the stone wall. I have to listen with all that I am to the taps and scratches behind the wall, which are very faint. Listening deeply to the taps and scratches, I arrived at a nowhere, which is beyond all the places I have dwelt in, at a place where I had to bid a good-bye to my quest for certainty, to my frustration with all forms of contradiction. Our ignorance is vast, and there will always be things we do not know. Even science will never grasp the whole of reality. A theory of everything will not be able to explain how a living cell can arise out of matter or how the human mind really works.[24] Thus, also for the modern scientific mind, the ever more subtle and insightful unknowing of Nicholas of Cusa is a worthy goal.

The scavengers have welcomed me home to the deeper dimensions of my inwardness and put me in touch with myself. I am happy among these strangers. Loving them has changed me in ways that I will never fully understand. Their giving me access to their interior life was a gracious opportunity to learn much about humanity up close and personal. It has changed me even if I did not want to be transformed. It was all there in the garbage dump I have made my home—the important things that make me feel real, make me experience the oneness of all that is—nostalgia and bitterness, poverty and redemption, affection and hopelessness, innocence and malice, awe and violence, ringing with the sweet-sour fierceness of the truth amidst the decaying garbage.[25] The God of Abraham, Isaac, and Jacob, the

God of Peter, James, and John, the God of Teilhard de Chardin, Thomas Merton, and Mother Teresa is present in the garbage dump if we know how to look. He is the same God I encounter in religious experience, the ultimate mind, the creative designer, the God who is consuming fire. In this encounter, I find reasons to believe that the cosmos is rationally ordered; it has a purpose; it is conducive to the realization of beauty and goodness, truth and creativity, and, finally, reasons to believe that the idea of a Creator God is coherent, plausible, and existentially satisfying.

The very core of my being was seared by thirty years of staying in the garbage dump. I have long since stopped asking what I can do for the people of Smokey Mountain. Now I am asking who I can be for them. And in my old age, I continue to burn with the call to spread the flame of justice, peace, and the integrity of creation into young hearts waiting like dry tinder for a spark of hope, a flame such as the prophet Jeremiah describes: "within me there is something like a burning fire shut up in my bones. I am weary with holding it in and I cannot" (20:9). As Elvis Cole, private investigator in the novel, says, "The Darkness frightens me, but what it does to us frightens me even more. Maybe this is why I do what I do. I chase the darkness to make room for the light."[26]

These are the defining moments of who I am as a priest and as a human being. I have to be true to this inner light, this burning desire within me—the desire not to allow the weak to be ground down by the cruel and the ruthless. The work will never be complete, and I will always remain a sinner, but I am not free to desist from doing it. Locking myself inside a garbage dump made me free, free from meaninglessness and boredom—boredom especially. The moments of grace I experienced in the dump site make it all worth it. The profound desire to find access to the transcendent in the garbage dump has overcome my moody, introspective self-preoccupation. The moments of grace make me live to the full Steve Jobs' advice: "Your time is limited, so don't waste it living someone else's life," he said. "Don't be trapped by dogma—which is living with the results of other people's thinking. Don't let the noise of others' opinions drown out your own inner voice."

God can only be encountered by those who have been set

free. If your theology does not set you free, it is not the right theology. If you want to liberate the poor, allow them first to set you free. I have chosen to live my life in this manner—to live for a cause greater than myself. I have to listen closely to the music of the spheres with all that I am and all that I have. And as I do, I experience the intimate touch of the Trinity's creative and redemptive power. In such a manner, I find the meaning of why I am in the universe.

The scavengers did not want anything from me. They just wanted me to be there with them. With the scavengers, I did not always have to be in charge, to be the winner all the time. It is in acknowledging their pain, my brothers and sisters in the garbage dump, and listening to them that I have achieved a measure of humanity. As one of my favorite "theologians," James Lee Burke, wrote in his short story, *The Convict*, many years have to pass before we learn that "it is our collective helplessness, the frailty and imperfection of our vision that ennobles us and saves us from ourselves." For an illumined heart, darkness holds no fear. And so, filled with the sense of boundless possibilities, I join hands with everyone engaged in building the earth. As Teilhard de Chardin declared, "It is our duty to proceed as though the limits to our abilities do not exist." I know I will never lose my soul again. The scavengers of Smokey Mountain have taught me how to chain my soul to myself wherever I go.

A UNIVERSE ON FIRE

There came to Abba Joseph, Abba Lot and said to him, "Father, according to my strength, I keep a modest rule of prayer and fasting and meditation and quiet, and according to my strength, I purge my imagination: What more must I do?" The old man, rising, held up his fingers against the sky, and his fingers became like ten torches of fire, and he said, "If thou wilt, thou shalt be made wholly a flame."
    —The Sayings of the Desert Fathers

The universe began 13.7 billion years ago as a cosmic ball of fire. Human creativity has been accelerating since the dawn of human history. Science and technology are getting more and more creative, much faster than our moral evolution. Teilhard de Chardin, in whom the evolutionary history of the cosmos inspired a deeply spiritual vision and a radiant hope for the future, grounded his thought in science yet proclaimed a deeply religious understanding of the universe. He showed us that faith can embrace the scientific account of our origins as its own sacred story without losing any of its spiritual power. He believed that creation is the preordained unfolding of life and spirit from primordial matter, matter charged with emergent possibilities within an evolutionary spirituality. The triune God who is consuming fire is God with us: "By means of all created things, without exception, the divine assails us, penetrates us and molds us. We imagine it as distant and inaccessible, whereas in fact we live steeped in its burning layers." We are the sentinels of the divine flame, living in hope for the moment when the universe will end in spiritual fire at the end of time.

In *The Phenomenon of Man*, written from a personal commitment to faith in an evolving universe, de Chardin wrote that in the beginning was Power, intelligent, loving, energizing: "In the beginning was the Word, supremely capable of mastering and molding whatever might come into being in the world of matter. In the beginning, there was not coldness and darkness: there was Fire." He went on to say that, "Once again the Fire has penetrated the earth . . . the flame has lit up the whole world from within . . . so naturally has it flooded every element, every energy, every connecting link in the unity of our cosmos that one might suppose the cosmos to have burst spontaneously into flame." He ended with this prayer: "Lord . . . you who are divine energy and living, irresistible might: since of the two of us it is you who are infinitely the stronger, it is you who must set me ablaze and transmute me into fire that we may be welded together and made one."[27]

One who has not experienced being wretched in the literal meaning of the term—overwhelmed by misery, darkness, looming menace—has only scratched the surface of what it means to be human. It is solely by risking life that freedom is obtained. Only if there are empty graves can there be a Resurrection, Nietzsche wrote. If God did not choose to work in ways that confound us, grace would not be amazing. We are stewards of the mystery but we have to bear our cross. The Russian monk Macarius of Optino remarked, "In order for people to recognize their spiritual wounds, they must undergo bitter sorrows, which purify the heart and restore to health the stricken soul." In engaging in solidarity and prophetic dialogue with the poorest of the poor, we have to learn to find ways to combine our different worlds and values (sometimes the warring parts of our selves) so that we can become more expansive, not more diminished, human beings. We can make our weakness and our pain a source of creativity as we burn with zeal for peace and justice.

And so, we have to be set aflame. Being on fire ignites the capacity for initiative, exploration, and endurance. I have tried to understand the significance of my faith in the evolutionary and processive movement of a universe on fire. This sense of presence in an evolving cosmos nurtures both contemplation and energizes action. It fosters a mindfulness that balances silence and activity, personal holiness and social transformation through compassion. Beauty, truth, and goodness are the keys to unlocking the secrets of the evolving universe, but we have to be set on fire, pure, hard, demanding fire. We can then protest against injustice, war, and the ravaging of the earth without suffering from burnout, without running away from the battle.

Being on fire provides us with the opportunity of experiencing beauty, truth, and goodness in their purest forms. Being on fire inflames the imagination about what it means to be a human being in an evolving cosmos. We can create the future if it is imagined and realized by burned men and women who work and sacrifice for a human future, who will make a stand for timeless human values like love, integrity, solidarity, creativity, respect for the dignity of every human being, and caring for the weak and disadvantaged. These burned women and men must oppose those who argue that these values are obsolete, meaningless, or a hindrance to progress. We have a chance to create a future we want to live in with these timeless values only if we have been set on fire to struggle for the good, the true, the beautiful.[28]

Hope in the God who is consuming fire is an active waiting: "For in hope we have been saved, but hope that is seen is not hope; for why does one also hope for what one sees?" (Rom.

8:24). We do deeds of justice and peace while we await the end-time as hope ignites new visions of freedom and responsibility. Hope sets our souls ablaze to burn away the dross of our despair and weakness. It fans the flames of a life of passion, deep meaning, and unassailable faith, a faith shaped by discipline and the constant awareness of death and rising again. Hope is future oriented and is grounded in a view of reality in which all things evolve towards ever-increasing beauty in a genuinely open adventure. We are limited only by our own capacity for growth and transcendence. Change is not a threat but an opportunity if we accept the responsibility to help make the future happen. The responses of human beings vary greatly under dangerous circumstances, observes the *I Ching*: "The superior man stands up to fate, endures resolutely in his inner certainty of final success, and bides his time until the onset of reassuring odds."

Bertrand Russell wrote that we can build the habitation of our soul only on the firm foundation of unyielding despair. Christians proclaim their unyielding hope and their expectation of future transformation as founded in the Galilean's promise who emptied himself so that we can be made full. This is the answer of Christians to Stephen Hawking's question in *A Brief History of Time*: Why does the universe go to all the bother of existing at all if it does not have to? The universe is the outward symbol of a deep inner purpose which is the reason why we are here. We have to discover the triune God in the universe. We can never find the God who is consuming fire anywhere else. And so Christians look at the universe through the eyes of hope and behold the inwardness of things and the authentically new that emerges in cosmic history in order to see the divine promise in the deepest dimensions of the cosmos.

St. Catherine of Siena called on everyone to "set the world on fire" with their love. Hope's sources sustain us along the way: "In the continuous and far-reaching labor of the moral life, hope is the sense of possibility that generates and sustains moral agency. Hope's object provides an impetus for action, a sense of direction, and a cause that renders process meaningful."[29] Hope is the defining feature of the Christian faith since our hope has a definite shape—the resurrection of the body and life everlasting in ultimate communion with the one and triune God.

"Between the forces of terror and the forces of dialogue, a great unequal battle has begun," Albert Camus wrote. "I have nothing but reasonable illusions as to the outcome of that battle. But I believe it must be fought." Camus also said that hope is awakened, revived, nourished by millions of solitary individuals whose deeds and works every day negate frontiers and the crudest implications of history. Each and every person, he continued, on the foundations of his or her own sufferings and joys, builds for all. I also believe that the battle has to be fought, and I have nothing but unreasonable hope that the forces of dialogue will vanquish the forces of terror in the end. Hope is purpose united to faith. In the transcendence of the God who is consuming fire, faith is carried by the forward momentum of anticipation and openness to what is new, carried forward into hope by the transcendence of the future. Hope, said Archbishop Desmond Tutu, is an inner light that can strengthen our resolve to create a better world and help us navigate the darkness of our times.[30] In hope's light and warmth, the human race shall overcome its tendency toward disunity and self-destruction.

Christianity is a religion of hope because of its expectation of a final future fulfillment. It therefore has the ability to think differently, to be creative enough to see reality from a wider perspective in order to engender intellectual convictions, ethical responses, and spiritual strength. With commitment to a common hope—scientific, ethical, and personal—we can overcome the many crises of poverty, disease, conflict, instability, and unsustainability that confront us. This is what the scavengers on Smokey Mountain mean by *pagkamakasaysayan* as a value, being historical—to be embraced by history and yet touch history too by personal acts of courage, compassion, and creativity to leave the world a better place than when one came into it. What each of us will decide as history embraces us and will mark the future for us all. We who have encountered the triune God in hope can never be intimidated by the singularity, by gene manipulation or by cybernetics because hope tells us the future will even be more wonderful than we can ever imagine.

In the transcendence of hope, we encounter the triune God in helping the abandoned, the widow, and the orphan in combatting the devastation of ecosystems and in nurturing peace in the face of perpetual conflict. Hope has to be rooted in action. Hope provides us with visions of the truly new and unanticipated. "Therefore, since we are receiving a kingdom which cannot be shaken, let us have grace, by which we may serve God acceptably with reverence and godly fear. For our God is a consuming fire" (Heb. 12:28-29).

NOTES

[1] The Second Vatican Council was called to session in 1962 to come to terms with this more dynamic understanding. *Gaudium et Spes* is the document The Church in the Modern World. The document starts with "The joys and the hopes, the griefs and the anxieties of the world." Pope John XXIII said that the council was convened to open some windows to let in some fresh air into the church and open it to the modern world. *Gaudium et Spes, 5*, declared that the world has moved from a static to a dynamic view of the world, from being to becoming.

[2] In his message to the Pontifical Academy of Sciences concerning evolution (October 22, 1996), Blessed John Paul II said that new knowledge has led to the recognition of the theory of evolution as more than just a hypothesis. See Gereon Walter's "The Catholic Church and Evolutionary Theory," for a discussion of the conflicts and congruences of Catholic faith and evolution in *Proceedings of the Pontifical Academy of the Sciences: Scientific Insights into the Evolution of the Universe and of Life, 31 October–4 November, 2008*, ed. Werner Arber, Nicola Cabibbo, and Marcelo Sanchez-Sorondo (Vatican City: Ex Aedibus Academicis in Civitate Vaticana, 2009), 450-69. See also Kenneth R. Miller, *Finding Darwin's God: A Scientist's Search for Common Ground between God and Evolution* (New York: HarperCollins, 2000). Miller says that God created a material world in which truly free, truly independent beings could evolve. See also Karl W. Giberson, *Saving Darwin: How to Be a Christian and Believe in Evolution* (San Francisco: HarperOne, 2008).

[3] See Lisa Randall, *Warped Passages: Unraveling the Mysteries of the Universe's Hidden Dimensions* (New York: HarperCollins, 2005), for an introduction into the fuzzy and warped universe of modern physics. For those who are more into the visual aspect, see *What the Bleep? Down the Rabbit Hole*, a DVD production of Captured Light Distribution that explores the metaphysical world of quantum mechanics and the fascinating link between science and spirituality.

[4] Krista Tippet, *Einstein's God: Conversations about Science and the Human Spirit* (New York: Penguin Books, 2010), 35. In Paul Davies, *The Mind of God: The Scientific Basis for a Rational World* (New York: Simon and Schuster, 1993), Davies, a theoretical physicist, noted that scientists are increasingly being driven by the new physics to probe more deeply into theories of cosmic

origin and destiny, space, and time, creation by design or chance. He claimed that by doing their work, scientists end up thinking about God more than theologians. God has also become a question for physicists.

⁵Ray Kurzweil defines singularity as "a future period during which the pace of technological change will be so rapid, its impact so deep, that human life will be irreversibly transformed." See Ray Kurzweil, *The Singularity Is Near: When Humans Transcend Biology* (New York: Penguin, 2006).

⁶See Keith Ward, *Pascal's Fire: Scientific Faith and Religious Understanding* (Oxford: One World Publications, 2006); Keith Ward, *The Big Questions in Science and Religion* (West Conshohocken, PA, Templeton Foundation Press, 2008), for a discussion of current issues in the science-religion debates. See also John F. Haught, *Science and Religion: From Conflict to Conversation* (New York: Paulist Press, 1995).

⁷For further discussions on the dialogue between science and theology, see Philip Clayton, ed., *The Oxford Handbook of Religion and Science* (New York: Oxford University Press, 2008); Peter Harrison, ed., *The Cambridge Companion to Science and Religion* (Cambridge: Cambridge University Press, 2010). See also Harold Attridge, ed., *The Religion and Science Debate: Why Does it Continue?* (New Haven, CT: Yale University Press, 2009).

⁸Parker Palmer, *To Know as We Are Known: A Spirituality of Education* (San Francisco: HarperOne, 1983), 37. He says that, "The truth we are seeking, the truth that seeks us, lies ultimately in the community of being where we not only know but are known" (ibid., 90).

⁹L. Gregory Jones, "Baptism: A Dramatic Journey into God's Dazzling Light—Baptismal Catechesis and the Shaping of Christian Practical Wisdom," in *Knowing the Triune God: The Work of the Spirit in the Practices of the Church*, ed. James J. Buckley and David S. Yeago (Grand Rapids: William B. Eerdmans Publishing, 2001), 163.

¹⁰While doing research for my dissertation, I visited George Gallup, Sr., at Princeton. He gave me a lot of research material he compiled while doing research on religiosity in America. From the results, I have reasons to conclude that many Catholics and evangelicals in the United States likewise do not have a deep understanding of the theological terms enumerated above.

¹¹Using the rigorous methods of modern sociological research, Rodney Stark documented the startling rise of Christianity in the early centuries. See Rodney Stark, *The Rise of Christianity: How the Obscure, Marginal Jesus Movement Become the Dominant Religious Force in the Western World in Four Centuries* (San Francisco: HarperOne, 1997). See also Rodney Stark, *The Rise of Christianity: A Sociologist Reconsiders History* (Princeton, NJ: Princeton University Press, 1996).

¹²Lewis Thomas, *Late Night Thoughts on Listening to Mahler's Ninth Symphony* (New York: Viking Press, 1983), 157.

¹³Keith Ward, *God, Faith and the New Millennium: Christian Belief in an Age of Science* (Oxford: Oneworld Publications, 1998), 11. See also Keith Ward, *Re-thinking Christianity* (Oxford: Oneworld Publications, 2007).

¹⁴Ibid., p. xiii.

¹⁵Timothy Keller, *The Reason for God: Belief in an Age of Skepticism* (New York: Riverhead Books, 2008), 226.

[16]"The Inexplicable Monks," in *What Have You Changed Your Mind About? Today's Leading Minds Rethink Everything*, ed. John Brockman (New York: HarperCollins, 2009), 272-75.

[17]See John F. Haught, *Mystery and Promise: A Theology of Revelation* (Collegeville, MN: Liturgical Press, 1993). Without the fine tuning of physical constants at the Big Bang, there would never have been a universe that can give rise to life and consciousness.

[18]Joan Goodall recounts similar experiences of living outside the moment, moments of eerie luminosity in *Reason for Hope: A Spiritual Journey* (New York: Grand Central Publishing, 2000). See also Andrew Newberg, Eugene G D'Aquil, and Vince Rause, *Why God Won't Go Away: Brain Science and the Biology of Belief,* and *The Mystical Mind: Probing the Biology of Religious Experience* (New York: Ballantine Books, 2001). The human brain seems to be hardwired for the spiritual. There is a built-in desire for self-transcendence and for participating in ultimate meaning in us.

[19]Simon Singh, *Big Bang: The Origin of the Universe* (New York: Fourth Estate, 2004), 388.

[20]Diamante Maya was a student from the Intervarsity Christian Fellowship who stayed on Smokey Mountain the summer of 2006. She also discovered that it was the scavengers who ministered to her soul. This is from her journal: "The children were incredibly perceptive of my needs. Standing on top of a huge mountain of trash, not only was I ministering to these children, but they were ministering to me. Not only did I feel a deep love for them, but I knew they loved me. They were not sad and decrepit. They appeared to have a joy and sense of adventure that was not hindered by their circumstances. Perhaps it wasn't they that needed me, but rather me that needed them." Diamante also helped organize shows for the Smokey Mountain dancers when they went on an environmental concert tour to Los Angeles in the spring of 2010.

[21]For a multidisciplinary discussion backed by field research of the Filipino understanding of well-being, destiny, and anguish, see Consuelo J. Paz, ed., *Ginhawa, Kapalaran, Dalamhati: Essays on Well-Being, Opportunity/Destiny and Anguish* (Quezon City: University of the Philippines Press, 2008).

[22]The McCann Worldgroup survey showed that a significant number of young people wanted to be remembered as "a person who made everyone laugh."

[23]*On the Love of God,* 7, 22. As St. Thomas Aquinas already wrote in his Commentary on St. John's Gospel, "Spiritual things are not received unless they are desired, nor are they desired unless they are somehow known."

[24]This is the hope of some scientists, that a theory of everything based on the scientific method will answer all our questions. See Michael Brooks, *13 Things that Don't Make Sense: The Most Baffling Scientific Mysteries of Our Time* (New York: Vintage Books, 2009). He claims that scientists are stuck and cannot explain fundamental mysteries, but this can be a sign that they are about to make a great leap forward. Other scientists have lost hope of ever answering these mysteries at all. John Horgan claimed that science, especially pure science, the grand quest to understand the universe and our place in it, will yield no more great revelations or revolutions, but only incremental, diminishing returns. See John Horgan, *The End of Science: Facing the Limits*

of Knowledge in the Twilight of the Scientific Age (New York: Broadway Books, 1997). In the October 2006 issue of *Discover,* Horgan repeated his arguments in his article "The Final Frontier." Ian Tattersall also believes that it is highly unlikely that science will ever penetrate the ultimate mysteries in *The Monkey in the Mirror: Essays on the Science of What Makes Us Human* (New York: Harcourt, 2002), 4.

[25]Immaculee Ilibagiza, in Immaculee Ilibagiza and Steve Erwin, *Left to Tell: Discovering God Amidst the Rwandan Holocaust* (Carlsbad, CA: Hay House, 2006), shares her story about finding God amidst the hideous display of inhumanity to each other during the war between the Hutus and Tutsis. There is no place on earth where God cannot be found—even in garbage dumps and killing fields. The sacredness and dignity of the human person can be recognized most clearly when it is desecrated and trampled upon.

[26]Robert Crais, *Chasing the Darkness* (New York: Simon and Schuster, 2008).

[27]See Ursula King, *Spirit of Fire: The Life and Vision of Teilhard de Chardin* (Maryknoll, NY: Orbis Books, 1996), for a description of the powerful and inspiring vision of fire, a vision of divine love and its fiery energy that creates, connects, transforms, and sets free. It is also the foundation of enduring hope.

[28]Relevant here would be Sir Ken Robinson's book, *The Element: How Finding Your Passion Changes Everything* (New York: Viking, 2009). The "element" is where talent meets passion. Burnt men and women should arrive at the "element," so that they can feel most themselves and most inspired and achieve at their highest levels.

[29]Ellen Ott Marshall, *Though the Fig Tree Does Not Blossom: Toward a Responsible Theology of Christian Hope* (Nashville: Abingdon Press, 2006), xiii.

[30]Cited in David Krieger, ed., *Hope in a Dark Time: Reflections on Humanity's Future* (Santa Barbara, CA: Capra Press, 2003), xvii.

INDEX